1974

Jean Piaget in his office in the Palais Wilson, Geneva, Switzerland, summer, 1972.

Children in La Maison Des Petits.

HOW CHILDREN LEARN MATHEMATICS
Second Edition

TEACHING IMPLICATIONS OF PIAGET'S RESEARCH

Richard W. Copeland
Florida Atlantic University

Macmillan Publishing Co., Inc.
New York
Collier Macmillan Publishers
London

Macmillan Publishing Co., Inc.
866 Third Avenue, New York, New York 10022

Collier-Macmillan Canada, Ltd., Toronto, Ontario

Library of Congress Cataloging in Publication Data

Copeland, Richard W.
    How children learn mathematics.

    Includes bibliographical references.
    1. Mathematics—Study and teaching (Elementary)
I.   Title.
QA135.5.C5957   1974   372.7   73–1040
ISBN 0-02-324750-9

Printing: 1 2 3 4 5 6 7 8   Year: 4 5 6 7 8 9 0

Excerpts from the following books are reprinted in this volume by permission of the publishers:

Jean Piaget, *The Child's Conception of Number* (New York: Humanities Press, Inc.; London: Routledge & Kegan Paul Ltd., 1964).

Jean Piaget, *Judgment and Reasoning in the Child* (New York: Humanities Press, Inc.; London: Routledge & Kegan Paul Ltd., 1928).

Jean Piaget and Barbel Inhelder, *The Child's Conception of Space* (New York: Humanities Press, Inc.; London: Routledge & Kegan Paul Ltd., 1963).

Jean Piaget, Barbel Inhelder, and Alina Szeminska, *The Child's Conception of Geometry* (New York: Basic Books, Inc.; London: Routledge & Kegan Paul Ltd., 1960).

Preface

The second edition of this book modifies the first in a number of ways. It includes the results of research conducted in the Jean Piaget Archives at the University of Geneva in Switzerland in the summer of 1972 and interviews with Jean Piaget and his main writing associate, Barbel Inhelder. There are also new chapters based on books recently written or translated into English. These include a chapter on children's conceptions of time, a chapter on children's conceptions of fractions and proportions, and a chapter on the relation of mathematics to genetic epistemology.

Purpose

There are two major purposes. One is diagnostic—that is, the book should aid in discerning a child's stage of development as a basic for determining the type of mathematics for which he is ready. The second major purpose is to serve as a text or supplement in the "methods of teaching mathematics" courses in teacher education. The reader will find this book very different from other methods texts because it is based on *how children learn*, not on *how to teach*, and it should enable readers to see mathematics from the standpoint of the child as he progresses through the various stages of development.

The teacher, as described in this book, should be skillful in the interview technique, and many of the quotations included are actual dialogues between children and teachers. Questions are not answered for the children; they are designed so that the child can answer them himself when he is able. Teachers should also be familiar with the type of laboratory materials children need at the concrete operational level in order to learn mathematical concepts. These materials are described in the many illustrations and in the mathematics laboratory chapter.

A companion volume, *Diagnostic and Learning Activities in Mathematics for Children*,[1] may also be helpful as a practical, ready reference for the busy classroom teacher. It includes thirty-two diagnostic or readiness activities in four basic areas—space, number, logical classification, and measurement. For background information the activites are keyed to related chapters in this basic text.

Jean Piaget

Many mathematics educators recognize the importance of Piaget but also recognize that to implement his ideas is a monumental undertaking. One basic problem has been the language barrier. *The Child's Conception of Time*, for example, was not translated into English until 1969 even though it was written in French in 1946. Even in English, Piaget's books are not easy to understand. Another problem is that some math educators, although aware of Piaget's research, want additional research before restructuring the mathematics curriculum in the elementary school. The net result is that there has been little change in teaching mathematics.

As described by Rosenbloom:

> Strangely, American mathematics educators have neglected the work of Piaget. Until the last couple of years, no methods text in elementary mathematics has even mentioned his works, even though he has studied the thinking process of children and has published books since about 1926.[2]

> It is imperative that teachers and curriculum writers understand children's development and such theories as conservation.[3]

---

[1] Richard W. Copeland. *Diagnostic and Learning Activities in Mathematics for Children.* New York: Macmillan Publishing Co., Inc., 1974.
[2] Paul Rosenbloom. "Implications of Piaget for Mathematics Curriculum," *Improving Mathematics Education for Elementary School Teachers—A Conference Report*, edited by W. Robert Houston. East Lansing, Mich.: Michigan State University, 1967. Sponsored by the Science and Mathematics Teaching Center and The National Science Foundation, p. 44.
[3] *Ibid.*, p. 47.

Contents

5.   Logical Classification   51

6.   First Experiences with Number   81

7.   Addition and Subtraction   111

1 A Review of Theories of Intelligence

The nature of intelligence in man is of fundamental importance to those concerned with education. In order to educate, teach, or foster learning, one needs to know how intelligence functions.

Intelligence was first defined as "fixed" or static, since it is based on the inherited "genes" of the individual. The IQ (intelligence quotient) was therefore constant. With this assumption went another, that of "predetermined development" based on the growth and maturation of somatic and neural tissues. In this process, intellectual capacity unfolds naturally and automatically. One implication for education if this were true is that the child not be pushed but be allowed to unfold and develop naturally. Rousseau and Pestalozzi were influential in this line of thought and pedagogy.

The extent to which the view that intelligence was fixed and not influenced by teaching was evidenced by Burt, Jones, and Miller, who in the 1930s described intelligence as follows:

> By intelligence, the psychologist understands inborn, all-round, intellectual ability. It is inherited, or at least innate, not due to teaching or training; it is intellectual, not emotional or moral, and remains uninfluenced by industry or zeal; it is general, not specific, i.e., it is not limited to any particular kind of work, but enters into all we do or say or think.[1]

[1] C. Burt, E. Jones, and E. Miller. *How the Mind Works.* New York: Appleton-Century-Crofts, 1934, pp. 28–29.

It is ironic that Binet, whose tests have been used so widely to determine this static IQ, did not subscribe to such a view. He said

> Some recent philosophers appear to have given their moral support to the deplorable verdict that the intelligence of an individual is a fixed quantity. . . . We must protest and act against this brutal pessimism. . . . We say that the intelligence of children may be increased. One increases that which constitutes the intelligence of a school child, namely, the capacity to learn, to improve with instruction.[2]

One method of studying the importance of environment on intelligence is through the observation of identical twins raised apart. Since identical twins have the same genes, any significant difference in intelligence must be due to environment and not to heredity. In such a study, Newman, Freeman, and Holzinger[3] found differences in IQ as great as 24 points between identical twins.

The realization that environment or experience plays a part in IQ led to the need for new theories. One of these involved the idea of the mind as a set of mental "entities" or "faculties" that worked like muscles. It was thought that the mind could be "expanded" by exercise. This led to much rote activity in the schools in the form of mental exercises. It was said that practice in memorization would make it easier for a person to remember; and that making careful detailed drawings in science would make one a better observer.

Thorndike and others disproved these notions and replaced them with "connectionism"—the stimulus–response sequence in which the mind becomes a network of responses to various stimuli based on the effect of the stimuli on the organism. This somewhat automatic and oversimplified theory gave way to the realization of some conceptual process between stimulus and response that must take place in the mind.

As long ago as 1912, Hunter[4] argued that the mind must be capable of some kind of symbolic process. The idea that the mind is a central system capable of such a symbolic process was characterized by Newell et al. in 1958 as a system for information processing.

---

[2] A. Binet. *Les Idées modernes sur les enfants*. Paris: Ernest Flanarion, 1909. Cited from G. D. Stoddard, "The I.Q.: Its Ups and Downs," *Educational Record*, 20 (1939), pp. 44–57.
[3] H. H. Newman, F. N. Freeman, and K. J. Holzinger. *Twins: A Study of Heredity and Environment*. Chicago: University of Chicago Press, 1937, pp. 18–20, 325–327.
[4] W. S. Hunter. "The Delayed Reaction in Animals and Children," *Behavior Monograph*, 2(1) (1912), pp. 1–85.

We postulate an information-processing system with large storage capacity that holds among other things, complex strategies (programs) that may be evoked by stimuli.[5]

Hunt reports:

Their theory assumes that an organism consists of receptors, which take in information in coded form, of effectors, which engage in action, and of a control system joining these. They make three postulates concerning the nature of the control system: (a) It has a number of memories containing symbolized information that are inter-connected by various ordering relations; (b) it has a number of processes which operate on the information in the memories; and (c) it has a definite set of rules for combining these processes into programs of processing. . . . [6]

In short, the mind is thought to operate in a fashion similar to an electronic computer. It specifies a program for the organism to follow based on information received. Asking the computer to work its problems on paper approximates having a human subject proceed to solve his problem out loud.

The preceding summary leads us to the work of the Swiss psychologist, biologist, philosopher, logician, and mathematician Jean Piaget. The implications of his work for mathematics education will be studied in detail. Concerning Piaget, Hunt reports:

A conception of intelligence as problem-solving capacity based on a hierarchical organization of symbolic representations and information-processing strategies deriving to a considerable degree from past experience, has been emerging from several sources. These sources include observations of human behavior in solving problems, the programming of electronic computers, and neuropsychology. It is interesting, therefore, to find such a conception coming also from Piaget's observations of the development of intelligence in children.[7]

Hunt's description of problem-solving capacity based on "symbolic representation and information processing" is characterized by Piaget as thought at the **operational** level. According to Piaget, there are two stages of operational thought. The first is **concrete operational.**

[5] Newell, Shaw, and Simon. "Elements of a Theory of Human Problem Solving," *Psychological Review* (1958), p. 163.
[6] J. M. Hunt. *Intelligence and Experience*. New York: The Ronald Press Company, 1961, pp. 75–76.
[7] Ibid., p. 109.

At this level ideas must be abstracted from experiences in the physical world, such as by **actions** performed on objects. Young children explore and manipulate objects in order to learn about them. This level of thought is the main consideration in this book since most children are in or moving toward this level of thought during the time they are in elementary school.

At eleven to twelve years of age, children reach the second level of operational thought, at which time they can reason and consider ideas at the abstract level without having to rely on their experience in the physical world. This level of thought, **formal operational**, is characterized as hypothetico-deductive, since it is based on a deductive reasoning process from any arbitrarily chosen hypothesis or premise.

Unfortunately Piaget's early work generated little interest in the United States, because psychology was dominated by associationistic theories of learning and by content-oriented psychometrics. Now there is a cognitive trend in the literature as the search for a theoretical model moves away from the laboratory rat toward the electronic computer.[8]

Piaget's theory is cognitive rather than associationistic. It is more concerned with structure than content—with how the mind works rather than what it works on. It is more concerned with understanding than with the prediction and control of behavior.[9]

[8] John L. Philips. *The Origins of Intellect—Piaget's Theory*. San Francisco: W. H. Freeman and Company, 1969, p. viii.
[9] Ibid., p. 6.

2 Genetic Epistemology and Mathematics

He [Piaget] has approached heretofore exclusive philosophical questions in a resolutely empirical fashion and created epistemology as a science, separate from philosophy, but interrelated with all human sciences.[1]

Genetic epistemology deals with both the formation and the meaning of knowledge. The essential question is: By what means does the human mind go from a lower to a higher level of knowledge? The fundamental hypothesis of genetic epistemology is that there is a parallelism between the progress made in logic (or the rational organization of knowledge) and the corresponding formative psychological processes.[2]

An example is Cantor's development of set theory, which is based on the fundamental operation of one-to-one correspondence. Where did the operation of one-to-one correspondence come from? Cantor found it in his thinking, a part of his mental equipment long before he turned to mathematics. The most elementary psychological observations reveal that one-to-one correspondence is a primitive operation.[3]

[1] From citation in a Distinguished Scientific Contribution Award recently presented to Jean Piaget by the American Psychological Association.
[2] Jean Piaget. *Genetic Epistemology*. New York: Columbia University Press, 1970, p. 13.
[3] Ibid., p. 5.

Are there certain mathematical structures basic to all others? The Bourbaki group of mathematicians attempted to isolate the fundamental structures of all mathematics. They established three mother structures: an algebraic structure (the prototype of which is the notion of a group), a structure of ordering, and a topological structure. These were later modified to include the notion of categories.[4]

The question then arises: What is the relation of these fundamental mathematical or logical structures and the psychological structures in the minds of children? A group of mathematicians and psychologists met in Paris for a conference titled "Mental Structures and Mathematical Structures." Piaget reports that

> ... the mathematician Dieudonne, who was representing the Bourbaki mathematicians, totally mistrusted anything that had to do with psychology. Dieudonne gave a talk in which he described the three mother structures [in mathematics]. Then I gave a talk in which I described the structures that I had found in children's thinking, and to the great astonishment of us both we saw that there was a very direct relationship between these three mathematical structures and the three structures of children's operational thinking. We were, of course, impressed with each other, and Dieudonne went so far as to say to me: "This is the first time that I have taken psychology seriously. It may also be the last, but at any rate it's the first."[5]

Logic and Psychology

The same problem of cooperation was found between logicians and psychologists. In the book *Logic and Psychology* Piaget examines the mathematical and logical basis or model for human thought.

> Theoretically, it is important to ask what sort of correspondence exists between the structures described by logic and the actual thought processes studied by psychology.[6]
>
> The algebra of logic can therefore help the psychologist, by giving him a precise method of specifying the structures which emerge in the analysis of the operational mechanisms of thought.[7]

---

[4] Ibid., p. 3.
[5] Ibid., p. 26.
[6] Jean Piaget. *Logic and Psychology.* New York: Basic Books, Inc., 1960, p. xvii.
[7] Ibid., p. xviii.

However, at the present time there is little collaboration between logicians and psychologists. Indeed, there is a mutual distrust which makes cooperation difficult.[8]

Classical logic believed it was possible to discover the actual structure of thought processes. . . . Classical philosophical psychology, in its turn, considered the laws of logic and the laws of ethics to be implicit in the mental functioning of each normal individual.[9]

But with the development of the young science of experimental psychology logical factors were excluded; intelligence was explained by sensations, images, associations and other mechanisms. The reaction to this approach was unfortunate.[10]

At about the time that psychologists were trying to divorce their science from logic, the founders of modern logic or 'logistic' asked for it to be separated from psychology for similar reasons. It is true that Boole, the inventor of the algebra that bears his name, still believed he was describing "The Laws of Thought."[11]

The logician Evert Beth reviewed a work Piaget did on the operational mechanisms of logic and criticized it "very severely." Piaget then wrote to Beth and invited him to participate in a number of meetings to see if a mutually satisfactory assimilation of positions could be reached. The subject of the meetings was the psychological formation and development of certain elementary logical structures. Piaget reports that it was a measure of Beth's intellectual honesty that he did not refuse to take part in such a venture, which from his point of view was extremely risky.[12]   The result ten years later was a book co-authored by Beth and Piaget titled *Mathematical and Epistemology Psychology.*[13]   In this book Beth defines the problem of epistemology as finding out how human thought produces scientific knowledge.

Basic Mathematical and Psychological Structures

In children's thinking basic algebraic structures are most readily found in the logic of classes or logical classification (Chapter 5). The

[8] Ibid., p. xix.
[9] Ibid., p. 1.
[10] Ibid.
[11] Ibid., p. 2.
[12] Evert Beth and Jean Piaget. *Mathematical Epistemology and Psychology.* Dordrecht, Holland: D. Reidel Publishing Company, 1966, p. xii.
[13] Ibid.

psychological structure necessary to properly classify objects in relation to each other is the mathematical or logical relation of **class inclusion**. A six- or seven-year-old may agree that all ducks are birds and that not all birds are ducks, but asked if there are more birds or ducks he does not know. He does not yet have the necessary algebraic structure.

ducks +   other birds   = all birds

birds + other animals = all animals

Thus a hierarchy of classification is structured based on the logic of the inclusion relation.

Young children do not have reversibility by negation, such as: If all the birds died, would there be any ducks left; or if all the ducks died, would there be any birds left? (See Chapter 5.)

Second, the psychological structure, **seriation**, necessary for the mathematical structure of **ordering** is not present until approximately seven years of age. For example, before this age children, when asked to arrange a set of ten sticks in order of length or height will group them in pairs, such as putting two short ones together and two long ones together, or will arrange the sticks in sets of three. This is followed by a trial-and-error approach—trying first one and then another to see which stick is right. There is no over-all coordinated approach.

To be successful in ordering, the child must have the psychological structure necessary to understand the mathematical or logical relation of **transitivity**. If B is longer than A and C is longer than B, then logically C is longer than A. Younger children if asked how A and C compare will say that they have to "look" again, and they put stick C by stick A to "see" that C is longer. (See Chapter 6.)

The third type of basic mathematical structure according to the Bourbaki group is **topological,** even though historically (and in school) the first type of geometry studied was Euclidean. Piaget also finds children able to solve topological problems before Euclidean ones. For example, children can make inside and outside distinctions and differentiate open from closed figures before they can differentiate Euclidean shapes such as circles and squares. (For further discussion see Chapter 12.)

Biology and Intelligence

Piaget, in studying intelligence, adopted the biological model of **adaptation**, a model more popular fifty years ago than now. Intelligence is studied through the general process of adaptation, and adaptation is studied as **behavior**.

Piaget and the rigid behaviorist school of psychology differ sharply in their ideas about behavior. For Piaget, studying behavior involves studying the total organization of the person or other organism. The most relevant aspect of intelligence is not what the person *does* (as an external action) but the rules or organization within the individual that control or govern the action. This is a much broader view than the stimulus–response (S–R) approach, for example, in which the action itself as a response is studied. The more limited mechanistic S–R approach was more conducive to carefully controlled laboratory-type experimentation, but it does not give us the important answers.

Piaget was able, like Darwin or Freud, to systematize his empirical observations of children by discovering structures where others saw nothing but inconsequential childish activities.[14] Einstein summarizes Piaget's developmental approach as "the idea of a genius, such simplicity."[15] It was these very procedures or experiments that were branded "unscientific" and not "controlled" and not large enough "samples" that led to a slow acceptance of Piaget's theories.

Intelligence, biologically speaking, is not a special biological organ but a way of behaving, being determined by the general laws of evolution and adaptation. The intelligence of man, as different from animals and children, is seen in the simple act of driving a nail into a piece of wood. Both the child and the ape may be able to hold and swing the hammer, but they do not have the internal coordination of spacial coordinates (vertical and horizontal) that will allow them to correct their actions as necessary. Later, the child can. (See Chapter 15.)

Piaget, Skinner, and Performance Objectives

Present trends in American education toward "behavioral" or "performance" objectives probably align themselves more with a

---

[14] Hans G. Furth. *Piaget and Knowledge*. Englewood Cliffs, N.J.: Prentice-Hall, Inc., 1969, p. 172.

[15] Ibid., p. 6.

"Skinnerian" than a "Piagetian" approach to education. Piaget's comments on this approach:

> In more or less close connection with the Pavlovian school of Soviet reflexology American psychology has evolved a certain number of theories of learning based on the stimulus-response view . . . the most recent of the great American learning theorists, Skinner, the author of some remarkable experiments with pigeons . . . convinced of the inaccessible nature of the intermediate variables [the mind] decided to confine his attention to stimuli or inputs that could be varied at will and to observable responses, or outputs, and then to take account only of the direct relationships between them, ignoring the interval connections. This "empty box" conception of the organism, as it has been called, thus deliberately thumbs its nose at all kinds of mental life, and confines itself solely to behavior in its most material aspects.[16]

The principle of programmed learning involves in effect beginning with certain preliminary definitions. From these the student must draw the correct conclusions in the form of several choices offered to him. If his choice is correct, he proceeds in the work sequence. If not, the exercise is repeated.

The value of this teaching method Piaget summarizes as follows:

> In cases where it is a matter of acquiring a set body of learning as in the teaching of languages, the machine does seem to be accepted as of undeniable service. In cases where the idea is to reinvent a sequence of reasoning, however, as in mathematics, though the machine does not exclude either comprehension or reasoning on the student's part, it does channel them in an unfortunate way and excludes the possibility of initiative.[17]

Also cited is the Woods Hole conference of mathematicians and physicists, who received Skinner's ideas with "no more than limited enthusiasm."[18]

Our concern with knowledge at the logico-mathematical level Piaget considers to be largely an internal rather than external process. The "empty box" theory is rejected because it is the box or structure of the mind that is the prime consideration in intellectual activity. Also, **repetition** or **external reinforcements** as practices in the programming

---

[16] Jean Piaget. *Science of Education and the Psychology of the Child.* New York: Orion Press, 1970, p. 76.
[17] Ibid., p. 78.
[18] Ibid.

approach to correct errors will not correct errors, since repetition or external reinforcement cannot build or modify the necessary intellectual structures to consider successfully such mathematical ideas as the inclusion relation or transitivity. That this is true will be demonstrated in the chapters to follow.

Mathematical Models for Children's Thinking

Piaget postulates that mental activity is mathematical in character. A basic mathematical model is that of the **group**. A group may be thought of as a mathematical system involving the properties of closure, commutativity, associativity, an identity element, and reversibility (an inverse element or operation).

The property of reversibility, for example, is necessary for understanding number and logical thinking. Yet it does not usually occur in children's thinking until six to seven years of age. It will be discussed at length in the chapters to follow. Reversibility is necessary for the idea of conservation, also to be discussed at length. For example, children observe liquid being poured into different-shaped containers and think there is more or less liquid based on the shape or the number of containers. Perception or what they "see" is their rationale. They cannot reason that the liquid could be poured back (inverse) and would then be the same as it was originally (identity).

Concerning children's thinking, Piaget uses the term "operations" for activities of the mind. Children pass through two basic stages of ability to think logically: the **concrete operations** period, from approximately seven to eleven or twelve years of age, followed by the **formal operations** period. The basic difference in the two periods is that in the concrete operations stage children's logical thinking must be based on actions performed on objects or things (concrete), while at the formal operations level children can reason at the abstract or hypothetical level using symbols and not requiring physical experiences. These stages are explored in detail in Chapter 4 and are mentioned here simply to refer to the mathematical or logical thinking involved at each level.

Concrete Operations

At the stage of concrete operations children do not have all the thought structures characteristic of the mathematical group. The logical structures they do have, however, are called "groupings" and include the logic of class inclusion and the logic of relations, such as the transitive relation, which allows ordering. Consider the transitive relation "taller than." If Jane is taller than Sue and Ruth is taller than Jane, then logically it can be concluded that Ruth is taller than Sue. (If $B > A$ and $C > B$, then $C > A$.)

The idea of class inclusion or hierarchical classification is also an extremely important grouping. Animals include birds and birds include ducks. Classes may be added to form larger classes. ($A + A' = B$.) This additive composition of classes is a powerful notion with which we classify all objects in our physical universe in relation to each other based on their individual and collective properties.

Formal Operations

At the formal operations level, beginning around eleven or twelve years of age, children can consider some arbitrarily chosen hypothesis or proposition and make the necessary deductions as to the possible outcomes without resorting to the physical world. They can use the logic involved in that of groups and lattices. Adolescent thought is described by Piaget using the "four group," or INRC group, developed by the Bourbaki school of mathematics. INRC represents identity, negation (inverse), reciprocal, and correlative transformations.

Children do not understand the mathematical idea of proportions until they reach the formal operations level of thought. Involved in understanding proportion is the logic of the INRC group.

Applying this idea to a problem of a balance scale used for weighing, weights are placed at different distances along the balance beam or cross bar. The child is asked to make the weights balance the scale. At about seven years of age the child realizes that weights can be subtracted (inverse) as well as added as one way of achieving balance. The procedure at the concrete operations thought level is largely trial and error, however. But at about twelve years of age, at the formal operations stage, the child can use the logic of proportion—that the horizontal distance from the fulcrum is inversely related to the weight.

The INRC group describes the proportional schema. If a weight destroys the balance, the weight can be taken off (negation). Or an equal weight can be added at an equal distance on the other arm (reciprocal). Or a heavier weight can be added closer to the fulcrum or a lighter weight farther away (correlation). Or all the weights can be removed to restore the balance to equilibrium (identity).

These ideas can be expressed in symbolic logic in terms of p and q, as can the more sophisticated structure known as a **lattice** (Jean Piaget, *Logic and Psychology*). The lattice may be understood better by the reader who is not a logician or mathematician by using an example at the concrete level. Consider the problem of the school administrator faced with integration involving every possible grouping of white and black boys and girls.[19] If the principal is operating at the formal operations or hypothetico-deductive level, he can consider all the possibilities in the lattice, which involve sixteen possible combinations of four binary propositions, ranging from none of them (null set) to all four of them. These would include:

1. No children at all
2. White boys only
3. White girls only
4. Black boys only
5. Black girls only
6. White boys and white girls
7. Black boys and black girls
8. White boys and black girls
9. Black boys and white girls
10. Girls only, white and black
11. Boys only, white and black
12. White boys and girls, and black boys
13. White boys and girls, and black girls
14. Black boys and girls, and white boys
15. Black boys and girls, and white girls
16. White boys and girls, and black boys and girls

Piaget and Inhelder tested children's ability to use this lattice structure using four similar flasks filled with different liquids, all colorless. A bottle of potassium iodide was provided which would make one combination of the liquids turn yellow. Only at twelve to thirteen years of age (the formal operations level) can the child work out a system to check all the possibilities.[20]

Since children will only be on the threshold of the formal operations level of thinking as they leave the elementary school, the primary concern in this book will be the concrete operations level of thinking. The junior high school science teacher may be asking too much of the elementary school teacher when he says: "If you don't teach them anything else, teach them how to use a proportion."

---

[19] Mary A. S. Pulaski. *Understanding Piaget.* New York: Harper & Row, Publishers, 1971, p. 70.
[20] Barbel Inhelder and Jean Piaget. *The Growth of Logical Thinking from Childhood to Adolescence.* New York: Basic Books, Inc., 1958, p. 117.

3 Jean Piaget: Biography and Views on Education

[Of great concern] is the ignorance in which we still remain with regard to the results achieved by our educational techniques.[1]

Piaget's Biography

Jean Piaget was born in 1896 in Switzerland. He first became a biologist and later a psychologist. At the age of ten he published his first article, concerning a rare albino sparrow, in the *Journal of Natural History of Neuchatel*.

Later, as a university student majoring in biology, Piaget became interested in philosophy and psychology. The writings of Bergson, identifying God with life, caused Piaget to write:

> It enabled me to see in biology the explanation of all things and of mind itself. . . . I got the impression of an ingenious construction without an experimental basis: Between biology and the analysis of knowledge I needed something other than philosophy. I believe it was at that moment that I discovered a need that could be satisfied only by psychology.[2]

[1] Jean Piaget. *Science of Education and the Psychology of the Child.* New York: Orion Press, 1970, p. 5.
[2] Henry W. Maier. *Three Theories of Child Development.* New York: Harper & Row, Publishers, rev. ed., 1969, p. 84.

14

Because of his mother's poor mental health, he was interested in psychoanalysis and pathological psychology, but he much preferred the study of normalcy and the workings of the intellect to that of the tricks of the unconscious. He studied in the psychological laboratories at the University of Zurich in 1918 and in the experimental laboratory of Alfred Binet in Paris from 1919 to 1921. During this time he attended lectures of Pfister, Jung, and Freud.

His first major works were published during 1924–1932. One of these was *Judgment and Reasoning in the Child*, published in 1928. He received wide recognition from university centers in Europe and the United States during this period, but his early works were criticized because he drew conclusions from children's answers at the verbal level. He reports:

> I well knew that thought proceeds from action, but I believed then that language directly reflects acts and that to understand the logic of the child one had only to look for it in the domain of conversations or verbal interactions. It was only later, by studying the patterns of intelligent behavior of the first two years, that I learned that for a complete understanding of the genesis of intellectual operations, manipulation and experience with objects had first to be considered.[3]

From 1929 to 1939 he formulated the psychological concept of **groupings**, which was to tie together his theory of cognitive development. During and following the World War II years Piaget continued his research—lecturing and writing in three capacities as the professor of the History of Scientific Thought at the University of Geneva, as Assistant Director of the Institute of J. J. Rousseau, and as Director of the Bureau of the International Office of Education. Jean Piaget is now Professor of Experimental Psychology and Genetic Epistemology at the University of Geneva. He retired from active teaching in 1972 to devote full time to writing.

The writer had the honor of visiting Dr. Piaget in Geneva in the summer of 1972. The color photos in the front and the back of the book were taken in Dr. Piaget's office as he dictated answers to correspondence. The first personal contact in the form of a letter written in 1968 to obtain quote permissions is a reminder that Dr. Piaget does not speak English even though he reads widely in a number of languages.

[3] Ibid., p. 86.

UNIVERSITÉ DE GENÈVE
SCHOLA GENEVENSIS MDLIX

FACULTÉ DES SCIENCES

Genève, le　18 mars 1968

Monsieur Richard W. Copeland
Professor of Education
Florida Atlantic University
BOCA RATON,　Floride 33432

Monsieur,

　　　　J'ai bien reçu votre lettre du
26 février et vous informe que je suis
tout à fait d'accord avec les extraits
que vous désirez faire des 4 volumes que
vous citez.

　　　　Veuillez croire, Monsieur, à l'expression de mes sentiments distingués.

J. Piaget

Publications

Piaget has probably written more books and had more books writ-ten about him than any man living today. Since his primary concern has been the development of logico-mathematical intelligence, many of his books are of interest to the mathematics educator.

For an overview of Piaget's ideas the books *The Psychology of the Child* and *Genetic Epistemology* are recent and also less difficult to understand than some of his other works. His views on education are described in *Science of Education and the Psychology of the Child*.

For the researcher interested in visiting Switzerland there is a Jean Piaget Archives collection of materials in various languages on the fourth floor of the Ecole de Psychologie et des Sciences de l'Educa-tion in Geneva. It is open only in the mornings.

The books of most value in preparing this manuscript were as follows:

	Published in English	Recent Publisher
Piaget, *The Child's Conception of Number*	1952	W. W. Norton & Company, Inc., New York
Piaget and Inhelder, *The Child's Conception of Space*	1956	W. W. Norton & Company, Inc., New York
Piaget, Inhelder, and Szeminska, *The Child's Conception of Geometry*	1960	Basic Books, Inc., New York
Piaget and Inhelder, *The Early Growth of Logic in the Child*	1964	W. W. Norton & Company, Inc., New York
Beth and Piaget, *Mathematical Epistemology and Psychology*	1966	D. Reidel Publishing Company, Dordrecht, Holland
Piaget and Inhelder, *The Psychology of the Child*	1969	Basic Books, Inc., New York
Piaget, *The Child's Conception of Time*	1969	Basic Books, Inc., New York
Piaget, *Genetic Epistemology*	1970	Columbia University Press, New York
Piaget, *Science of Education and the Psychology of the Child*	1970	Orion Press, New York

Piaget As a Genetic Epistemologist

With reference to Piaget's position in the field of psychology, his works are now receiving wide attention and study. His theories are being tested in many laboratory situations. Only recently has this become so, partly as a result of the earlier lack of English translations. Also, by ignoring existing learning theory research, he did not encourage some support. As described by Maier:

> The striking absence of any reference to learning theory research is best described by John H. Flavell: "it is important to realize that it is (Piaget's) philosophy of science rather than laziness or experimental naivete, which dictates the informal quality of his research." Piaget concerns himself with the organizational activities *within* the individual rather than with the stimulating environmental cues which are the concern of most learning theorists. Wayne Dennis writes: "We turn to Piaget for ideas, not for statistics."[4]

[4] Ibid., p. 90.

Another difficulty is described by Isaacs:

> The main impediment lies in certain understandable resistances to his work which merit examining just because they further bring out its transforming effect and value.
> ... most of the fundamental structural ideas which ... philosophers regard as abstruse philosophic mysteries (reality, causality, space, time, number, the forms and laws of logic, etc.) have a long observable history of psychological growth behind them. And this history is one which starts from their virtual absence or negation [in the minds of children] and goes through a succession of transformations [before they reach the forms of deductive logic found in adults].... Philosophers may feel that they can continue to ignore this, but psychologists cannot [pp. 30–31].[5]

As an answer to this observation by Isaacs, Piaget is now classified as a **genetic epistemologist**, since he is concerned with the nature of knowledge and the structures and processes by which it is acquired. This is in contrast to his not being a child psychologist in the practical sense, concerned primarily with child growth and development. His main concern is to show, according to Elkind,[6] that in all discussions of the development of knowledge the roles of maturation and experience are not sufficient but must include also a mental logical structure called **equilibration**: "Piaget argues that much of our knowledge comes not from without but from within by the force of our own logic ... a fact often forgotten in education."[7]

As Isaacs points out,[8] Piaget's work is crucial for educational philosophy as well as psychology because it shares with progressive education an approach to the child in terms of action, process, and growth. Educational philosophy, for which true education is growth, finds in Piaget's psychology the foundation and framework it most needs.

[5] With acknowledgment to the late Nathan Isaacs, from whose pamphlet *Some Aspects of Piaget's Work* (published by the National Froebel Foundation, London, 8th ed., 1965) we have permission to quote.
[6] Jean Piaget. *Six Psychological Studies.* New York: Random House, Inc., 8th ed., p. xviii, Introduction.
[7] David Elkind. *Children and Adolescents—Interpretative Essays on Jean Piaget.* New York: Oxford University Press, 1970, p. 25.
[8] Isaacs, op. cit., pp. 30–31.

Professional Education

Asked to evaluate the development of education and teaching for the period 1935 to 1965, Piaget is most pessimistic and alarmed by

> The immensity of the efforts that have been made and the absence of any fundamental renewal in our methods, in our programs . . . in pedagogy as a whole considered as a guiding discipline.[9]

The first observation that comes to mind "is the ignorance in which we still remain with regard to the results achieved by our educational techniques."[10]

Education has not developed into a science. Governmental officials in education have no impartial and objective discipline with the authority to supply principles and factual data. The result is a government deciding on principles to be applied in education. Public educators then serve as civil servants to implement the principles and policies decided by government officials. This is in contrast to governmental officials in health who have the medical profession to furnish basic principles and policies. "Our school system has been constructed by conservatives who think more in terms of fitting children in the molds of traditional learning than in terms of training inventive and critical minds."[11]

Training Elementary Teachers

> Cut off from the scientific trends and the atmosphere of research and experiment that could have injected new life into them, teachers plug along through the required credits in education and go through the motions of performing a single piece of research, which they hand in with a sigh of relief, never to undertake any more.[12]

The fundamental problem is that educators are more interested in teaching than they are in children. Their concentration, their training, is upon methods and curriculum rather than child psychology. Teachers want to teach and have children listen.

---

[9] Piaget, *Science of Education*, op. cit., p. 3.
[10] Ibid., p. 5.
[11] Ibid., p. 124.
[12] Mary A. S. Pulaski. *Understanding Piaget*. New York: Harper & Row, Publishers, 1971, p. 196.

The British infant schools described briefly in the math laboratory chapter have attempted to implement Piaget's ideas. Children are allowed to move freely about, to talk with each other, and to investigate materials on their own. There is a variety of material—buttons, beads, string, material to measure, and commercial materials such as mathematical balancies—to explore many kinds of problems involving mathematics.

A disadvantage of the teachers' training college is that it shuts the primary teaching body in on itself or creates a closed social entity.[13] The psychological training so necessary to primary-grade teachers cannot be obtained unless the students have the opportunity to engage in research themselves. One cannot learn child psychology without participating in research. It is useless to limit courses to exercises or practical work toward already known results.[14]

This research is found only in universities, and a university is the only place in which school teachers can learn to become researchers and to rise above the level of mere transmitters.[15]

At the University of Geneva, research programs are planned in yearly stages by the professors and conducted by the assistants. The assistants go every afternoon to work with children. Students go with the assistants in groups of two or three. They learn (1) to record facts, (2) how to question children, and (3) to make periodic reports on the progress of research. "In a word it is by and through research that the teachers' profession ceases to be merely a trade." [16]

Early Childhood (Preschool) Instruction

Piaget reports that when intelligence was conceived as arising from the interplay of perceptions or sensations, a "sensory education" was presumed to be the answer. Froebel, with his exercises, provided a basic model. Montessori later used the same principles, but "added a fair amount of action even though it was channeled in advance by previously assembled apparatus." [17]

Piaget, Dewey, and Montessori would agree on the need for exploratory activity on the part of children. They endorse an activity-type

---

[13] Piaget, *Science of Education*, op. cit., p. 125.
[14] Ibid., p. 126.
[15] Ibid.
[16] Ibid., p. 130.
[17] Ibid., p. 98.

program allowing for physical exploration of objects. Piaget and Dewey, however, criticize Montessori's highly structured materials as being used only in preplanned ways. As expressed by Dewey,

> [The Montessori] demand is for materials which have already been subjected to the perfecting work of mind . . . That such material will control the pupil's operations so as to prevent errors is true. The notion that a pupil operating with such material will somehow absorb the intelligence that went originally to its shaping is fallacious. Only by starting with crude material and subjecting it to purposeful handling will he gain the intelligence embodied in finished material.[18]

Piaget makes the same criticism of the Cuisenaire rods. Children must be allowed to explore the rods and develop for themselves the mathematical ideas involved. This is in contrast to structured lessons telling the children how to fit the rods together to get the right answers.

Emphasis should be on a sensory-motor type of education at the preschool level, and systematic learning in the fields of reading, writing, and arithmetic should be deferred. Piaget adds that sensory-motor activities prepare the child for logical operations in as much as logic is based on the general coordination of actions before being formulated at the level of language.[19]

There is considerable pressure today to begin academic instruction in early childhood (Bruner's hypothesis). The argument is that this period is critical for intellectual growth. Elkind asks the question: What is the evidence that preschool instruction has lasting effects upon mental growth? The answer is that there is none.[20] Not only is there no clear-cut longitudinal data on the lasting nature of such instruction, but there is evidence in the opposite direction. Several workers suggest a negative correlation and in turn suggest a hypothesis that the longer we delay formal instruction, up to certain limits, the higher the ultimate level of achievement.[21]

Elkind contends on the basis of the stages of development outlined by Piaget that it is the elementary school years that are most crucial to intellectual growth. Most of this time, that is, from six or seven to twelve years of age, the child is in the concrete operational stage, the first stage of real logical thought.

---

[18] John Dewey. *Democracy and Education: An Introduction to the Philosophy of Education.* New York: The Macmillan Company, 1916, p. 232.

[19] Piaget, *Science of Education,* op. cit., p. 98.

[20] Elkind, op. cit., p. 129.

[21] Ibid.

Teaching Aids

Piaget takes a dim view of many teaching aids, in that educators with insufficient psychological backgrounds confuse "active" methods with "perceptual" or intuitive methods. Films and television, for example, may produce "figurative" processes rather than operational or logical processes. Perception, or what we "see," produces a mental copy or impression of what is seen, but that may be all that it is, a copy. This is in contrast to producing a flexible, reversible, stable understanding of the principles involved. Films as such are simply a presentation which may be somewhat better than a lecture or verbal explanation in that two senses are involved (visual and auditory) rather than only the auditory sense. There are no physical actions on the part of the learner in either case.

Similarly, Skinner's teaching machines are successful if by success is meant the verbal reproduction of the desired answer:

> These machines have performed at least one great service for us, which is to demonstrate beyond all possible doubt the mechanical character of the schoolmaster's function as it is conceived by traditional teaching methods. . . .[22]   (See pp. 9–10 for Piaget's evaluation of the Skinner position.)

Motivating the Learner

Of prime concern to the teacher is whether or how to motivate the learner. What is the psychological basis for the "need" for cognitive activity?

Piaget rejects the notion of external forces as the prime factors in motivating cognitive activity. In doing so he rejects the concept of "reinforcement" which is central to behaviorism and learning theory.[23]

Motivation for cognitive activity comes primarily from within the individual, not from without. Once the necessary cognitive structures are functioning there is an intrinsic tendency to assimilate and accommodate the environment.

[22] Piaget, *Science of Education*, op. cit., p. 77.
[23] Barry J. Wadsworth. *Piaget's Theory of Cognitive Development*. New York: David McKay Company, Inc., 1971, p. 24.

The principal motive power of intellectual activity [is] the need to incorporate things into the subject's schemata. . . .[24]

Social Interaction versus Individualized Programming in Lesson Planning

Stress has been placed on children's being allowed to perform actions on objects as a basis for developing the necessary intellectual structures or elaborations. The math laboratory is one vehicle that shows promise in this direction.

But should the children work only individually in the mathematics laboratory? Piaget remarks that

> . . . without interchange of thought and cooperation with others the individual would never come to group his operations into a coherent whole . . .[25]

There is a necessity of action with people as well as action upon objects in the educational process. In lesson planning provision should be made for group activity, which encourages questions and the interchange of ideas. It may be advisable to have the children work in groups in the mathematics laboratory as well as on individual projects.

[24] Jean Piaget. *The Origins of Intelligence in Children.* New York: International Universities Press, 1952, p. 46.
[25] Ibid., p. 193.

4 Piaget's Theory of Intellectual Development

Words are probably not a short cut to understanding; the level of understanding seems to modify the language that is used rather than vice-versa.[1]

This chapter describes basic stages of development in children's thinking and factors affecting this development. These are related to three basic types of knowledge and to learning, memory, and language development. Three basic mathematical structures found in children's thinking as a basis for developing logico-mathematical knowledge have already been outlined (Chapter 2).

Stages of Development

Piaget identifies four basic stages in the development of mental structures. In each of these there are substages, which will not be described here. The reader interested in studying each substage in detail may like to read *The Psychology of the Child* by Jean Piaget and Barbel Inhelder (New York: Basic Books, Inc., 1969).

[1] Eleanor Duckworth. "Piaget Rediscovered," in E. Victor and M. Lerner, eds. *Readings in Science Education for the Elementary School.* New York: The Macmillan Company, 1967, p. 319.

To avoid confusion, it should be noted that Piaget uses the term "stages" in two contexts. The following "stages" might better be called "periods" in the life of a child. Although they are not numbered, they occur in the order described. Later we will talk about "stages" in terms of numbers, as stage 1, stage 2, and stage 3. These numbered stages refer to the levels of understanding of a particular concept. Stage 1 is no understanding, stage 2 is partial understanding, and stage 3 is complete understanding (see pp. 84–87).

Sensory-motor Stage

This first stage, from birth to one and one-half years, is a preverbal, presymbolic period. It is a direct-action period—actions of sucking, looking, grasping, which at first are uncoordinated actions and then gradually become coordinated—grasping and looking at an object, for example. This action type of intelligence may be partially inherited, a reflex action—sucking, for example—but there must still be a coordination of actions, as can be observed in the baby searching for the nipple, at first a random search but later a coordinated one. Reflex actions can also be observed as parents use various kinds of stimuli to make the baby laugh or smile, such as tickling his foot or swinging him in the air.

There is a progression in the sensory-motor period from spontaneous movements and reflexes to acquired habits and from these to intelligence. One of the first habits is thumb sucking. This is not a reflex action but a habit that the child discovers and finds satisfactory.

Such habits may grow out of the child's actions or be the result of conditioning imposed from outside. A famous example of conditioned behavior was that of Pavlov's dog, who salivated when he heard a bell (as long as food continued to follow the bell).

At about one year of age there is a new element in the child's behavior. He can establish an objective, such as getting a ball that is out of reach, and then develop a procedure for obtaining the ball. For example, if the ball is on a rug he can reach, he may note that moving the rug moves the ball, so he pulls the rug (and the ball) toward himself.

Such an act Piaget characterizes as intelligence, an act of intelligence being defined as one in which there is first purpose or end and then a search for appropriate means to that end. The search for a means may involve schemes never before used. The means are first determined by experimental physical or external groping, such as happening to pull the rug. Later the means result from mental (internalized) consideration of possibilities.

Preoperational Stage

This period, beginning at one and one-half or two years, lasts until approximately seven years of age. Brighter children will move to the following stage a year or two earlier than seven, however, and less intelligent children a year or two later than seven. This period of preoperational intelligence may be characterized as the stage of **representation** or **symbolism**. During the first period, the sensory-motor phase, there is no use of words or symbols to represent things, no imagining, playing "let's pretend," or playing at "keeping house" with dolls. To engage in these activities, thought is present at the representational level. Words are being used to **represent** things. Playing "let's pretend" involves imagining—the ability to represent something such as mother cooking or mother dressing the baby.

In the sensory-motor stage the child is restricted to direct interaction with his environment, but in the preoperational stage he begins to manipulate symbols or representations of the physical world in which he lives. The preoperational period is often described as lasting from two to seven years of age. However, this is only a rough guide, as will be observed in the following chapters. For some mathematical concepts, children do not leave the preoperational stage until nine or ten years of age.

During the end of the sensory-motor or during the first part of the preoperational period there is semilogic, logic of one-way mappings. In psychological terms the child realizes that pulling a cord opens the curtain or pulling a blanket on which there is a ball is a way to get the ball. This cause–effect relation is still an action type of intelligence aimed at getting results.

There is as yet, however, no reversible thought process that will allow for a type of logic which can be used in the next stage, that of concrete operations.

Concrete Operational Stage

The third stage, from approximately seven to eleven or twelve years of age, is that of concrete operations. It is particularly important to the elementary school teacher, because most of the time that children are in the elementary school they are in this stage of development.

This stage marks the beginning of logico-mathematical thought. The child is said to be "operational" in his thinking. The stage is called "concrete operational," since the necessary logical thought is based in part on the physical manipulation of objects. The child no longer uses perception or sensory cues as a basis for answering questions requiring logical thought.

Piaget studied the concrete operational stage using the concept of **conservation** or **invariance**, which is a basic characteristic of this stage. For example, a child is shown two glasses containing the same amount of water.

Figure 4-1

The water in one glass is then poured into a taller glass with smaller diameter.

Figure 4-2

When the child understands that the amount of water is still the same and rejects what perception tells him (one looks like more), he is using logic and has arrived at the concrete operational thought level for this concept.

That the amount of water is conserved or remains invariant after the pouring operation is referred to as the concept of **conservation** or **invariance**. To arrive at this stage the child must realize that the process can be reversed—that if the liquid is poured back into the original container, the amount should be the same. The psychological criterion for a reversible operation is that of conservation. $+A$ is reversed by $-A$.

This is a **concrete** operational stage because the child is obtaining ideas from actions on such concrete objects as water and clay. At the beginning of the concrete operational level the ideas of the child are still based on observation and experience with objects in the physical

Figure 4-3. Shonda, 6, is preoperational for conservation of quantity concept. She thinks the amount of liquid changes when poured into a different shaped container because it "looks" like more.

world, but he is beginning to generalize or break away from manipulation of objects as a way of "knowing." When these generalizations are complete and correct, the child is at the concrete operational level.

Figure 4-4. Some children like Robert, 6, like to establish equality of liquid themselves in beginning conservation task.

   This level is important mathematically as well as psychologically because many of the operations are mathematical in nature. For example, these operations at the concrete level include, according to Piaget, those of "classification, ordering, the construction of the idea of number, spatial and temporal operations, and all the fundamental operations of elementary logic of classes and relations of elementary mathematics, of elementary geometry and even of elementary physics." [2]

   Operations at this level involve a mathematical structure Piaget calls "grouping"—putting objects together to form a class, separating a collection into subclasses, ordering elements in some way, ordering events in time, and so on.

   Ordering or seriation involves, for example, the ability to order ten objects by length. This requires the mathematical idea of the transitive property—if B is longer than A and C is longer than B, we can logically conclude that C is longer than A. The preoperational child is unable to use this logic and will put stick C by stick A to satisfy himself that C is longer than A.

   The idea of class inclusion is also impossible for the preoperational child. He is unable to consider which is larger, a class or group of birds or a class of ducks. (See Chapter 5.)

Figure 4-5.   Misty, 7, preoperational for hierarchical classification of ducks, birds and animals. She cannot make the necessary classifications.

[2] Jean Piaget. "Development and Learning," *Journal of Research in Science Teaching,* 2 (1964), p. 3.

Figure 4-6. Susan and John, both 9, are concrete operational. They can make the necessary classifications for a hierarchical classification.

The idea of linear measurement is also impossible for the preoperational child. He thinks the length of a stick changes when it is moved. (See Chapter 14.)

Formal Operations Stage

The last or fourth stage is the **formal operations** stage or the hypothetic-deductive operational level. This does not usually occur until eleven to twelve years of age. The child now reasons or hypothesizes with symbols or ideas rather than needing objects in the physical world as a basis for his thinking. He can operate with the form of an argument and ignore its empirical content. He can use the procedures of the logician or scientist—a hypothetic-deductive procedure that no longer ties his thoughts to existing reality. He has attained new mental structures and constructed new operations.

These new structures include the propositional combinations of symbolic logic—implication (if–then), disjunction (either–or, or both), exclusion (either–or), reciprocal implication, and so on.[3]

---

[3] For a full discussion, see Jean Piaget and Barbel Inhelder, *The Psychology of the Child*. New York: Basic Books, Inc., 1969, Chap. 5.

At the formal level it becomes possible to establish any relations between classes bringing together elements singly, in twos, threes, and so on. This generalization of classification and relations of order culminates in a combinatorial system—combinations and permutations. This combinatorial system is of prime importance in the extension of the power of thought.[4]

Children's understanding of combinations can be investigated with different-colored counters by asking how many different ways the counters can be grouped or combined in smaller groups of two or three, for example. Children's understanding of permutations can be investigated by showing them a row of different-colored objects and asking them in how many ways the row can be arranged. Children at the concrete operational level do an incomplete job, being unable to make the necessary generalizations. At the formal operational level, around twelve years of age, the child is able to develop a complete method of solving the problems (first combinations and a little later permutations) without, of course, discovering the formulas.[5] (See also pp. 12–13.)

The child can now also consider the powerful mathematical idea of a proportion, which allows him to make maps reduced to an arbitrary scale—to solve problems of time and distance, problems of probability, and geometrical problems involving similarity.

Factors Affecting Mental Development

There are **four** factors affecting mental development as the child proceeds through the stages of development just described—**organic growth** (maturation), **experience, social interaction** or transmission, and **equilibration.**

Organic Growth Factor

The first of these factors is organic growth, especially maturation of the nervous and endocrine systems. Maturation consists essentially of opening up new possibilities and is a necessary but not sufficient condition for the appearance of certain behavior patterns. For example, although vision is coordinated at about four and one-half months, the organic conditions for visual perception are not fully realized until adolescence.[6]

[4] Ibid., p. 133.
[5] Ibid.
[6] Ibid., p. 154.

Experience Factor

With reference to the experience factor, there are two types of experience that are different from a psychological standpoint and important from a pedagogical standpoint. First there is a physical experience, and second there is a logical mathematical experience. The act of weighing two objects to determine if they have the same weight would be a physical experience. Weight is a property of an object or objects, such as pebbles.

The logical mathematical experience in contrast comes not from the object or objects themselves but from the action of the learner on the objects. For example, a child under seven is given a set of pebbles and asked to place them in a row. He is asked to count them in one direction and then in the other. He then places the pebbles in a circle and counts them in one direction and then the other. He then tries another arrangement. He discovers that the number is always the same and is independent of the order. He discovers a property of his actions on the pebbles and not a property of pebbles. This is quite another form of experience and marks the beginning of mathematical abstraction. The subsequent deduction is "interiorizing" the action carried out on the pebbles so that pebbles will no longer be necessary.

Similarly, the child can be asked to weigh three objects: A, B, and C. This is a physical experience. But if B is heavier than A and C is heavier than B, can the child predict which is heavier—C or A—or will he have to weigh C and A again?

The logical or mathematical structure of transitivity necessary to realize that C must be heavier than A involves a logical or mathematical experience. Although we can provide a physical environment and physical knowledge by having children do things such as weigh objects, the mathematical structure of transitivity is not "taught." This idea is discussed again later in the chapter in Piaget's reaction to experiments by Smedslund.

Social Transmission Factor

The third factor, that of social transmission or educational transmission, involves the imparting of knowledge by language. This factor is important, but only when the child has a "structure" that allows him to understand the language being used. And it is at this point that a child often becomes lost, the teacher not realizing that he does not yet have the necessary structures. The relation "brother of" or "sister of" may mean something different to the young child, for example. He sees the other children as his brothers and sisters but does not see himself as a "brother of" the other children in the family. The reversibility of the "brother of" or "sister of" relation is not yet understood. The child can think in only one direction.

Equilibration Factor

The fourth factor, equilibration or self-regulation, is the fundamental one, according to Piaget. One form of equilibration is the coordination of the first three factors. But there is another form. The child having passed through the necessary stages of maturation is shown two balls of clay the same size. With the verbal guidance of a teacher, the child is asked to flatten one ball and is then asked if there is more in one than the other. He is not sure and compensates for the action of flattening by restoring the flat clay to its original form. He realizes that they are the same. It is this compensation type of action or reversibility that leads him eventually to a stage of equilibrium in which he knows that transformations in shape do not change the amount. This process of equilibration is an active process involving a change in one direction being compensated for by a change in the opposite direction. The term **equilibration**, or self-regulation, is used in the sense that it is used in cybernetics—processes with feed back and feed forward, of processes that regulate themselves by progressive compensation of systems, in a sense like an electronic computer.

Children of less than seven are usually unable to reconcile apparent contradictions such as that when one stick is placed above another it looks longer, yet placed side by side the sticks are found to be of the same length. Older children are able to accommodate to this information—that the position a stick occupies does not determine its length. A new mental "equilibrium" has been established.

For this equilibrium to occur, the child must act or "operate" himself on objects. It is not sufficient to explain why if ideas are to become a part of his own mental structures.

Piaget would agree with Dewey that the child must experience things for himself. Good pedagogy will involve providing an environment in which children can try things out for themselves and find their own answers. Piaget went so far as to say:

> If they read about it, it will be deformed as is all learning that is not the result of the subject's own activity. . . . teaching means creating situations where structures can be discovered; it does not mean transmitting structures which may be assimilated at nothing other than a verbal level. . . . a teacher would do better not to correct a child's schemas, but to provide situations so he will correct

them himself. . . . words are probably not a short cut to understanding; the level of understanding seems to modify the language that is used rather than vice-versa.[7]

Equilibration as a Biological Process

The idea of "instinct" as a way of knowing or knowledge has not been acceptable in psychology. In an evolutionary, biological orientation, instinctual or innate knowledge is acceptable—a knowledge that develops over thousands of years of development of a species. In such a context, individual learning can be seen as a special case of biological learning that is at the center of the living process of evolution.

Piaget would hold with Darwin that this evolutionary knowledge results from environmental pressures and chance gene mutations. But also very important is a dimension of this development that has received little attention.

Within this evolutionary and individual development framework, Piaget postulates that there is a regulatory and organizing factor, a self-regulatory factor already referred to as **equilibration**. In the lower level of the animal kingdom this factor of internal coordinating movements is quite rigid, even though it may be quite complex (e.g., bees locating honey). Behavior patterns in mammals are not given or predetermined genetically. Patterns of behavior are not specific and not necessarily triggered by a sensory cue. Animal behavior is not rigid in its adaptation. One of the best examples of non-specific motor activity is the human hand. By acting on and manipulating objects a child begins to develop a knowledge of his environment.

In man, evolutionally, there is a breaking of instinctual patterns of behavior, and these are replaced by a hereditary programming in favor of two new kinds of self-regulation or adaptation that are more flexible and constructive, assimilation and accommodation. **Assimilation** involves treating, filtering, or modifying data from the physical world in such a way as to incorporate it into the mental structures of the individual. When new data conflict with old, the modification of internal schemes to fit or accommodate to this new data is called

---

[7]Duckworth, op. cit., pp. 317–319.

accommodation. These processes involve revising partial understandings, broadening concepts, and relating one idea to another.

Piaget insists that these organizing mechanisms of assimilation and accommodation are primarily internal activities. They are ignored in the school of psychology that bases intelligence on the mechanism of association, an external process. Association involves control or development of the mind by "chaining," a series of external stimuli or connections. The mind is then simply a response mechanism. Piaget contends, however, that the mind can and does operate on its own.

All man's past history is a prelude to his capacity for logical thinking today. But in the individual the ability to think logically is developmental, involving stages of development through which each child must go before he reaches the operational or logical level of thought.

Psychological and Mathematical Operations

To know an object or event, according to Piaget, is not simply to look at it or hear about it and make a mental copy or image of it. Knowledge is not a copy of reality. To know an object is to act on it, to modify it or transform it, and, in the process, to understand the way the object is constructed. Such an act is called an **operation.** An operation is the essence of knowledge. It is an interiorized (mental) action that modifies the object. As such it is a psychological operation.

The term **operation** also has a special meaning in mathematics. The fundamental processes of arithmetic, such as addition, are operations. In the sentence $3 + 2 = 5$, the symbol + represents an operation on the numbers 3 and 2, which produces the number 5.

Whereas in mathematics, addition and subtraction may be thought of as different operations, in the psychological sense addition and subtraction are a *reversible* operation, and addition is not meaningful to the child unless the operation can be reversed. If $3 + 2 = 5$, then 5 is equal to what two numbers?

Children may be introduced to addition at the concrete level by joining sets of objects and noting the resulting number. This "joining" of sets is still another mathematical operation, called **union** of sets.

Definition of an Operation

Piaget defines an operation in terms of four fundamental characteristics:

1. An operation is an action that can be internalized, that is, carried out in thought as well as physically.
2. An operation is an action that is reversible—that can take place in one direction or the opposite. Time, for example, is not reversible, but addition is. Add 1 and 1 which is 2, and then subtract 1 from 2 which is 1 again. There are two types of reversibility. One is by inversion or negation: $+A - A = 0$ or $+1 - 1 = 0$. The second type of reversibility is that of reciprocity, which is a reversal of order rather than a negation. If $A = B$, then $B = A$ (symmetry).
3. An operation supposes some conservation or invariance, even though it is a transformation or action. In addition, for example, we can transform the way we group the addends, such as $4 + 1$ or $3 + 2$, but the sum remains the same.
4. An operation does not exist alone but is a part of a larger structure or a system of operations, such as the whole numbers, that includes many mathematical structures, such as the additive group and the rules for associativity, commutativity, transitivity, and closure.

Similarly, in logic, a logical class does not exist in isolation but is a part of the total structure of classification. To classify using the **inclusion relation**, for example, consider a city such as Miami, Florida. Miami is in or "included" in Florida, Florida is "included" in the United States, the United States is "included" in North America, North America is "included" in the northern hemisphere, the northern hemisphere is "included" in the sphere or earth, which is "included" in the solar system, and so on. Thus a hierarchy of classification is built. It is these operational structures of classification that are the natural psychological reality and basis for the development of human knowledge.

Biology, Mathematics, and Three Types of Knowledge

The meaning of knowledge, particularly "logico-mathematical" knowledge as related to biology, is the subject of one of Piaget's latest books, *Biology and Knowledge*.[8]   His focus on logico-mathe-matical knowledge makes the book of particular interest to mathe-matics educators.

Most biologists, according to Piaget, have taken the position that knowledge consists basically of information drawn from our environ-ment (acquired experience) and of figurative or motor responses to sensorial stimuli.[9]   This is the familiar stimulus–response mechanism or connection S–R, the brain simply being a response, recording or registering data from outside the organism.

In contrast to this commonly held and oversimplified view, Piaget claims that intelligence and knowledge are only meaningful if con-sidered in terms of the level of development of the human organism.

The basic types of cognitive functions include

1. Instinctive or reflex actions whose programming is inherited—sucking, blinking, jerking, and so on.
2. Perceptual or sensory activities—seeing colors, feeling surfaces, and so on.
3. Acquired behavior involving conditioning (Pavlov's dog), the formation of habits, and various types of memory.
4. Logico-mathematical structures.

Exercising these cognitive functions in man results in three forms of knowledge.   The first, **instinctive**, is very limited in man but very complex (although rigid) in some members of the animal kingdom, for example bird migrations.   The second and much broader type of knowledge is that of **physical experience**—experi-ence of physical objects in space—that is, noting facts about ob-jects such as that wood floats and water freezes.   The third type of knowledge, **logico-mathematical knowledge**, is an extension of the second, and this knowledge achieves an independence of ex-perience; and even where it is bound up with objects, the knowl-edge springs from **actions** performed on the objects rather than the objects themselves.

As an example of logico-mathematical knowledge, Piaget[10] cites a mathematician friend whose first interest in mathematics came as a child when he arranged a set of pebbles in a row and found that the sum was the same no matter from which end he began to count. The order was not in the pebbles; it was **he** who put the pebbles in a line.

[8] Jean Piaget. *Biology and Knowledge*. Chicago: University of Chicago Press, 1971.
[9] Ibid., p. 2.
[10] Jean Piaget. *Genetic Epistemology*. New York: Columbia University Press, 1970, pp. 16–17.

Neither was the sum in the pebbles; it was **he** who united them. The physical objects could just as well have been beans or buttons.

The actions just described Piaget characterizes as individual actions—throwing, pushing, touching, and so on. The result of such action on objects may be a simple type of abstraction.

A second type of abstraction, however, reflective abstraction, is based not on individual actions but on coordinated actions. Coordinated actions may be of several types:

1. They can be joined together (additive coordination).
2. They can succeed each other (ordinal or sequential coordination).
3. A correspondence between two actions.
4. Intersections among actions.

All these coordinated actions have parallels in logical structures and are the basis of logical structures as they develop later in thought.[11]

These logico-mathematical structures involve activities largely internal, as contrasted to the largely external nature of perception and conditioning as a type of intelligence.

It is, of course, the logico-mathematical structures that the mathematics educator is particularly interested in. More important, if these processes are largely internal, what part does the teacher play? The conditioning processes so often used are certainly not appropriate.

Learning

The preceding discussion dealt with "knowledge," defined by Piaget as a **spontaneous process** of total development involving the physiological, emotional, and mental systems. In contrast, a teacher or psychologist would describe learning as a limited process that is **provoked** rather than spontaneous—limited to a single problem or structure. A basic theory of learning (Thorndike) has been based on a stimulus–response sequence or schema. Piaget rejects this theory in that it omits the vital intermediary of the mental "structures" of the learner:

> I think the stimulus–response schema, while I won't say it is fake, is in any case entirely incapable of explaining cognitive learning.

---

[11] Ibid., p. 18.

Why? Because when you think of a stimulus–response schema, you think usually that first of all there is a stimulus and then a response is set off by this stimulus. For my part I am convinced that the response was there first. . . . a stimulus is a stimulus only if it is significant, and it becomes significant only to the extent that there is a structure which permits its assimilation, a structure which can integrate this stimulus and at the same time set off a response. I would propose that the stimulus response schema be written in a circular form—in the form of a structure or schema *which is not simply one way.* . . .[12]

In the stimulus–response schema, the fundamental relation is that of **association**. In contrast to this, Piaget considers the fundamental relations to be **assimilation** and **accommodation**, defined as the integration of any sort of reality into a mental structure, and thinks this to be of primary pedagogical importance. His conception of intelligence differs markedly from that of the designers of many of the intelligence tests. Piaget's theory implies a natural, ordinal scale of intelligence that contrasts in important ways with the view of a more-or-less fixed IQ.[13]

As to how organized knowledge is acquired, then, Piaget finds both the maturational and learning theory approach inadequate. Maturation processes are not in themselves enough to explain learning. Neither is the stimulus–response learning theory sufficient. Neither is the combination of these two theories sufficient to explain learning. Piaget believes that a third kind of developmental process, which he calls **equilibration**, must occur.

As an example, the child acquires some unorganized ideas through social learning or experience with the environment, but at some point these ideas or "schemas" conflict, and forces must be set in motion to harmonize these conflicting ideas. This is the process of equilibration, which occurs at a certain stage in the development of children. It is a logico-mathematical process. The child at about age seven is often able to reject the impression of appearance. He substitutes the logic that if two sticks placed side by side are the same length to begin with, although one may look longer if moved, the process can be reversed and the stick placed in its original position; hence logically the sticks must remain the same length.

[12] Duckworth, op. cit., pp. 329–330.
[13] J. M. Hunt. *Intelligence and Experience.* New York: The Ronald Press Company, 1961, p. 39.

Stendler summarizes Piaget's theory of intelligence or cognitive development as follows:

> For Piaget, intelligence is not something that is qualitatively or quantitatively fixed at birth, but rather, is a form of adaptation characterized by equilibrium. Part of man's biological inheritance is a striving for equilibrium in mental processes as well as in other physiological processes. Twin processes are involved: assimilation and accommodation. The child assimilates information from the environment which may upset existing equilibrium, and then accommodates present structures to the new so that equilibrium is restored.[14]

Acceleration of Learning

To what extent, then, can these mental structures be affected, or their development accelerated, by learning? Can the concept of conservation, for example, be accelerated?

A six-year-old child observes two sets of objects and says the number is the same. He counts and finds "five" in each set.

Figure 4–7

The objects are then spread apart in one set.

Figure 4–8

The child now says there is more in the spread-out set. Number is still meaningless.

---

[14] Celia B. Stendler. "Piaget's Developmental Theory of Learning and Its Implications for Instruction in Science," in E. Victor and M. Lerner, eds., *Readings in Science Education for the Elementary School.* New York: The Macmillan Company, 1967, p. 336.

Piaget answers:

> This question [of accelerating learning] never fails to amuse students and faculty in Geneva, for they regard it as typically American. Tell an American that a child develops certain ways of thinking at seven, and he immediately sets about to try to develop those same ways of thinking at six or even five years of age. Investigators in countries other than America have tried to accelerate the development of logical thinking, and we have available today a considerable body of research on what works and what doesn't work. Most of the research has not worked. It hasn't worked because experimenters have not paid attention to equilibrium theory. The researchers have tried to teach an answer, a particular response, rather than to develop operations. They have tried to teach the child that of course the hot dog (shaped piece of clay) will weigh as much as the clay ball; just put both on a two-pan-balance and you'll see. But the child is completely unconvinced unless he shuffles the data around in his mind, using one or more of the operations I've described. Learning a fact by reinforcement does not in and of itself result in mental adaptation.[15]

Mildred Almy confirms the conclusions of Piaget: "Taken as a whole such attempts have been rather unsuccessful."[16] Experience is a factor, but it is not the major factor.

> So far as the conservation of the number of objects in a set is concerned, the most obvious way to teach the child is to have him count before and after the objects are rearranged. If he does this often enough, with appropriate reinforcement to help him recognize that the correct answer is the same number regardless of the arrangement, one would expect him to shift eventually to conservation. (Piaget contends, on the other hand, that such counting is meaningless. . . .)[17]

The child must first develop to the stage of conservation of number, usually six and one-half to seven years of age, before he can be "taught" number.

Similarly, a youngster observes two balls of clay that have the same weight. One ball is then pressed into the shape of a sausage and the child is asked if they still weigh the same. Has the weight been conserved? Not until eight or nine years of age is the average child able

---

[15] Ibid., p. 343.
[16] Mildred Almy. *Young Children's Thinking.* New York: Columbia University Teachers College Press, 1967, p. 42.
[17] Ibid., pp. 42–43.

to rationalize this idea. The conservation of volume is not achieved until eleven to twelve years of age.

Piaget describes the work of an American psychologist, Smedslund, who conducted experiments with children on the conservation of weight and the transitivity of weights; that is, if *A* weighs as much as *B* and *B* weighs as much as *C*, then *A* weighs as much as *C*. Smedslund was successful, in conducting a series of weighings, to get five- and six-year-old children to generalize that the weight was not changed when the shape was changed. The children, however, resisted the idea of transitivity and could not generalize it. In evaluating this research, Piaget states:

> He successfully obtained a learning of what I call physical experience (which is not surprising since it is simply a question of noting facts about objects), but he did not successfully obtain a learning in the construction of the logical structure. *This doesn't surprise me either since the logical structure is not the result of physical experience. It cannot be obtained by external reinforcement. The logical structure is reached only through internal equilibration, by self-regulation, and the external reinforcement of seeing that the balance did not suffice to establish this logical structure of transitivity.*[18]

A study by Elkind[19] corroborates Piaget's findings concerning the age at which children are able to conserve quantity, weight, and volume.

In the foreword to *Young Children's Thinking*, Piaget restates his position:

> In the area of logico-mathematical structures, children have real understanding only of that which they invent themselves, and each time that we try to teach them something too quickly, we keep them from reinventing it themselves. Thus, there is no good reason to try to accelerate this development too much; the time which seems to be wasted in personal investigation is really gained in the construction of methods.[20]

Jerome Bruner classified Piaget as "unquestionably the most impressive figure in the field of cognitive development,"[21] but Piaget

[18] Stendler, op. cit., p. 330.
[19] David Elkind. "Children's Discovery of Mass, Weight and Volume," in I. E. Sigel and F. H. Hooper, eds., *Logical Thinking in Children*. New York: Holt, Rinehart and Winston, Inc., 1968, p. 17.
[20] Almy, op. cit., p. vi.
[21] Jerome Bruner. *Toward a Theory of Instruction*. Cambridge, Mass.: Harvard University Press, 1967, pp. 6–7.

does not agree with him on acceleration. In a speech at New York University in March 1967, he commented as follows:

> A few years ago Bruner made a claim which has always astounded me; namely, that you can teach anything in an intellectually honest way to any child at any age if you go about it in the right way. Well, I don't know if he still believes that. . . . it's probably possible to accelerate but maximum acceleration is not desirable. There seems to be an optimum time. What this optimum time is will surely depend on each individual and on the subject matter.[22]

Piaget concluded:

> Learning is subordinated to development and not vice-versa. . . . No doubt you will object that some investigators have succeeded in teaching operational structures. But when I am faced with these facts, I always have three questions . . . first, is this learning lasting? What remains two weeks or a month later? . . . Second, how much generalization is possible? What makes learning interesting is the possibility of "transfer" to a new situation . . . [and third] what was the operational level of the subject before the experience and what more complex structures has this learning succeeded in achieving?[23]

This may seem discouraging to the teacher, that there is a readiness stage that the child must reach before logical concepts can be taught or rather learned. The teacher can, however, be instrumental in structuring an appropriate environment in which children will develop as they are able.

Piaget does qualify his remarks on the teaching of logical concepts by saying some can be taught if the structure you want to teach can be supported by simpler, more elementary, logical mathematical structures already possessed by the child. For example, can a child be "taught" conservation of number? As an experiment he is given seven blue tokens and he is asked to put down as many red tokens. At the preoperational stage he puts a red token opposite each blue token, but if the red tokens are then spread out, he no longer thinks there are the same number of blue as red. The conservation of number in this experiment is not achieved usually until six or seven years

[22] Frank Jennings. "Jean Piaget, Notes on Learning," *Saturday Review*, May 20, 1967, p. 82.

[23] Jean Piaget. "Development and Learning," in E. Victor and M. S. Lerner, eds., *Readings in Science Education for the Elementary School*. New York: The Macmillan Company, 1967, pp. 332–333.

of age. But a simpler experiment may speed the process—for example, a child is given a pile of beads and asked to put one in each of two jars and then to continue the process. If one of the two jars is hidden from his view as he continues the process, will he conserve the number idea? Is there still the same number in each jar? The four-year-old will not want to make a prediction or generalize, but the generalization will be made at about five and one-half years of age—thus at an earlier age than the generalization about the red and blue tokens. But Piaget would qualify any such acceleration by simpler experiment by saying that the generalization "may" occur and that the influence "may not be immediate."

Language and Intelligence

Man, the most highly developed mammal, has the most highly developed language or ability to communicate. Communication has been extremely important in extending the knowledge of mankind. However, at the level of the five- to twelve-year-old child, language is another matter.

There is a commonly held view that language has a thought-structuring property or that language produces thought; hence through language one can teach children concepts. Piaget, as Furth points out,[24] is one of the few scholars, if not the only one, who does not think language is intrinsically necessary for operational thinking. The phrase "operational thinking" refers to logical thought or reasoning ability and not ability to recall a fact such as "Richmond is the capital of Virginia." The meaning of "capital" would, however, involve operational thought.

There is a close relationship between language and thought at the highest operational level of development (the propositional or hypo-thetico-deductive thought stage), but this stage does not usually occur until around twelve years of age. This means, if Piaget is correct, that most children of five to twelve do not achieve operational thinking or reasoning ability through words but must do so through their own operations on objects in the physical world, as in a laboratory setting.

[24] Hans G. Furth. *Piaget and Knowledge.* Englewood Cliffs, N.J.: Prentice-Hall, Inc., 1969, p. 109.

Language may direct attention to pertinent factors in a problem by asking "Would this help?" Language may also control perceptual activities by saying "Look at this." Thus language can prepare an operation but is neither sufficient nor necessary for the formation of thought at the concrete operational level.[25]

Piaget restated his position in a symposium in 1963 as follows: "There is little relation between the two domains of verbal comprehension and concrete reasoning, as if at this stage [concrete operations] one had to do with two different processes."[26]

As arguments for this position, Piaget[27] cites first that there is a sensory-motor type of intelligence that appears around one year of age, while language appears around the middle of the second year. This sensory-motor type of intelligence is characterized as an action or practical type of intelligence aimed at getting results. For example, the baby develops a way of getting a toy on a blanket, such as by pulling the blanket. Such intelligence is capable of being repeated and generalized (a schema). Piaget finds in this sensory-motor intelligence a certain logic of inclusion, ordering, and correspondence which will be foundations for later logical and mathematical structures. There is also a conservation and reversibility characteristic. At around one year of age the child realizes that an object hidden from view still exists (object permanence).

A second argument is based on children whose thinking is logical but who do not have language available to them—the deaf and dumb. These children are delayed with respect to normal children but not as much as blind children. Blind children have the great disadvantage of not being able to make the same coordinations in space.

A third argument is based on the work of Chomsky. He has reversed the classical view that logic is derived from language. Instead, language is based on intellectual structures. Logic is not derived from language; language is based on a kernel of reason.

A fourth and final argument is based on the work of a psycholinguist, Hermine Sinclair. One experiment involved linguistic training for a group of children who had not reached the stage of conservation. She found only minimum progress after linguistic training, that is, by about 10 per cent of the children.

While words do not "give" understanding at the concrete operational level, the words used by children are often indicative of their level of understanding. Thus for very young children any man may

[25] Ibid., p. 130.
[26] Ibid., p. 129.
[27] Piaget. *Genetic Epistemology*, op. cit., pp. 45–49.

be "Daddy." This is a logically correct classification as far as sex is concerned. Daddy is a man, but of course not all men are Daddy.

Children at the preoperational level often use words as absolutes. For example, in comparing two quantities, one larger than the other, the child says there is "a lot" or there is "a little." One is "small," the other "big." The relation between the two quantities is not stated. In contrast, children at the concrete operational level often use words that better express the **relation between** the two quantities, such as saying there is "more" or "less" in one than the other. They may also express two properties in one sentence; in comparing two pencils, one short and thick, the other long and thin, the response may be one is "longer and thinner" than the other.

Social Interaction

Having possibly downplayed the importance of language, Piaget did say "Without interchange of thought and cooperation with others the individual would never come to group his operations into a coherent whole. . . ." [28]

Although language does not structure thought, it may provide ideas for thought which otherwise might not be considered. There is an importance of action with people as well as action upon objects.

The word "cooperation" in the quotation above is worth noting. Emphasis should be placed on cooperation in the learning process rather than on competition.

Memory and Intelligence

Memory is often thought of as a storing of information, but this oversimplifies its true meaning. Knowledge enters the organism in two ways, either by evolutionary means (a biological memory or memory of the genes) or developmentally through the individual. Biological memory is often described as instinctual, such as that which causes bird or fish migrations. The amazing amount of knowledge necessary for bees to signal directions to other bees for a source

---

[28] Jean Piaget. *The Origins of Intelligence in Children.* New York: W. W. Norton & Company, Inc., 1963, p. 193.

of nectar is considered to be a biological memory. It involves ability, for example, to transpose angles and to consider the position of the sun even when it may not be visible.[29]   Our concern, however, is more with knowledge as it occurs in the individual on a developmental basis.

Piaget rejects the common notion of memory as a "copy" of reality. There does not even need to be an internal image for the first level of memory, that of recognition. Recognition is a part of every sensory-motor habit. The baby "recognizes" his mother or the feeding bottle and starts to suck without being able to construct a mental image.[30]

There are three levels of memory; the first, **recognition**, which is a sensory-motor response, has just been described. The second and third levels do involve the common notion of memory as the ability of "recall," but to "recall" what? The second level of memory is an imitative one based on sensory impressions.

This second level of memory, which is based on an ability to accommodate or organize sensory data or impressions, Piaget calls **"figurative"** knowing. A child draws or imitates a triangle based on remembered sensory impressions. This is in contrast to the third level of memory, which necessitates thought at the operational level. At this level the child "operates" on reality and transforms it into an object as he "knows" it. It is this third level of memory or knowing— **true understanding**—that is the main concern of the teacher. Can the child still draw a triangle after the immediate sensory impressions are lost? Has he abstracted the idea of a triangle as any three-sided figure?

The differences in the second and third levels of memory are easy to demonstrate. Piaget used a simple but ingenious experiment of showing children a picture of a wine decanter partially filled with red wine and tilted.

Figure 4-9

[29] Furth, op. cit., p. 149.
[30] Ibid., p. 150.

Children of six and seven years of age are able to make a drawing or copy of this picture with little difficulty. An hour later the majority of the children can still make a correct "copy." However, a week later they remember the tilted wine bottle but are not able to draw the liquid correctly.

The figurative knowledge or memory has become weaker and the child must now rely on his operational understanding of the phenomenon of level or horizontal. Since not until around the age of nine does the child develop the concept of horizontal in space, the six- and seven-year-olds now draw the liquid as

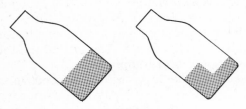

Figure 4–10

When the child reaches the operational level, he can remember how to draw the liquid correctly regardless of how the bottle was tilted or how long ago he "saw" the bottle tilted. These stages of development are discussed more fully in Chapter 11.

A similar result can be obtained by showing six- and seven-year-olds line segments arranged in order of length.

Figure 4–11

At first they can make a copy correctly based on remembered sensory perception, but later, when the image fades, they are unable to "order" unless they have reached the operational level of understanding of "seriation" or "order." The operational structure of seriation or ordering is fundamental in mathematics and is discussed more fully in Chapter 6.

Piaget and IQ Tests[31]

In studying intelligence, what are the similarities and differences between the Piagetian developmental approach and the mental test or psychometric approach?

Similarities

Both viewpoints hold that mental ability is at least in part genetically determined. And from this assumption both recognize the importance of maturation processes.

Neither approach uses the experimental method as it is usually conceived. Most psychometric tests are correlational in character, relating test scores of children and parents, twins, and so on. No attempts are made to modify intelligence. Neither did Piaget use the experimental approach, because it was not appropriate for the problems he wanted to study. He used a natural history type of inquiry in which relevant phenomena were carefully observed and classified. In so doing he exposed "dark sides" of children's minds, which the adult often has difficulty believing.

A third commonality is what each considers intelligence to be. The psychometricians, as represented by Jensen, characterize intelligence as the ability to generalize and abstract or to determine relations. Although intelligence tests do measure language and perceptual skills, the central idea is rational thought. Piaget, of course, is primarily concerned with reasoning ability and logical thought, which he calls knowledge at the logico-mathematical level.

Differences

The differences in these two approaches are essentially (1) the type of genetic causality, (2) the description of mental growth, and (3) the contributions of nature and nurture.

The psychometric conception of intelligence assumes that intelligence is randomly distributed in a given population and that such distributions should resemble the normal probability of the bell-shaped curve. This allows for ease of comparison of an individual with the rest of the population.

Piaget, in contrast, is more concerned with the nonrandom factors in the genetic determination of intelligence—the biochemical organ-

---

[31] This section is taken primarily from David Elkind, "Two Approaches to Intelligence," *Children and Adolescents—Interpretative Essays on Jean Piaget.* New York: Oxford University Press, 1970, pp. 115–135.

izers and organization centers and how they work in sequence as the child moves from one developmental stage to the next. This sequence, he maintains, is invariant. Piaget is more concerned with intraindividual changes in the course of his development, whereas the mental-test approach is more concerned with interindividual differences in ability or comparing one individual to others.

In considering the chronology of mental growth, the psychometric approach is to plot a learning curve. Given an IQ score at age eight, for example, the curve predicts what the intelligence will be at any given later date. In so doing these scores do not say anything about the amount or quality of the knowledge, but only that from what a child has at a given age a prediction can be made as to what he will have at a future time.

Looking at the problem from the Piaget standpoint, mental growth means the formation of new mental structures and consequently new mental abilities. From the standpoint of utility, the Piaget approach is **qualitative**, which makes it particularly useful in diagnosing learning difficulties. The IQ test, in contrast, is primarily quantitative and is of practical value in predicting school success.

The IQ tests do have items that test the various levels of intelligence, but the levels or qualitative differences are ignored by assigning equivalent point scores to the various test items regardless of the mental processes involved.

Psychometrizing the Piaget Tasks

Intelligence scales and intelligence tests are now being built more consistent with the Piaget tasks. What will be the value of such tests? Elkind[32] considers them of little value at this time, since the general intelligence tests look at human abilities in a broader sense. They measure language ability, rote memory, perceptual motor coordination, and reasoning ability.

Tests of educational achievement are generally geared to what is taught in the schools, and they measure, with some fidelity, school progress. The Piaget tasks, in contrast, assess those concepts that a child learns more or less on his own. The curriculum must be restructured before the Piaget tasks can be of much use in measuring school achievement.

[32] Ibid., p. 133.

5 Logical Classification

> Our hypothesis is that the construction of number goes hand in hand with the development of logic and that a pre-numerical period corresponds to the pre-logical level. . . . Logical and arithmetical operations therefore constitute a single system . . . the second resulting from generalization and fusion of the first under the complementary heading of "inclusion of classes." [1]

A prelogical and prenumerical level lasts for many children until approximately seven years of age. That they are at a prelogical and prenumerical stage can be shown by their inability to classify and through the lack of understanding of the conservation or invariance concept. The inclusion relation will be considered in this chapter and conservation of number will be discussed in Chapter 6.

Counting is often the first mathematical idea taught to children, but as such it is a rote-memory type of activity. The idea of number should grow out of an understanding of the inclusion relation as outlined in the quotation above. Classification serves as a basis, psychologically speaking, for the development of both logical and mathematical concepts.

[1] Jean Piaget. *The Child's Conception of Number.* New York: Humanities Press, Inc., 1952, p. viii.

In a recent work Piaget concludes on the basis of genetic data that

> The development of number does not occur earlier than that of classes (classificatory structures) or of . . . transitive relations [at seven to eight years of age on average].[2]
>
> This parallelism between the evolution of number, classes and seriation [ability to order], is thus a first piece of evidence in favour of their interdependence as against the view that there is an initial autonomy of number.[3]

First Experiences in Logical Classification

As children explore the world in which they live, they learn to recognize and name the various objects they see. Among the first objects recognized, for example, are mother and the feeding bottle. Later, other objects are pointed out and named, such as car, horse, or dog. These objects are recognized on the basis of certain physical properties, such as color, size, shape, or certain patterns of behavior.

In being able to recognize an object, the child has **classified** it into a certain category different from the many other objects, based on certain unique characteristics or properties. The study of the physical world (science) becomes one of classification—plants and animals being two of the most basic classifications. As new objects are discovered, they must be classified in relation to the objects already discovered.

Simple Classification

Some of the first classification experiences for school children are of a sorting type. Children should put objects back where they belong after they have finished playing with them. There are many objects in an elementary classroom and each has a place it "belongs to."

[2] Evert W. Beth and Jean Piaget. *Mathematical Epistemology and Psychology.* Dordrecht, Holland: D. Reidel Publishing Company, 1966, p. 259.
[3] Ibid., p. 261.

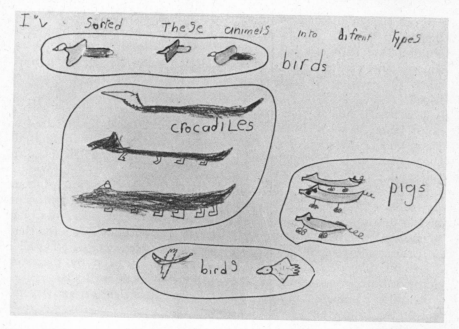

Figure 5-1. A collection of animals is sorted by a 6-year-old into categories. It is not clear why there are two separate lots of birds. From: *Mathematics Begins*, Nuffield Junior Mathematics Project. (Courtesy: John Wiley & Sons, New York, N.Y.)

The idea of sorting or classification is based on the idea of a **relation**. A child is playing with a doll that "belongs to" Susan. "Belongs to" is a relation of the doll to Susan. Because of this relation, the doll should be returned to Susan. Similarly, coats "belong on" the coat rack, tablets "belong in" the desk, and so on.

As children investigate objects, the objects may be classified or related in many ways. Some are heavier than others. This relation of "heavier than" can be investigated with scales. Some are "larger" than others. Some have a relation of "the same color." Some "float in water." Some do not. Children even classify in terms of "objects I want to play with" and "objects I do not want to play with." In geometry they will classify "objects with three edges" as triangles.

In performing such classification children are learning about the world in which they live. From such classification will later come definitions such as "a triangle is . . . ," "a family is . . . ," "a mother is . . . ," and "a river is . . . ."

From a psychological standpoint perceptual structures may be sufficient to solve a simple classification problem.   For example, if children are shown a set of objects such as cardboard cutouts of squares and circles in two colors and two sizes, sensory cues may allow the child to put the same shapes together or the same colors together.

It is worth noting that children will usually sort by shape before color, and last of all by size.   In asking the children to sort the objects, two boxes should be provided and the restriction made that **all** the objects must be put in the two boxes and also that **all** those in the same box must be alike in some way.

Children of about four years of age begin the classification arbitrarily, such as first by color and then switch to shape.   The categories or classes are not sharply defined and there is no overall plan.   If a plan is chosen, such as beginning with "the little round ones," such a classification will result in some of the objects not being classified at all.

Around five or six, children make the classification by shape or color or both.   Classifying by size is somewhat more difficult.

Another somewhat more difficult Piaget classification activity involved the following:

Figure 5-2

The method of sorting used by the children follows an age progression.   The youngest, less than five years old, make some sort of graphic or geometric display of the objects, arranging them in some kind of pattern, such as a square or house.   They are unable to classify the objects in accordance with some property, such as color, shape, or size.

At the next stage, ages five to nine, the geometric display of the objects is no longer the prime consideration by the child. He now attempts to classify by some property, such as color or shape. He is partially successful but does not realize that there is a hierarchy of classification. An eight-year-old is able to place or classify the objects into four different sets based on the property of shape. He then puts together the curved shapes classifying them as "*all* the 'rounds'."[4]

Relations Between Sets or Classes

Whereas the simple classification tasks just discussed may be solved by perceptual structures, the logic of class inclusion and hierarchical classification will require intellectual or logical structures. As expressed by Piaget, "A class cannot be constructed by perception but only by logic, for it pre-supposes a series of abstractions and generalizations from which it derives its meaning."

The necessary logical structure, from a teaching standpoint, will not be conveyed to the child by verbal explanation, good visual aids, repetition, or the like. The prelogical child will insist that a duck is a duck and not a bird, not being able to understand the logic of inclusion.

Children should have many experiences in determining properties of sets and relationships between sets. Such a study involves mathematics. Number, for example, is a **property** of a set of objects, and because of its importance in this book it is considered in Chapters 6, 7, and 8.

To properly classify objects, their **relation** to other objects already studied must be known. For example, consider a set of horses. Are they animals? To show such a relationship as a basis of classification, two circles may be drawn, one to represent horses, the other animals. The relative position of the circles shows the relation that exists between horses and animals. Logically, there are several possibilities.

---

[4] Barbel Inhelder and Jean Piaget. *The Early Growth of Logic in the Child.* New York: W. W. Norton & Company, Inc., 1969, p. 55.

If all horses are not animals, then the diagram should be drawn as

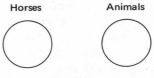

Figure 5-3

If some horses are animals and some not,

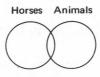

Figure 5-4

If **all** horses are animals, then

Figure 5-5

The third drawing expresses the relation correctly. The set or class of animals **includes** the set of horses. The **inclusion relation** is important in logic and mathematics. It is an idea used very often by Piaget as "class inclusion."

The illustrations shown are often called Venn diagrams. They provide a convenient and powerful way of expressing the relation between two or more sets. Our whole physical world can be structured into a hierarchy of classification.

In comparing any two sets of objects, the relation between them will always be one of three types:

1. Disjoint sets: those sharing no elements (boys and girls, ducks and fish).

2. Intersecting sets: those sharing some elements (blue-eyed girls and brown-haired girls).
3. One set a subset or included in the other (flowers include roses).

The last relation of inclusion was investigated at great length by Piaget and Inhelder in *The Early Growth of Logic in the Child.*[5] It is fundamental to building a hierarchy of classification.

Figure 5-6. Shonda, 6, is pre-operational for the inclusion relation concept. She says there are more daisies than flowers.

Children's understanding of the quantifiers "all," "some," and "none" will also be explored, since they are fundamental to correctly describing or understanding the inclusion relation. Are, for example, all horses animals? And are all animals horses?

[5] Ibid.; first translated into English in 1964.

The Inclusion Relation

Objects are included in a set based on certain common properties. For example,

The set of objects I like includes . . . .
The set of heavy objects includes . . . .
The set of red blocks includes . . . .
The set of objects that belong to Susan includes . . . .
The set of animals includes . . . .

In mathematics one set of numbers may include another; for example, the whole numbers include the odd numbers and the integers include the whole numbers. In geometry the set of quadrilaterals includes squares, rectangles, rhombi, and parallelograms. The idea that the set of people who live in Florida (circle F) includes the set of people who live in Miami (circle M) may be illustrated as

Figure 5-7

As children consider objects that belong to more than one class, or classes that overlap, the terms "some" and "all" become important. With these verbal tools children begin to describe the way classes overlap or include other classes. Thus "all" Miamians are Floridians but only "some" Floridians are Miamians. That children do not grasp such relations easily is evidenced by the following discussion.

The Family and the Inclusion Relation

1. A child, aged seven, is asked: "What is a family?" "It means people who live together."
2. Another child, aged nine, is asked: "What is a family?" "A father, mother, and children."
   "Does your father have a family?" "No, when he was little he had a family."

The child with his egocentric pattern of thought sees the family only as belonging to him. He does not see all members of the family as "included" in the family. The family is a relation only to him.

The Country and the Inclusion Relation

Are you Swiss? "No. I'm Genevan."

Up to the age of nine, according to Piaget, 75 per cent of the children deny being both Swiss and Genevan. Using Venn diagrams the child sees that Geneva is "in" Switzerland but does not comprehend the "part-to-whole" realtionship.

Figure 5-8

Switzerland simply surrounds Geneva. It is the shaded area in the illustration. The child "juxtaposes" or places Switzerland alongside Geneva. The child thinks of the part by itself, not in relation to the whole. As he thinks of the **part** in which he lives, Geneva, he is unable to see its **relation** to the **whole**, Switzerland.

The inclusion relation involves both logical and arithmetical operations not yet present in these children.

The Quantifiers "All," "Some," "None," and "One"

To solve classification problems it is necessary to realize that a class involves **two** kinds of properties or relations:

1. Properties that are **common** to a given class and the other classes to which it belongs (ducks are birds as well as ducks since they "have feathers," "can fly," and so on).
2. Properties that are **specific** to the given class that differentiate it such as "web feet," "color," and "shape."

The part-to-whole relations are conveyed by the quantifiers "all," "some," "none" and "one." The difficulties children have with such concepts are surprising to many teachers in training. Yet such difficulties must be realized for effective teaching.

All and Some

The words "all" and "some" are crucial in logical thinking. Not until a child is nine to ten years old is he usually able to use these words correctly in a logical sense for classification.

To test children's understanding of the words "all" and "some," Piaget used a set of objects that included red squares, blue squares, and blue circles but no red circles. The child is asked to identify the colors and shapes.

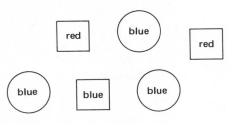

Figure 5-9

The child should then be asked:
"Are all the circles blue?"
"And are all the blue ones circles?"

A four- or five-year-old when asked "Are all the circles blue?" responds that they are not because "There is a blue square." He cannot make the distinction between "Are all the circles blue?" and "Are all the blue ones circles?" He is unable to establish logical classes and will usually be unable to do so until nine or ten years old.

The Singular Class

The concept of the singular class is not operational until eight or nine years of age,[6] and the empty or null class is not operational until ten to eleven years of age.[7] In investigating the singular class, such as "the sun" or "the moon" or the one that is different, Piaget used a set of three to six triangles all the same color except one. On the back of the one that is different is marked an X. The child is asked to pick out the one with an X on the back. Most are unable to do so until eight or nine years of age.[8]

---

[6] Ibid., p. 120.
[7] Ibid., p. 146.
[8] Richard W. Copeland. *Diagnostic and Learning Activities in Mathematics for Children.* New York: The Macmillan Company, 1974.

Figure 5-10. John, 9, is able to select the singleton set or one that is different (the circle).

The Empty or Null Set

The empty or null set is the set whose number of elements is zero. For example, the set of people 14 feet tall is an empty or null set or class. The idea of the empty set is not too difficult an idea for the adult to accept, but how about the child? Here is another example of an idea presently being introduced to children before they have the logical structure necessary to understand it.

Piaget and Inhelder used as an experiment a set of cards, some of which were pictures of houses, some with trees, some apples, and other items, and some blank cards. The children are asked if the cards can be classified into two sets.

> The children's reactions were very clear. It is only at 10-11 years that children adopt the classification which seems most natural to us: a division into blank cards versus cards with pictures. Until then we find three separate types of reaction, although these do not represent different levels of maturity: (1) the blank cards may be classified by a different criterion from the others, i.e. shape, instead of content; (2) they may be slipped in with the collections containing pictures; (3) they may be ignored and left in disorder while only

the picture-bearing cards are classified. In all three cases, the subject is refusing to construct a null class.[9]

The conclusion is

Concrete operations are bound up with the objects to which they apply. This supposes that these objects do exist, and so the notion of an empty class is excluded. Formal thinking, on the other hand, deals with structures independently of their content, and this is true even in the realm of classification. Thus what seems natural to children of 10-11 years, or to us, may not seem natural at 5-7 or even at 7-9. . . . That is why the null-class is rejected right up to the time when the structure of inclusion relations begins to be separated from their concrete content, at 10-11 years.[10]

Figure 5-11. John, 9, unable to make a null set classification, uses the blank cards as front yards for the houses.

Hierarchical Classification

To test children's understanding of a hierarchy of classification, Piaget used a set of 16 flowers. This set included 8 primulas, 4 of

[9] Inhelder and Piaget, op. cit., p. 147.
[10] Ibid., p. 149.

which were yellow. Logically, flowers include primulas and primulas include yellow primulas, but many children of less than nine or ten years are unable to consider correctly the transitive relationship of A to B to C. Asked the question, Are there more primulas or more flowers?, they respond that there are more primulas.

That A includes B or that there are more flowers than primulas was answered correctly by less than half of the seven-year-olds, by two out of three of the eight-year-olds, and by almost all nine- to ten-year-olds.

Using two questions—(1) Are there more primulas or more yellow primulas? and (2) Are there more flowers or more primulas?—correct responses to both questions were given by 26 per cent of the seven-year-olds, 61 per cent of the eight-year-olds, and 73 per cent of the nine- to ten-year-olds.[11]

As developed more fully on pages 113–114, once a set such as flowers is considered in terms of its subsets, such as primulas and yellow primulas, the primulas and yellow primulas may be compared successfully, but the child is unable to reverse the thought process from primulas back to flowers and hence to consider the relation of primulas to flowers.

Neither can the child consider successfully the transitive relation involved, that if A includes B and B includes C, then logically A must include C.

Multiple Classification

The idea of the classification of an object or objects in two or more sets simultaneously is often called multiple classification. This idea in mathematics, intersection, and in logic, conjunction, is discussed in a following section on logical connectives. Multiple classification is also discussed in Chapter 8 and in *Diagnostic and Learning Activities in Mathematics for Children.*[12]

Logical Classification Games

The teacher may use blocks of wood or cardboard in several shapes and paint them in three colors. There are also commercial materials

[11] Ibid., p. 109
[12] Copeland, op. cit.

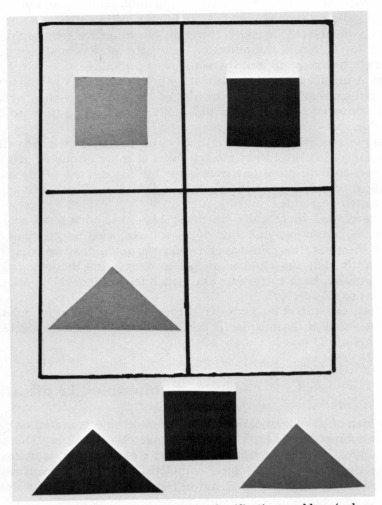

Figure 5-12.   Sample multiple classification problem (color
and shape).   Pick object from bottom that best fits empty
space. (Dark triangle.)

available, such as the Dienes attribute or logic blocks, which provide
games in classification and logical relations.[13]   These are plastic

[13] Z. P. Dienes and E. W. Golding. *Learning Logic, Logical Games*. New York:
Herder and Herder, Inc., 1966.

geometric models that involve four properties—size, color, thickness, and shape. Children enjoy playing with such blocks and will sort or classify the blocks in terms of some property or attribute, such as color or shape.

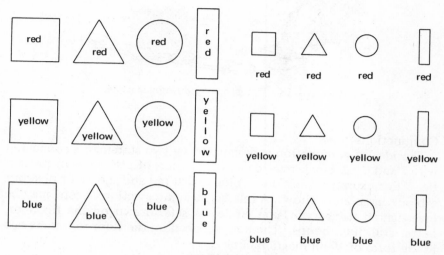

Figure 5-13

A sample game is the one-property-difference game, which involves a child picking out a block from the set that is a mixture of shapes, colors, and sizes. The next child must pick out another block that is exactly one attribute or property different from the first block. For example, if the first child picks a large, thick, red square, the next child may pick a large, thick, red circle. The third child must correct the second child if he is wrong in his selection. If not, he picks out another block. The game may be varied in many ways, such as picking out a block different in two attributes.

The blocks may also be used in studying the logical operations of intersection and union of sets.

Logical Connectives

To extend activities in logic may involve the logical tools of conjunctions, disjunctions, negations, and implications. Again logic blocks may be used.

Figure 5-14. Two property difference game.

Conjunctions

The idea of conjunction is designated by two statements connected with "and." A block may be a conjunction of attributes or properties. For example, pick out a block both red **and** square or pick out a block large **and** yellow. A related idea, intersection of sets, may be investigated using two large circles as sets, drawn on the floor, or, better still, hula hoops. The hoops placed on the floor represent sets in the form of Venn diagram circles.

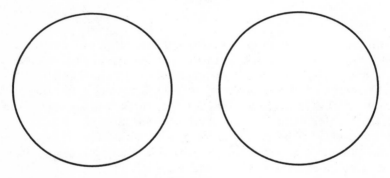

Figure 5-15

If one hoop or set is designated as containing all "red" blocks, all red go in it. If the other set contains all "triangles," then all triangles go in it. The problem is what to do about classifying the "red triangles," since these blocks belong in both sets. To solve the problem, one hoop partially overlaps the other and the red triangle blocks are placed in this overlap area.

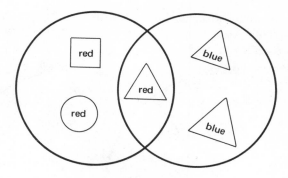

Figure 5-16

Mathematically the "intersection" of these two sets is the set of red triangles. This overlap area may be described as the **conjunction** of the two sets, usually indicated by the conjunction "and"—the set of blocks both red **and** triangles.

Figure 5-17. Eight year olds have difficulty with "intersection" of sets problem. From: Richard W. Copeland, *Mathematics and the Elementary Teacher*, p. 40. (Courtesy: W. B. Saunders Co., Philadelphia.)

The conjunction or intersection game can be varied from simple to complex. The intersection of three sets may be considered by more advanced children as shown.

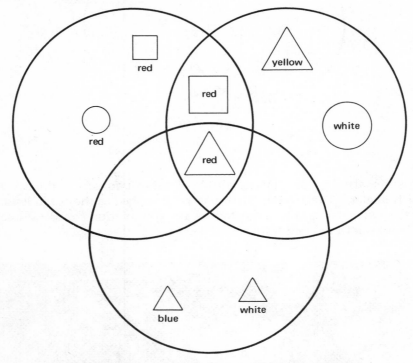

Figure 5-18. Intersection of 3 sets—large, red, triangle.

The idea of conjunction or intersection of two sets is also referred to by Piaget as **simple multiplication** and is discussed more fully in Chapter 8. Again, the idea is not as easy to understand as the adult might think. Consider, for example, a picture of a row of leaves of different colors and a column of green objects placed in a position so that the end of the row and column intersect.

The child is asked to pick from another collection of objects the object that "fits" both the row and column. At age nine Piaget found 50 per cent of the children still unable to complete the task of double classification simultaneously.[14]

---

[14] Inhelder and Piaget, op. cit., p. 184.

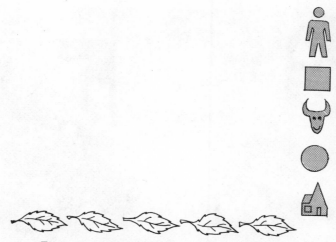

Figure 5-19. Intersection of greens and leaves.

Disjunctions

Children have greater difficulty with the idea of disjunction, usually designated by "or," than with the idea of conjunction. The game is now to place in the hoop or set all blocks that are red or triangles. The resulting union set consists of all blocks either red or triangles. This idea in mathematics is often referred to as the **union** of sets (red and/or triangles).

Implication

In considering an example involving only the two properties "red" and "triangle," if a block is picked that is **not red**, it must be a triangle.

If not red, *then* a triangle.

This is the logic of implication. If there are two possibilities and it is not one (red), then it must (logically) be the other (triangle).

The logic of implication uses the connective "if . . . , then . . . ."

Negations[15]

The idea of "not red" may also be called a negation. Children may be asked to pick out blocks that are "not red" or flowers that are "not roses."

---

[15] For a comprehensive study of children's understanding of negation, see Piaget and Inhelder, ibid., pp. 137–142.

Figure 5-20. John, 9, is successful with negation, picking out the not triangles, not blues, not smalls, etc.

The negation game can be combined with conjunction or disjunction games. For example, pick out all the blocks that are

yellow or not square   (disjunction and negation)
yellow and not square   (conjunction and negation)

Logical Symbolism

Using symbols to consider ideas represented at the concrete level with blocks may be investigated as follows. Sets are given letter names, for example,

red set	R
square set	Sq
thick set	Th
thin set	Tn

The symbol for the conjunction "and" in logic is $\wedge$. The symbol for the disjunction "or" in logic is $\vee$. Hence

R	$\wedge$	Sq	means red and square
R	$\vee$	Sq	means red or square
NR	$\wedge$	Sq	means not red and square

These games for children involve picking out the appropriate set, if given the symbolism, or they may be given a set of blocks and asked to describe the relations in logical symbolism.

Such games in logic can be played by children because the variables in this universe are not difficult to recognize—color, shape, size, thickness—and are limited to blocks. But as the variables and relations become more abstract, children have great difficulty.

"Brother of" and "Right and Left of" as Logical Relations

Mathematics and logic involve a study of **relations**. It is a basis for classification. As we have seen, this is very difficult for the child. In the preceding section we explored the idea of logical classification based on logical relations that exist between objects or sets of objects. Sorting of objects that belong together for some reason such as color or shape or size was one example. "Belong to" is one relation. Another relation is "the same color as." Such activities are a beginning in logical classification.

The child, however, will not be operating on a fully abstract logical level until eleven to twelve years of age. We shall now discuss difficulties children have with other relations that seem easy to the adult.

Two logical relations are considered—"brother of" and "right and left of." The ability to grasp the relation or relationship of ideas is fundamental to reasoning. The inability of children to grasp the **relationship** of notions or ideas is a principal obstacle to the development of their reasoning.

The "Brother of" Relation as a Symmetric Relation

Do children understand the "brother of" relation as a type of classification? Piaget[16] investigated this question by asking boys if there is any thing wrong with the sentence "I have three brothers, Paul, Joe, and myself." (For girls, girls' names are substituted and the word "sisters" substituted for the word "brothers.")

Typical Responses:

1. Age 10:   "I have three brothers, Paul, Joe, and I," thus concluding he can be a brother to himself.

[16] Jean Piaget. *Judgment and Reasoning in the Child*. New York: Humanities Press, Inc., 1928, p. 74.

2. Age 9:   "There is nothing silly in the sentence." This child
               interprets "I have" to mean "We are three brothers,"
               thus replacing the logic of the "brother of" relation
               by the simpler logic of membership or inclusion in the
               family.
3. Age 9:   "He has two brothers; he is not a brother. Each of
               the other brothers has only one brother." The sym-
               metric relationship that if he is my brother, then I
               am his brother is not admitted or understood. The
               child views the situation from only one position, his
               own.
4. Age 9:   The child tries to find out how many brothers each
               brother has. "Paul has two brothers, Joe two, and
               myself two, and we don't know what the last one is
               called. There are four in the family."
5. Age 9:   Right answer. "He only has two brothers if he counts
               himself as a brother."

If there are two brothers in a family (between the ages of five and
nine) and one is asked if he has a brother, the answer will be yes, but
then if he is asked whether his brother has a brother, the answer may
be no.

The **symmetric relation** between brothers is often not understood,
even though the idea of **inclusion** or membership in the family of
each brother may be understood. (See Chapter 7 for a further study
of this relation.)

The **symmetric** relation between two ideas A and B means that the
relation of B to A is the same as A to B. If A and B are brothers,
"the brother of" relation is symmetric in that B is the brother of A
and A is the brother of B. All relations are not symmetric. For
example, consider the "taller than" relation. If A is taller than B,
then B is not taller than A. Neither is "the brother of" relation symmetric for a sister and brother. Tom may be the brother of Sue. But
Sue is not the brother of Tom.

The child often sees brothers only in relation to himself, not the
relationship of himself to them. Psychologically it is egocentrism of
thought that does not allow the child to think from but one point of
view. Also, until he reaches the operational thought level he is unable to reverse the sequence of thought. He can think "Paul is my
brother" but is unable to reverse the idea, that logically then "I am
Paul's brother."

The symmetric property is also an important idea in number. For
example, consider the "equals" relation. To say that $3 + 2$ is equal

to 5 states a relation of 3 + 2 to 5. The equals relation has the sym-metric property. If 3 + 2 is equal to 5, then 5 is also equal to 3 + 2. Again the child has difficulty reversing this sequence. He does not yet have reversibility of thought. No wonder the first-grade teacher has difficulty teaching numbers in other than rote fashion.

The Right-and-Left Relation

The young child views left and right as absolute rather than as relations to each other. If a pencil is placed to the left of a pen, the child may say the pencil is left, but left becomes absolute rather than a relation between objects. This is easily demonstrated by first considering two objects, such as

$$A \qquad B$$

The child identifies A as left, but if a third object C is added,

$$A \qquad B \qquad C$$

most children ten years old or less will not admit that B can be left of C. Thus the idea left of or right of is not a relative notion but absolute. Not until the age of eleven will 75 per cent of the children pass such a test. Care must be taken to be sure the meaning of left as a relation to right is understood. We found some children inter-preting left to mean "remain"; thus B is left, if A and C are removed. For example, see last item of illustration, pages 198–200.

In studying this relation Piaget concludes:

> At the earliest ages the child says that the first of these objects [considered B] is "in the middle," and disputes the possibility of [the same object] being both to the left and to the right [depend-ing on which of the other objects are considered]. Later on, how-ever—and our experiments showed this very clearly round about the age of 11–12—the child will acquire a sufficiently relative notion of the relations of right and left, one that is sufficiently removed from the immediate point of view, for the relation to remain the same, whatever the point of view. Henceforward, there is reciprocity of view-points, and consequently, complete reversibility of thought [a basic characteristic of deductive logic].[17]

[17] Ibid., p. 193.

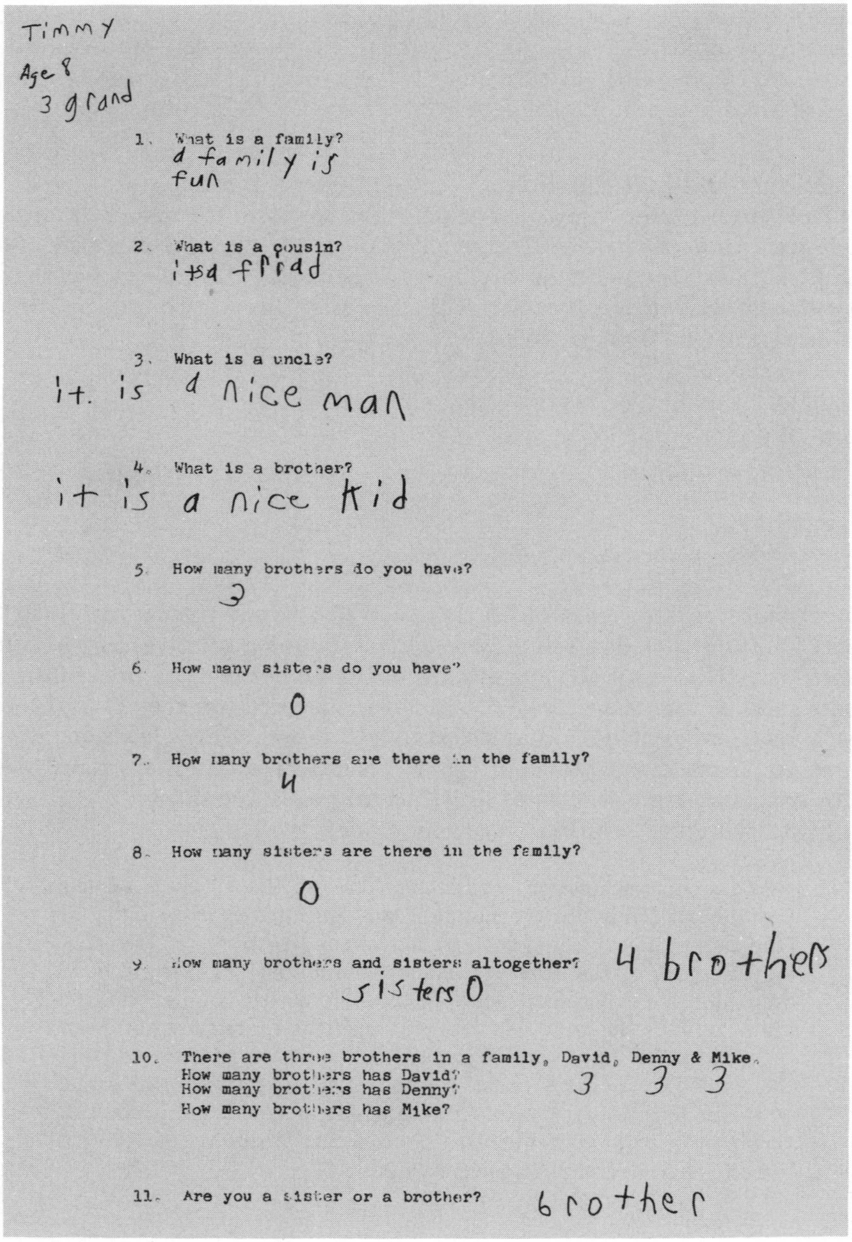

Timmy
Age 8
3 grand

1. What is a family?
d family is
fun

2. What is a cousin?
it sa ffrad

3. What is a uncle?
It. is a nice man

4. What is a brother?
it is a nice kid

5. How many brothers do you have?
3

6. How many sisters do you have?
0

7. How many brothers are there in the family?
4

8. How many sisters are there in the family?
0

9. How many brothers and sisters altogether?   4 brother
sisters 0

10. There are three brothers in a family, David, Denny & Mike.
How many brothers has David?   3   3   3
How many brothers has Denny?
How many brothers has Mike?

11. Are you a sister or a brother?   brother

Figure 5-21. 4 samples of childrens' work.

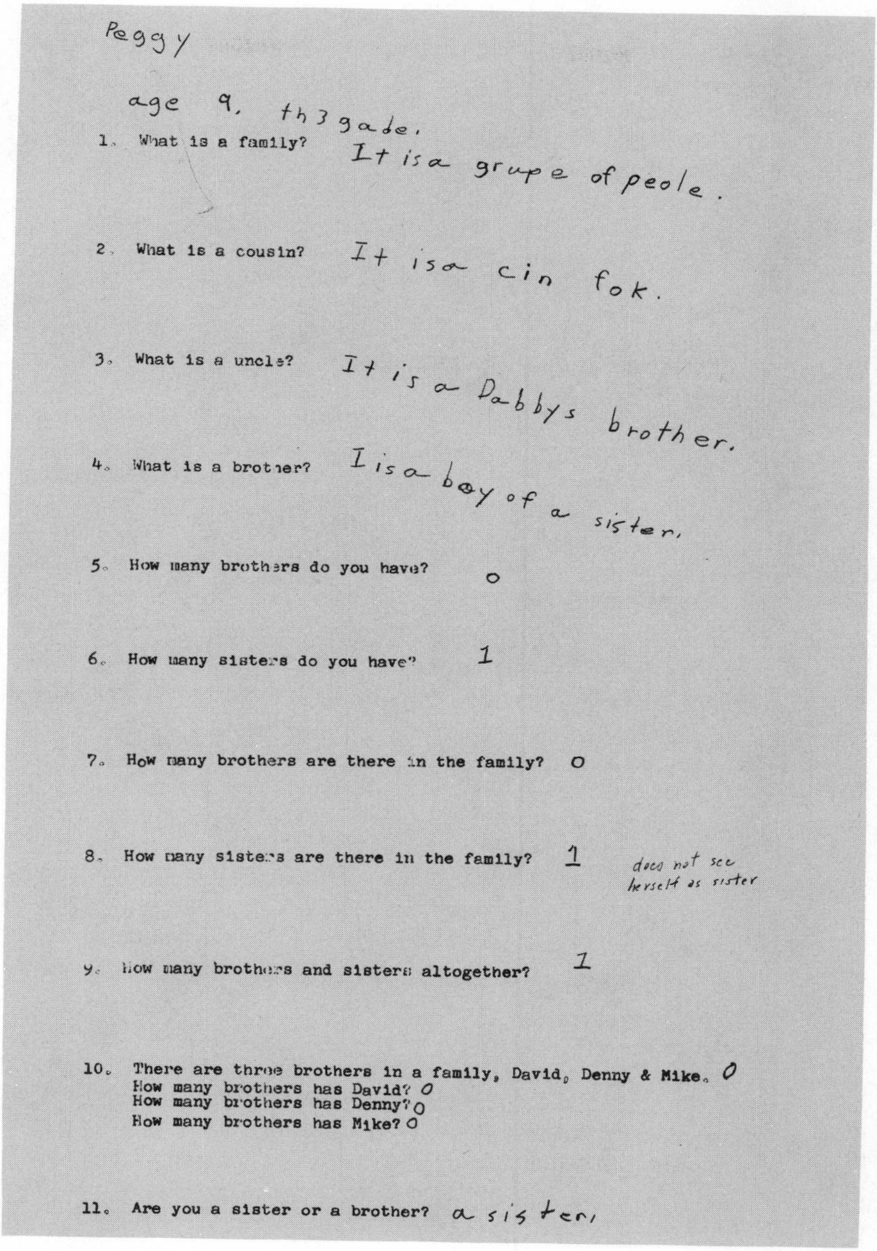

Peggy

age 9, th 3 gade.

1. What is a family? *It is a grupe of peole.*

2. What is a cousin? *It is a cin fok.*

3. What is a uncle? *It is a Dabbys brother.*

4. What is a brother? *I is a boy of a sister.*

5. How many brothers do you have? *0*

6. How many sisters do you have? *1*

7. How many brothers are there in the family? *0*

8. How many sisters are there in the family? *1*   *does not see herself as sister*

9. How many brothers and sisters altogether? *1*

10. There are three brothers in a family, David, Denny & Mike. *0*
How many brothers has David? *0*
How many brothers has Denny? *0*
How many brothers has Mike? *0*

11. Are you a sister or a brother? *a sister.*

Figure 5-22

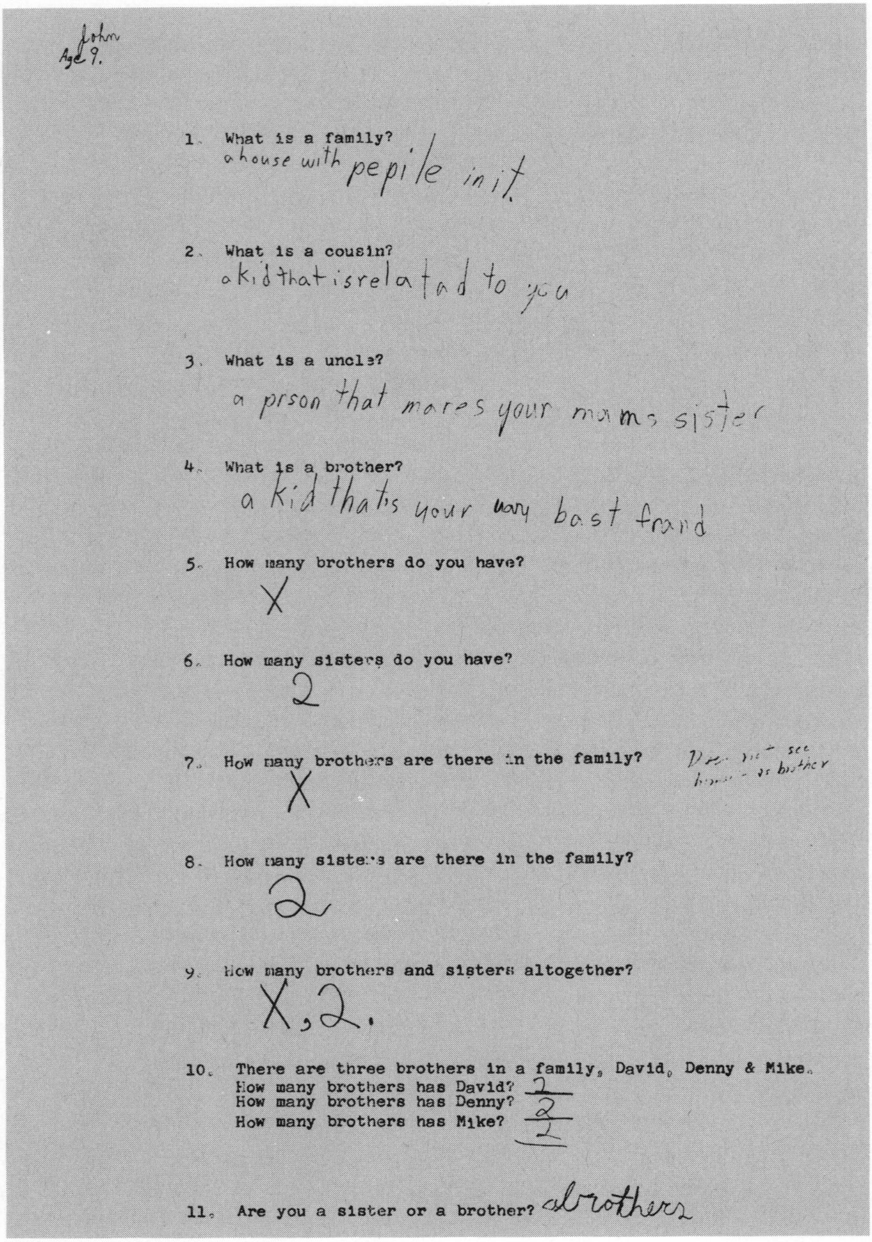

John
Age 9.

1. What is a family?
a house with pepile in it.

2. What is a cousin?
a kid that is related to you

3. What is a uncle?
a prson that mares your mama sister

4. What is a brother?
a kid thats your very bast frend

5. How many brothers do you have?
X

6. How many sisters do you have?
2

7. How many brothers are there in the family?
X
Dos not see
hom - or brother

8. How many sisters are there in the family?
2

9. How many brothers and sisters altogether?
X, 2.

10. There are three brothers in a family, David, Denny & Mike.
How many brothers has David? 2
How many brothers has Denny? 2
How many brothers has Mike? 2

11. Are you a sister or a brother? a brother

Figure 5-23

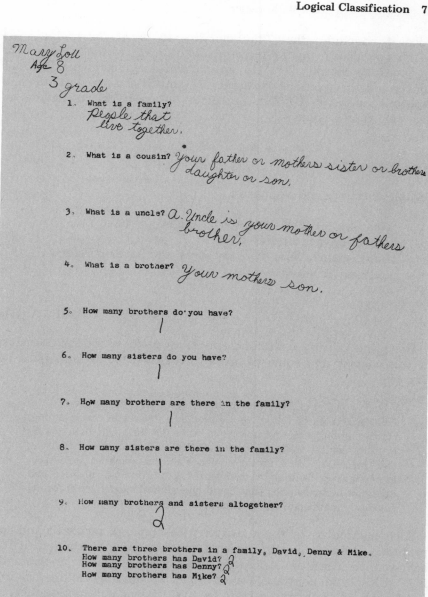

Mary Loll
Age 8
3 grade

1. What is a family?
   People that
   live together.

2. What is a cousin? Your father or mothers sister or brothers
   daughter or son.

3. What is a uncle? A Uncle is your mother or fathers
   brother.

4. What is a brother? Your mothers son.

5. How many brothers do you have?
   1

6. How many sisters do you have?
   1

7. How many brothers are there in the family?
   1

8. How many sisters are there in the family?
   1

9. How many brothers and sisters altogether?
   2

10. There are three brothers in a family, David, Denny & Mike.
    How many brothers has David? 2
    How many brothers has Denny? 2
    How many brothers has Mike? 2

11. Are you a sister or a brother?
    Yes.

Figure 5-24

Piaget concludes that *"the inability to grasp the relativity of notions or ideas is one of the principal obstacles to the development of childish reasoning."*[18]   He constructed a test involving 12 items concerning the relations "brother of" and "right and left of" and reported the test as a genuine predictor of age based on the percentage of correct responses.

Years:	4–5	6–7•	8–9	10–11	12
Percentage correct:	19%	24%	55%	87%	100%

Sample questions and responses:

> What is a brother? "A brother is a boy." (Age 7)
> Are all boys brothers? "Yes."
> All of them? "No, there are some who have no sisters."

Implications

The place in early childhood education of the activities described in this chapter and some of those to follow is well summarized by Bruner:

> One wonders ... whether it might be interesting to devote the first two years of school to a series of exercises in manipulating, classifying and ordering objects in ways that highlight basic operations of logical addition, multiplication, inclusion, serial ordering and the like. . . . Such an early science and mathematics precurriculum might go a long way toward ... the kind of intuitive and inductive understanding that could give embodiment later in formal courses in mathematics and science.[19]

Such manipulative-type activities with concrete materials and appropriate questions by the teacher provide a much firmer basis for achieving the operational thought level necessary for real understanding.   This is in contrast, for example, to training children in the symbolism of the empty set or the addition and subtraction facts in first grade.   Such training involves little understanding, as will be demonstrated in Chapters 6 and 7.

---

[18] Ibid., p. 96.
[19] Jerome Bruner. *Process of Education*. Cambridge, Mass.: Harvard University Press, 1963, p. 46.

The Psychology of the Inclusion Relation and Teaching Mathematics

The inclusion relation involves both logical and arithmetical operations. Yet many children six to nine years old do not have the necessary mental operations to relate the part to the whole either in a qualitative or quantitative way. Serious study must be given to the restructuring of the mathematics program, particularly for grades K-3.

This chapter precedes the next chapter, "First Experiences with Number," since a full understanding of number by the child is a gradual process and must involve an understanding of classification and the inclusion relation. This is not to say that a partial understanding of number does not precede an understanding of classification. For example, a child at six may be able to compare successfully the numbers of two sets of objects and determine which is "more," even though the arrangement of the objects in the sets is changed. The same child may not be successful until a year later with the inclusion relation necessary for the classification or comparison of primulas to flowers.[20]

Without the concept of the inclusion relation, if the child in considering a set of five objects as four objects and one object can only compare the four to the one and not the five, then what meaning can addition have?

As stated previously Piaget concludes on the basis of genetic data that

> The development of number does not occur earlier than that of classes (classificatory structures) or of . . . transitive relations [at seven to eight years of age on the average].[21]
> This parallelism between the evolution of number, classes and seriation [ability to order], is thus a first piece of evidence in favour of their interdependence as against the view that there is an initial autonomy of number.[22]

Seriation (Ordering) and Classification

Seriation is considered in the next chapter as a part of first experiences with number. As a psychological development, it should be compared with the ability to classify. The ability to seriate or order, such as from smallest to largest, or to count at the operational level, that is, with true understanding of the inclusion relations involved,

---

[20] Inhelder and Piaget, op. cit., p. xvii.
[21] Beth and Piaget, op. cit., p. 259.
[22] Ibid., p. 261.

develops usually at seven to eight years of age. Although children at the sensory-motor level may be able to "order" a set of objects by size, it is a trial-and-error procedure and not the result of operational thought.[23] That seriation develops slightly earlier than classification is partially due to the fact that a **relation** such as size can be perceived while a class as such cannot. But perception is still not sufficient to solve seriation problems, as will be seen in the next chapter.

Exercise

Bring a group of five- to eight-year-olds to class or visit an elementary school and, as a game for the children, test their level of understanding using some of the tests described. The same procedure is suggested for the other chapters.

Chapter 11 is an extension of this study of the growth of logical thought in children for those who would like to continue it at this time.

---

[23] Inhelder and Piaget, op. cit., p. 247.

6 First Experiences with Number

It is a great mistake to suppose that a child acquires the notion of number and other mathematical concepts just from teaching. On the contrary to a remarkable degree, he develops them himself, independently and spontaneously. . . . Children must grasp the principle of conservation of quantity before they can develop the concept of number.[1]

Many children, especially in grades K–2, are being "taught" number before they can understand it. A systematic learning about numbers, including the basic addition facts and the concept of place value, should possibly be deferred until children can master the diagnostic tests to be described.[2] For the average child this will be around six and one-half to seven years of age. Even then, teaching cannot be done by "telling," as pointed out by Piaget in the quotation above. The teacher should provide a learning situation that will provoke the desired learning by the child when he is ready. This will involve concrete materials and a proper questioning technique in order that the child may disengage for himself the mathematical structure involved as he handles or manipulates objects.

---

[1] Jean Piaget. "How Children Develop Mathematical Concepts," *Scientific American*, Nov. 1953, p. 74. Copyright © 1953 by Scientific American, Inc. All rights reserved.

[2] For a complete listing of tests, see Appendix A. For a handbook of such tests, see Richard W. Copeland, *Diagnostic and Learning Activities in Mathematics for Children*. New York: The Macmillan Company, 1974.

Class and Number

Counting is one of the first number ideas taught to children, but the numbers they recite often have little meaning for them. Children learn many things about the physical world in which they live before they abstract the idea of number. The study of number should grow out of their classification experiences with the physical world.

As a child looks about and sees the many things around him—many shapes, sizes, and colors—he begins to classify or recognize objects based on certain properties or qualitative characteristics of the objects. Parents praise him as he points out and names objects such as "car," "house," "Mother." He may recognize a car as "something he rides in," "something in the street," "something that moves," an object that has a certain "shape," "size," and "color." As he sees other cars, he begins to generalize and to develop ideas about a set or class of "cars." He begins to arrange or classify his world into classes of people, houses, animals, dogs, and so on. Many science activities are concerned with such classification of objects in our physical world, beginning in biology with the general classes of plants and animals. In this discussion the meaning of "class" and "set" is the same.

Classification is based on **properties** shared in common by a given set of objects, such as size, shape, color, or warm-blooded. Number is also a **property** of any class or set of objects, but it is not a physical property such as those just named. Numbers present a special challenge to children, since they are not physical objects like a horse or a car.

Conservation of Number

Children are taught to determine the number of a set by **counting,** which is learning a set of number names in order 1, 2, 3, 4, . . . , and matching these numerals with the set of objects to be counted.

Figure 6–1

Does the child who can count by matching number names to objects being counted understand the real meaning of number?

A youngster observes two sets of beads displayed as follows:

Figure 6-2

He agrees they are the same (in number).   Then if one set is spread out as follows, would he still say they are the same?

Figure 6-3

Most children five or six years of age respond that there are more in the spread-out set.   The spatial configuration of, or space occupied by, the beads is to the child the number idea.   The beads that are spread out occupy more space, so there must be more beads.   These children have not reached the stage of **conservation** or **invariance of number.**

Figure 6-4.   John, 6, concrete operational, has concept of conservation of number.

The extent of this lack of understanding of conservation of numbers can also be demonstrated by having a five- or six-year-old take beads from a pile with both hands, placing one bead at a time in each of two jars, a jar for each hand.

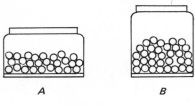

A   B

Figure 6-5

Even though he has placed a bead in jar *A* for each bead placed in jar *B*, he thinks there is more in jar *B*. Even if the child can count and says there are, for example, 30 or 100 in each container, he still says there are more in *B* because the beads are higher in *B*.

Stages of Development

The term **stages**, when numbered 1, 2, and 3, as in the following sections, refers to levels of understanding of a particular concept, stage 1 being no understanding, stage 2 partial understanding, and stage 3 complete understanding. These numbered stages should not be confused with the stages or periods in the life of a child described in Chapter 4 as sensory-motor, preoperational, concrete operational, and formal operational (see pp. 24-30).

These two sets of stages may be related, however. Stage 1, or no understanding, may be characterized as preoperational; stage 2, or partial understanding, is transitional between preoperational and concrete operational; and stage 3, full understanding, is at the concrete operational level. For some conceptions there is a stage 4, which refers to complete understanding at the purely abstract or formal operations level.

Stages of Learning Equivalence

True or lasting equivalence of two sets means that the two sets have the same number of objects regardless of how arranged. Piaget maintains that *"although one-to-one correspondence is obviously the tool used by the mind in comparing two sets, it is not adequate, in its original form or forms* [children in the first two stages] *to give true equivalence to the sets."* [3]

Since one-to-one correspondence or matching is less difficult in comparing elements of sets that are complementary, such as a set of dolls to a set of dresses or a set of napkins to a set of children, complementary sets should be studied first. Later, sets of elements that are of the same quality are matched, such as one set of dolls to another set of dolls or one set of marbles to another set of marbles.

Test first with sets that are complementary. Piaget used a set of 6 bottles and a set of 12 glasses.

Figure 6-6

Learning of one-to-one correspondence and equivalence may be divided into three stages. In stage 1 the children cannot match objects in one set with objects in another set (determine exact correspondence). This is usually at four to five years of age.

A four-year-old is asked to pick out as many glasses as bottles or to pick out a glass for each bottle. He takes all 12 glasses and places them near the bottles but in a shorter row.

Figure 6-7

[3] Jean Piaget. *The Child's Conception of Number.* New York: W. W. Norton & Company, Inc., 1965, p. 80.

Asked if there are more glasses or more bottles, he responds that there are more bottles. Asked to put one glass for each bottle, he makes the two rows the same length.

Figure 6–8

He now thinks there are as many glasses as bottles. If the bottles are then spread out more than the glasses, he again thinks there are more bottles.[4]

The youngster at this stage cannot establish one-to-one correspondence (match each glass to a bottle). Evaluation is in a "global" sense based on the length of the set of objects or the space the whole set occupies rather than their number. Six bottles are "more" than 12 glasses when they are spread wider apart.

In stage 2, one of transition, the youngster can match objects in one set with objects in another but still does not have the idea of "lasting equivalence" or conservation when the objects in one set are spread farther apart. His is a trial-and-error approach.

A youngster at stage 2 is asked to pick out a glass for each bottle. He estimates that he needs 9 glasses to match the 6 bottles, but as he matches the bottles and glasses realizes he has 3 extra glasses and removes them. But if the glasses are then put closer together and the bottles spread apart, he thinks there are now more bottles. He does not yet fully understand the invariance of number.

This youngster at stage 2 is working at a level called "intuitive," that is, basing his judgment on the way the whole thing "looks" to him or on the basis of sensory perception. Thus he makes the same mistakes as the youngster at stage 1, believing the spread-out set contains more objects. But as he matches the objects in the two sets he sees that is wrong and is confused by the contradiction. Thus by trial and error he may arrive at the right answer. He uses his sense of "touch" to manipulate the objects to verify his ideas and then his sense of vision to judge the result. He is not working at the abstract or purely intellectual level as is the case in the third stage.

[4] Ibid., p. 43.

In the third stage the youngster has mastered both the idea of matching or one-to-one correspondence and also the idea of lasting equivalence. He matches 6 glasses with 6 bottles and maintains they are the same in number even if the sets are rearranged. In this stage the operation or idea of one-to-one correspondence as a basis for equivalence has developed and triumphs over mere intuition or visual comparison. Number is no longer a function or dependent on the shape or configuration of the set of objects. He no longer needs to use a trial-and-error approach to determine the correctness of his answer, but answers on the basis of the logic of invariance.

The extent or range of misconception and the subtleties involved in a single number problem for the four- to six-year-old are almost unbelievable from the standpoint of the adult. Only with careful questioning can the many possible interpretations of the child be determined. For example, one five-year-old, given 3 pennies and 3 flowers and told he can buy a flower for each penny, is asked how many flowers he can buy for 3 pennies. He replies that he can buy 3 flowers, but if the flowers are spread out he no longer believes he can buy 3 flowers. He no longer believes the two sets are equivalent. The global or space-occupied concept has triumphed. A six-year-old, facing the same problem but with 7 pennies and 7 flowers, even though he counts each set and finds "seven" for each set says "there are more pennies because there is one penny past the end (of the flowers)." It is clear that number is meaningless at this stage even though the youngster has mastered one-to-one correspondence.

Piaget concludes that what is extraordinary is that these children, even though they themselves make the exchange (of one penny for one flower), are incapable of assuming the equivalency of the two sets. Perception of space occupied (global comparison) carries more weight than verbal numeration or counting.[5]

Sets, Qualitatively the Same

The previous discussion and experiments involved a study of equivalence of sets and one-to-one correspondence at a lower level in that the objects to be matched were complementary. Also the child was given explicit directions to put an object from one set opposite an object in the other set with little reference to number per se but only using such questions as "which has more?"

In this study the elements of sets are not complementary, but qualitatively the same, all buttons or all beans, for example. More

[5] Ibid., p. 59.

important, rather than giving the child two specific sets to work with, he is shown one set of 15 buttons and asked to pick out "the same number" from a larger set.

Figure 6-9

While somewhat more difficult than matching complementary sets, the same three stages can be observed. The child at stage 1 arbitrarily picks out any number of buttons and spaces them out to resemble the model.

Asked how many are in the model (15), he says he does not know. Asked why the two sets are the same then, the child says because he looked (checked) twice.

Apparently, counting aloud and the actual mathcing of object to object will not enable the youngster at this stage to learn that two sets are equivalent. He still thinks there are more or less, depending on the space occupied by each set of objects. It may well be that the youngster is performing with no understanding, even though he can count. Thus 12 objects may be the "same number" as 15 if they occupy the same space. Careful questioning reveals that when the child says "same" he is, in fact, referring to the number of objects, not the space occupied.

An alternative procedure is to use closed figures, such as circles, squares, and rectangles made with counters.

Figure 6-10

A child at stage 1 in attempting to duplicate a circle of 10 counters, makes a circle of 14. Similarly, for a circle of 6 matches he makes one with 12 matches:

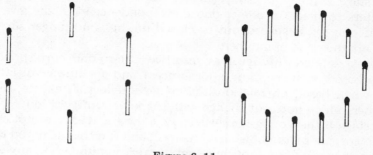

Figure 6-11

Asked if there are the same number of match sticks in each set, he says "Yes."

Another child, in attempting to duplicate figures whose shape depended on the number of elements, such as .·. or :: , is successful, but in attempting to copy a square of 9 counters,

Figure 6-12

he makes a square of 15 counters.

In attempting to copy a figure in a right-angle array such as

Figure 6-13

he uses more counters than shown in the figure.

The only quantification or number idea that a youngster is capable of at this level is "more" or "less," and this may be based on the space occupied by the counters and thus lead to a wrong conclusion.

In stage 2 the youngster can pick out the appropriate number of counters to place in one-to-one correspondence with the given set, but if one set is spaced out or closed up, he is no longer sure that they are the same in number.

Piaget defined this level as **intuitive** one-to-one correspondence when based on perception (appearances), and **operational** or intellectual when based on relationships of an intellectual nature, such as number, which does not change with shape or configuration.

In stage 3 the youngster realizes that the number does not change if the spacing of the objects is changed, and thus has achieved lasting equivalence. He can duplicate a set, correct in number, in any shape, such as a circle, square, right angle, or cross.

Reversibility of Thought

It is the freeing from perception at stage 3 that marks the beginning of an operation on the intellectual rather than perceptual level. The youngster has achieved reversibility in that if one of two equal sets is rearranged, such as from a row of objects to a pile or heap and the other from a heap to a row, he realizes that the number of each set has not changed, that is, from heap to row is the same as from row to heap as far as the number of the set is concerned.

Figure 6-14

Other transformations from one configuration to another should be considered. Examples might include circles, right angles, and crosses.

Figure 6-15

It is this lack of reversibility that characterizes the first and second stages of learning. Reversibility is also necessary for the additive concept. If the child knows that 3 + 2 = 5, can he also solve 5 = □ + □ or 3 + □ = 5? It is not surprising that first-grade teachers find it difficult to teach these ideas.

Piaget concludes:

> All the preceding experiments have shown that at a first level (usually at about the age of 4½–5), the child evaluates discontinuous quantities as if they were continuous [a set of marbles as having length] . . . His quantitative judgments are thus based only on the general shape of the set and on global relationships such as "more or less long," "more or less wide," etc. . . .
>
> The child who is asked to pick out "as many" counters as there are in a given set is in no way equipped by his intellectual structure to consider the set as being a union of units, i.e., 1 + 1 + 1 . . . etc., which would imply that he already possessed the notion of whole number. For the child, therefore, "as many" merely means a set similar to the model with respect to its overall qualities [size and shape]. . . .
>
> He cannot understand that when there is a change in the shape, and therefore in the distribution of the parts, something remains invariant, namely, the number of elements. The reason is that he has not yet acquired the notion of number, but only of perceptual wholes. . . .[6]

At stage 2, each part of the whole is considered as the child begins to coordinate what he sees. The number is counted and he is puzzled at the apparent contradiction of what he "sees" and what counting "tells" him.

A youngster at stage 2 counts 12 counters in each of two rectangles but is doubtful of their equivalence because in one, the longer side was horizontal, and in the other, vertical.

Figure 6–16

The same confusion exists when considering equivalent sets in two concentric circles even though each element in the outer set was opposite an element in the inner set.

[6] Ibid., pp. 86–87.

Figure 6–17

Children in stage 2 are slightly more precise and more mobile but are still restricted by perception or sensory intuition. It is a semi-operational stage. The child is still not capable of truly logical dissociations and compositions of elements in a set.

Stage 3 represents a definite progress. The child at this stage assumes the sets to be equivalent, no matter how the configuration of the elements in the set is changed. Lasting equivalence has been achieved.

Piaget concludes:

> The fundamental factor of this development is, in our view, the complete reversibility of the action involved in the child's procedure. The operation he performs is no longer immediately absorbed in the intuitive result obtained. It frees itself, as it were, and becomes capable of moving in reverse. [Thus] each transformation can be compensated by its inverse, so that any arrangement may give rise to any other, and conversely.[7]

Thus the child no longer relies on the shape of the figure but proceeds exclusively by reference to the one-to-one relationship that exists between the elements of the two sets. He succeeds for the first time in decomposing the wholes and coordinating the number relationship between the two sets. His actions constitute a reversible system of thought. He can consider the transformation of a set to different forms and knows the number remains the same.

Three Levels of Counting to Determine Number Relations

The idea of **relation** is important in the world of mathematics as well as in the physical world. It furnishes a basis of comparison of

---

[7] Ibid., p. 89.

ideas both in logic and in mathematics. Some of the first experiences in mathematics for children involve the comparison or relation of two quantities. Are they "the same as" or "equal" or is one "greater" than the other or "smaller" than the other? These relations—"greater than," "less than," and "the same as" or "equal"—furnish a basis for some first questions concerning quantity and number for children. In their various classroom or playroom activities, children are constantly faced with the problem of "enough" or "as many as." Are there enough sheets of paper, crayons, napkins?

To determine answers to these questions, it is necessary to "count." Teachers need to be aware of three levels of ability in "counting."

Rote Counting

Counting, as first learned by the child, is often a rote activity. Before entering school, his parents may have thought they taught him to count. He has memorized a sequence of sounds, "one, two, three, four . . . ," and therefore says that he can "count." However, if he is asked how many objects you hold in your hand, he may be guessing an answer. His counting is purely a rote-type or memory learning. He has not yet learned to establish a one-to-one correspondence by matching number names to the objects being counted.

Rational Counting

One-to-one correspondence or matching is fundamental to determining the number of a set, and children need many readiness activities of a matching sort, such as dresses to dolls, milk cartons to straws, children to pieces of paper, pencil to paper. The children may be shown two sets and asked to compare them by placing an object in one set by an object in the other set to see if there is more in one set.

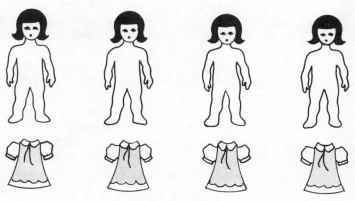

Figure 6–18

Such activities are appropriate prior to the concrete operational level. Children can see and handle objects. These activities in three-dimensional space are followed by worksheets or books in which there are pictures of sets and the children draw lines between pairs of objects in the two sets. This, of course, is moving toward the abstract, since pictures are two-dimensional representations of three-dimensional objects.

After matching objects to objects in pictures, children learn to match the number names or numerals to objects.

1   2   3   4

They may then be shown several sets, each containing a different number of objects, and asked to write the number of objects below each set.

Figure 6–19

When they can place the number names in one-to-one correspond-ence with objects in a set and tell you, for example, in which of the above sets there are "four" objects, they are then beginning to count rationally. The teacher may think they then understand the idea of number four. However, the idea of number is so subtle that if she shows them another set of four objects arranged in some different fashion such as spread out more, the children may say there is "more" in the spread-out set. These children have not reached the stage of conservation or lasting equivalence even though they can "count" correctly.

Counting with Lasting Equivalence (Conservation of Number)

Activities have already been described at length to determine whether a child uses counting at this level of true understanding. The question in determining equivalence of two sets is whether the child uses the logic of invariance of number or perceptual cues, such as one set looks like more because it is "bigger," "longer," and so on. More than one activity should be used, however. The child may be a conserver in comparing sets of four objects and yet be overwhelmed by perceptual factors in comparing sets of nine objects.

Other Types of Conservation and Age Levels

To relate the idea of conservation of number to other types of conservation to be considered in the chapters on measurement or metric geometry, it is worth noting that the various types of conservation do not occur at the same time in children's thinking. They do occur in the same order usually: first, conservation of number, then quantity, then weight, and finally volume at around ten to eleven years of age.   Although this is the order pattern, brighter children will move through the order probably two years before the average youngster.   Conservation of number, for example, may be achieved by the bright five-year-old as compared to seven years for the typical youngster.

One might guess that the following activity on conservation of quantity would be easier than conservation of number for children, but the reverse was found to be true. Measurement requires "operations" more difficult than counting.   To determine the amount of continuous sets, such as water, measurement rather than counting is necessary.

"If I give you some milk in one cup, will it be the same if I pour it into two cups?"

Figure 6–20

"I'll have a little more."
"Where?"
"In the two cups."

"Now if Mother gave you these two cups of milk and we pour the milk into that tall glass, which would you rather have?"

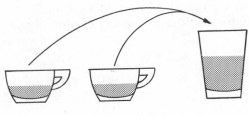

Figure 6-21

"The tall glass."
"Why?"
"Because there's more."
This dialogue with a five-year-old is typical. He is not ready to believe that a given quantity of liquid remains constant when its shape is changed. He does not yet understand what Piaget refers to as **conservation** or **invariance** of quantity. Perception, or what the child sees, triumphs over the logic of identity, that it is still the same quantity.

The same phenomenon will be observed in working with two balls containing the same amount of modeling clay. If the shape of one is changed to flat or lengthened or if the ball is made into smaller balls, the child no longer thinks the amount is the same.

Figure 6-22

1.   Which is more? Or are they the same? "They are the same."
2.   And now? "There is more." Where?

If the child does not think the original balls are the same, ask him to transfer clay from one to the other until he does think they are the same.

Seriation (Ordering), Transitivity, and Ordinal Number

> There is a very primitive ordering structure in children's thinking, just as primitive as the classification structure . . . the structure of seriation.[8]

This is the second basic part of the chapter, that concerned with number in its ordinal sense. The first part of the chapter was primarily concerned with cardinal number.

Seriation

The psychological structure necessary for the mathematical structure of **ordering** Piaget calls **seriation**. To study children's ability to order or seriate, he used a set of ten sticks, each a different length by $\frac{1}{8}$ or $\frac{1}{4}$ inch. This slight difference made the task difficult for a child working on the preoperational or perceptual level.

At the preoperational level children take a big one and then a little one and then repeat the procedure, or they may arrange the sticks in sets of three—small, middle-sized, and large. There is no over-all coordination.

At stage 2 or the end of the preoperational level, children are successful in arranging the sticks in a series by length, but it is a trial-and-error procedure—trying one and if that does not work trying another one.

At stage 3, around seven years of age, the concrete operational level, the procedure is an organized and exhaustive one. The smallest stick is found, then the next smallest, and so on. The child at this stage realizes the dual relation of the next stick—that it will be the next largest (compared to the preceding stick) and also the next smallest (compared to the stick to follow it).

It is also at stage 3 that the child is operational with respect to the necessary **transitivity** relation involved. If stick B is longer than A and stick C is longer than B, he realizes that stick C is also longer than A. Thus he coordinates the relations between all three sticks. This the preoperational child cannot do. He places stick C by A to check to be sure it is longer than A as well as B (trial and error).

The necessary conditions for seriation Piaget summarizes as

> Once two relations are co-ordinated, i.e., once at least three elements are related [A, B, and C], further co-ordination offers no new

---

[8] Jean Piaget. *Genetic Epistemology*. New York: Columbia University Press, 1970, p. 28.

problem. . . . Once this is overcome, both corresponding double seriations and isolated additive series are possible.[9]

The second part of this quotation cites a readiness for problems of
the next two sections, an additive series and a double seriation.
Although important from a mathematical and teaching standpoint,
they offer no new problems from a psychological standpoint.

The Relationship Between Ordinal and Cardinal Numbers

To perform a seriation task (as in the preceding section when sticks
were arranged in a series by height), numbers are not needed. In this
and the next section they are.

In its ordinal sense number refers to the position of an element in a
set—fifth, eighth, and so on. In its cardinal sense number refers to the
total number of objects in a set. Little attention has been given to the
relationship of these two number ideas as they develop in children.

To explore the understanding children have of ordinal number, or
ordination and cardination, Piaget used a geometric design for a
series of ten cards—a square, A; a rectangle, B, the same width but
twice as high; a rectangle, C, the same width but three times as high
as A; and so on.[10]

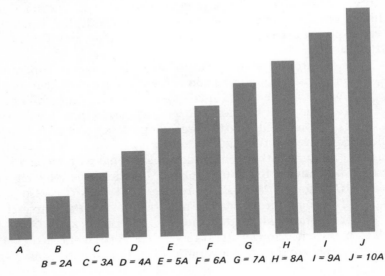

Figure 6-23

[9] Piaget. *The Child's Conception of Number*, op. cit., p. 105.
[10] Ibid., p. 123.

The child is given a mixed-up set of cards and asked to place them in order. After this has been done, he is asked how many cards like *A* he can make with *B*, with *C*, and so on. Thus $B = 2A$, $C = 3A$, and so on.

After this idea is mastered, a card is picked at random, such as *F*, and the child is asked how many *A*'s or units are in *F*.

Figure 6-24

If he knows the ordinal number names and can count, he knows that its position is "sixth." But can he then tell you, since *F*'s position or ordinal number is sixth, how many *A*'s or units are in *F* (which is the cardinal number 6). If so, he has grasped the relation between ordination and cardination. If, however, he needs to measure the height of the *F* card in units of *A*, by placing the *A* card on *F* or approximating with his fingers (see p. 98), thus finding 6 *A*'s or units in *F*, it is clear that he does not understand the relationship between ordinal and cardinal number.

At the preoperational level (four to five years of age), the child may be able to arrange the cards correctly in series by height and to respond to the question "How many cards like *A* are there in *B*?" by saying "Two," but he is soon lost, saying there are four in *C*, for example. Farther along in the series of cards he takes the *A* card and measures with his finger imaginary units the size of *A*, thus estimating an answer. Asked about the *I* or 9 card, he counts by measuring with his finger imaginary divisions on the card, "1, 2, . . . , 8." Asked about the *C* card, measuring, he counts, "1, 2, 3, 4, 5."

Thus children at the preoperational stage may count the cards in the series without hesitation and even understand, when two successive cards are compared, that the difference is A or 1. But when asked to say how many A's are in E, for example, they are unable to think that since E is the fifth card there must be 5 A's in E. Instead they measure or count along the E card to find how many A's in E.

Thus at the preoperational level we have a child who can say the number names in order or count by rote but who has no idea of the cardinal or ordinal number idea involved. Children at this level have systematic difficulty in grasping the relationship between cardinal and ordinal number, but once the two ideas are grasped (as in stage 3) they appear to be essentially linked one to the other.

At stage 3 or the operational level is Let, age six. He is asked to arrange the cards in order.

> How many cards are there?—*10*.
> How many like this one (A) can we make with that one (B)?—*2*.
> And with C?—*3*. (He counted on the card.)
> And with that one (D)?—(He began by counting on the card and
> then cried: *We can make 4.*)
> And that (E)?—*5, because I know how the figures go!* [11]

Let says, "I know how the figures go." He sees the ordinal and cardinal relationship. The interviewer can now skip around in the series picking any card and Let will note its position by counting from A. If its position or ordinal number is sixth, then the number of A's or units in it (cardinal number) is six. The cards can then be mixed up and a card chosen at random, such as G. Asked how many A's in G, Let orders the cards from A to G, counts them and says "seven." His reasoning is that since the ordinal number or position of G is seventh, then the cardinal number of G, expressed in number of A's or units, is seven.

Children at stage 3, the operational level, can immediately find the value of one of the cards, when pointed out at random or when the series is disarranged. The series is no longer rigid for them but is mobile or operational. Each card can be considered in its relation to the others, whatever the order. Some children will even count down or use decreasing order, indicating that G is seventh because counting from right to left "10, 9, 8, G is seventh."

Ordinal Correspondence

Our discussion of number has been primarily that of "cardinal" number and the relationship of cardinal number and ordinal num-

---

[11] Ibid., p. 139.

ber.   In fact, when one speaks of a number it is usually cardinal number that is meant.   The cardinal number of a set is the number of elements or members of that set.

$$n(a,\ b,\ c,\ d)\ =\ 4$$

Number may also be used to refer to the position of an element in a set.   The letter c occupies what position in the order of elements in the set above?   Reading from left to right, it is the *third* element. This is a number in its ordinal sense.   If the order of the elements in the set were changed to $(b,\ c,\ d,\ a)$, for example, the cardinal number is still 4 but the "third" element is now d, counting from left to right.

Although ordination and cardination ideas are different, each involves the other.   Piaget maintains that ordination always involved cardination, and cardination always involved ordination.   If the order of the elements in this set is changed to $(c,\ b,\ a,\ d)$, the cardinal number is still 4.   But to determine the cardinal number of the set (4), the elements must be considered in some order if each element is only to be counted once.   All one-to-one correspondence as a basis for finding cardinal number presupposes ordering the elements in some way.

To study the child's concept of ordinal correspondence Piaget used ten wooden dolls each of a different height and ten wooden sticks each of a different length.   The child is asked to arrange the dolls in order of height and then to arrange the sticks in the same manner. The child is then asked to choose the stick that goes with each doll. As a second test, ten plasticene balls of different sizes were used to match with the ten dolls of different heights.

Again three stages of development can be observed.   In the first the child (aged four to five) cannot use the method of double seriation, that is, cannot arrange both dolls and sticks in order from smallest to largest.   He arranges them in haphazard order.   He may be able to find the biggest stick for the biggest doll and the smallest but is unable to order the whole series.   Asked to find the ball for the smallest doll, he chooses the smallest ball but is again unable to order correctly the double series, dolls to balls.

In stage 2 the child can form the two series without help and match the appropriate dolls and sticks but uses a trial-and-error approach to the solution of the problem.   He makes mistakes and corrects them.

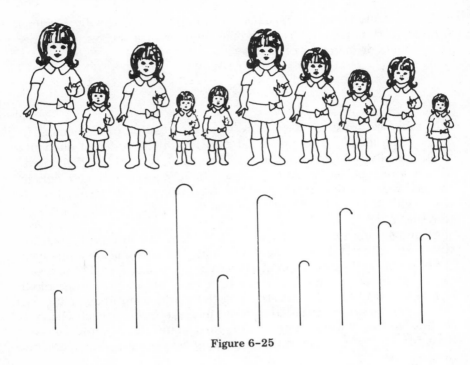

Figure 6-25

In stage 3 the youngster is at the abstract or "operational" level. His judgments are not just based on trial and error or perception as he moves the objects about. At this stage the youngster has no difficulty ordering the double series and matching correctly dolls and balls. He looks first for the biggest or smallest ball and may not even need to line up the balls by size in order to pick out the next smallest or largest. Asked to place the dolls and balls in two rows so that each doll has the right ball, he has no difficulty.

From Serial to Ordinal Correspondence

Such serial correspondence as the ability to arrange two sets of objects (dolls and sticks) in a double series can be done at the perception level. Ordinal correspondence or determining which stick goes with the seventh doll, for example, is more difficult.

The three stages of development leading to conservation of number are again apparent as ordinal correspondence is considered. In stage 1, if the objects in one set, such as the balls, are moved closer together while the objects in the other set (dolls) remain in the same position, the youngster can no longer visualize the correspondence between the elements of the two sets. The idea of which balls belong to which dolls is lost. A four-year-old says that ball 7 belongs to doll 8 if they are opposite each other.

In stage 2 the youngster can work more independently but still loses the idea of correspondence when the spacing between the elements of one set is changed. He has not reached the conservation stage.

Figure 6-26

In stage 3 the child realizes that the ordinal number relationship remains constant if the sets are spaced differently. To find the right ball for the seventh doll, he does not depend on perception and choose the ball opposite the seventh doll, which would be incorrect. Instead he counts from left to right to the seventh ball or from right to left 10, 9, 8, 7.

The children now use numeration or count to name a position correctly. The ideas of cardinal number and ordinal number are now correlated.

Place Value and Base Ten

Piaget did not investigate, at least in his published works, the child's concept of place value in our base-ten system of numeration. Yet historically the development of the concept of place value was considered a great invention.   As reported by the French mathematician Laplace:

> It is from the Indians that there has come to us the ingenious method of expressing all numbers in ten characters, by giving them, at the same time, an absolute and a place value; an idea fine and important, which appears so simple, that for this very reason we do not sufficiently recognize its merit. But this very simplicity, and the extreme facility which this method imparts to all calculation, place our system of arithmetic in the first rank of the useful inventions. How difficult it was to invent such a method one can infer from the fact that it escaped the genius of Archimedes and of Apollonius of Perga, two of the greatest men of antiquity.[12]

Laplace was crediting the Indians of India and our Hindu–Arabic system for this invention, although the Olmec and Mayan Indians of Central America had a place-value system before the time of Christ.[13]

That it took time historically to develop a place-value system and also a number to represent the idea of zero probably comes as no surprise to the teacher attempting to teach place value to children.

Introducing Place Value to Children

Beginning at the concrete level, children are asked to count out objects such as straws in sets of ten and to wrap each set of ten with a rubber band. Then the child is asked to write on the left side of a line the numeral representing sets of ten and on the right side of the line the sets of one or single straws left when there are no more sets of ten.

Thus the idea is established that the **place** a numeral is written determines whether it is sets of ten or sets of one. Later an abacus is used where a single object represents sets of ten.

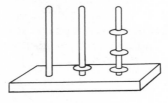

Figure 6-27

---

[12] Cited by Florian Cajori in *A History of Mathematical Notations*, published in 1928 by the Open Court Publishing Company, LaSalle, Ill.
[13] Richard W. Copeland. *Mathematics and the Elementary Teacher*. Philadelphia: W. B. Saunders Company, 1972, pp. 77–80.

Then at the symbol level expanded notation is used, 34, for example, being expressed as

$$3 \text{ tens} + 4 \text{ ones}$$
$$\text{or} \quad 3 (10) + 4 (1)$$
$$\text{or} \quad 30 \quad + 4$$

and, finally, the conventional notation, 34.

For three- and four-place numbers the same procedure is used. For example,

$$3{,}241 = 3 \text{ thousands} + 2 \text{ hundreds} + 4 \text{ tens} + 1 \text{ one}$$
$$\text{or} \quad 3{,}241 = 3 (1{,}000) \quad + 2 (100) \quad\quad + 4 (10) + 1 (1)$$
$$\text{or} \quad 3{,}241 = 3{,}000 \quad\quad\quad + 200 \quad\quad\quad + 40 \quad + 1$$

The concept of place value is fundamental to the operations of addition and multiplication, the subjects of the next two chapters.

Implications for Teaching

The activities described throughout this chapter are examples of the kind of experiences children should have between the ages of four and seven or eight in order to begin to learn about number. They may be used as readiness activities and also as diagnostic tests. Because of the different stages of development, each child should be tested individually.

Ordinal Number

The idea of ordering numbers (2 comes after 1 and before 3) is necessary in order to determine the cardinal number of a set. But before ordering numbers children should have practice in ordering elements in sets of physical objects.

The simplest form of ordering is to line up a set of objects in some way, such as a fork, knife, and spoon from left to right.

Figure 6-28

The child is given a duplicate set and asked to arrange them in the same order and then in reverse order. The same can be done with doll clothes or different-colored blocks.

Figure 6-29

Children may also be shown a less familiar set of objects in some order and asked to duplicate it with another set in the same order.

Figure 6-30

They should also be asked to reproduce the set in reverse order and other orders, such as circular.

Figure 6-31. Reverse ordering.

In such problems there is a definite **order** or arrangement of the elements, but no **relation** has been imposed such as "taller than" or "blacker than" or "fatter than." The children should then be asked to **order** a set of objects on which a relation has been imposed such as to arrange a set of objects from "shortest to tallest."

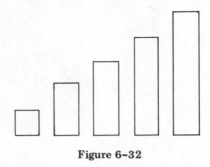

Figure 6-32

Later, numbers can be ordered as on a number line.

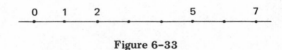

Figure 6-33

To be successful in problems of **seriation** or **ordering**, it is important to keep in mind the necessary psychological structures of

1. Reversibility of thought, or ability to order in two directions, such as forward and backward.
2. Transitivity—if B is greater than A and C is greater than B, then C is also greater than A, thus coordinating a series of relations (around seven years of age).
3. The dual relations involved for any given element in determining its position—that it must be larger than the preceding element and yet smaller than the element to follow.

Cardinal Number

If grouping procedures are used in teaching mathematics, children might be grouped in the three stages so well outlined by Piaget. Children at stage 1 are not yet ready for formal work and need many readiness activities in grouping sets of objects and comparing them to determine such relations as "the same" or "more" or "less." This necessitates matching or one-to-one correspondence activities. Children should be encouraged to match objects in one set with objects in another set, but they can do it only in very limited fashion, if at all.

Children at stage 2 are much more able to perform a matching of objects in one set with those in another, but as the configuration of one set is changed, they become confused about whether the number is still the same for each of the two sets, even though counting produces the same number. They are at a transitional stage as far as conservation of number is concerned. They need many experiences in comparing equal sets in which the configuration of one set is changed to see if they can conserve the number idea involved. They should also be shown one set of objects in various configurations and asked to pick out the same number from a larger set. The many activities described in this chapter and the accompanying booklet, *Diagnostic and Learning Activities in Mathematics for Children*,[14] provide appropriate activities.

Children at stage 3 have mastered the idea of the conservation or invariance of number and are ready for the more highly structured type of mathematical activities normally provided in the first and second grades. But since the average child does not reach the conservation of number stage until approximately six and one-half to seven, this means that many of the activities often presented in the first grade, such as meaning of numbers, place value, and addition and subtraction facts, should be deferred until the second grade. Many readiness activities at first-grade level with physical objects will provide a firmer foundation for the construction of number ideas than will algebra and symbolism, now taught in many first-grade classes—for example, $3 + \square = 7$. Such symbolism has no meaning for many first graders regardless of how hard the teacher works.

Many first- and second-grade teachers will be surprised if they test their children along the lines outlined in this chapter. They will realize that what they thought they were teaching, they were, in fact, not teaching, because (1) the children have not reached the necessary stage of development, and (2) the children needed more experience with physical objects to abstract the number ideas even if they were ready.

Number ideas must be abstracted by the children themselves, but the teacher should provide the concrete materials and proper questions when the child is ready. Some children reach the third or

---

[14] Richard W. Copeland. *Diagnostic and Learning Activities in Mathematics for Children.* New York: The Macmillan Company, 1974.

fourth grade and still do not have the concept of conservation of number. This seems to be particularly true for disadvantaged children. One can only conjecture as to the waste of time in number manipulation at the symbol level for such children and their teachers as they worked on "numbers" during the first few years of school.

In summary, activities and tests similar to those described in this chapter should be explored and mastered by children before going on to more concentrated work in the abstract arithmetic world of symbols. This may mean deferring some of the paperwork activities at the symbol or numeral level.

7 Addition and Subtraction

> We shall not here be concerned with investigating how the child learns addition and subtraction tables at school, learning which is frequently merely verbal.[1]   Additive composition comes late on the scene, in spite of appearances.[2]

As pointed out in this quotation, the ability to add or understand addition develops later than many parents and teachers think. Many first graders or six-year-olds are "taught" addition before they can understand it. The result is simply a verbal type of learning. Attention must be given both to methods of teaching and to stages of development of children if true understanding is to occur.

Grouping and the Inclusion Relation

Piaget uses the term "addition" as an operation on numbers and also as an operation on classes. Class grouping is a **qualitative** one, such as grouping in terms of children, beads, or flowers. This is in contrast to number grouping, which is **quantitative** in character. Grouping provides a basis for classifying objects in our physical world. It is also a basis for a study of ideas in logic.

[1] Jean Piaget. *The Child's Conception of Number*. New York: Humanities Press, Inc., 1952, p. 161.
[2] Ibid., p. 198.

Number can be related to logic. In fact, logic **concepts** and **numbers** have an important common basis, the grouping operation. In logic, a class may be considered in terms of its parts or partial classes. The class of children, for example, may be thought of as including the class of boys and the class of girls. Children may consider the class of animals in terms of classes of horses, cows, dogs, and so on, each class being included in the class of animals. This is a logical relationship—the inclusion relation. But to what extent is this logical relation of the part to the whole understood? Can the "inclusion" relation involved in a study of classes in logic be understood without understanding the addition of numbers? Piaget maintains that both class (in logic) and number result from the same operational mechanism of grouping and that one cannot be fully understood without the other.[3]

To investigate a child's understanding of such logical grouping, Piaget studied children four to seven years of age. He used a box of wooden beads, all of them brown except for two white ones, in order to determine to what extent children comprehended the inclusion relation.

Figure 7–1

Could the children use the mental process of logic to conclude that if the class or set of wooden beads included the set of brown beads and the set of white beads, then the set of wooden beads must then be larger than either the set of brown beads or the set of white beads?

Only the mathematical relation "larger than" is considered here in the study of the logic of the inclusion relation. (The numbering of each class and the study of addition of numbers is the subject of the next section.)

It is surprising that this idea is so difficult to grasp at the four-to-seven age level. At this first stage the youngster cannot visualize the

[3] Ibid., p. viii.

whole as being larger than its parts. Shown a set of wooden beads in a box, nine brown and only two white, and asked "Are there more wooden beads or more brown beads?" he replies "More brown ones." Asked if the brown ones are made of wood he replies "Yes," and asked "Are the white ones made of wood?" he replies "Yes." Yet when the question is repeated, "Well, then, are there more brown ones or wooden ones?" he again says "More brown ones." That he is only able to compare the parts, the brown to the white, is evidenced by his response that there are more brown because there are only two wooden ones (meaning the white ones).[4]   Asked which would make a longer necklace, the wooden beads or the brown beads, he replies that the brown beads would.

Children at stage 1 are unable to consider the quantity of wooden beads because the idea of the wooden or whole is lost when the parts—brown and white are considered. There is systematic difficulty for children less than seven or eight years old in comprehending what is referred to in mathematics or logic as the inclusion relation; the idea of the three classes, wooden beads, brown beads, white beads, could not be considered simultaneously.

The child understands the question but is simply unable to answer it correctly, which can be verified by other experiments. For example, the child can be shown a set of flowers in two colors. Piaget used 20 poppies and 3 bluebells.

Figure 7–2

[4] Ibid., p. 164.

What colour are they?—*They're red and blue.*—The red ones are poppies and the blue ones are bluebells.—*Yes.*—I want to make a very big bunch. Must I pick the flowers or the poppies?—*The poppies.*—Show me the poppies. (She pointed correctly.)—Show me the flowers.—(She made a circular movement to indicate the whole of the drawing.)—Then will the bunch be bigger if I pick the flowers or the poppies?—*If you pick the poppies.*—If I pick the poppies, what will be left?—*The bluebells.*—And if I pick the bluebells, what will be left?—*The poppies.*—And if I pick the flowers, what will be left?—(Reflection.) *Nothing at all.*—Then which will be bigger, the bunch of flowers or the bunch of poppies?—*I've told you already.*—Think (repeating the question).—*The bunch of poppies will be bigger.*—And what about the bunch of flowers?—*It won't be the same.*—Will it be bigger or smaller?—*Smaller.*—Why?—*Because you've made a big bunch of poppies.*[5]

This experiment can be varied using less of a contrast in numbers such as 2 white flowers and 5 red flowers and the result is often the same. (See photo p. 57.)

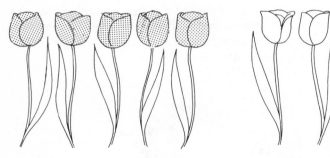

Figure 7-3

Then an experiment with a set of boys and a set of girls, using flannel cutouts or pictures, produces the same result. A child at this stage shown a picture of 2 girls and 5 boys and asked whether there are more boys or more children responds that there are more boys because there are only 2 girls. "Well, are the girls children?" "Yes." "Then are there more boys or more children?" "More boys." The idea that if both boys and girls are children then there must be more children than either boys or girls is not grasped.

[5] Ibid., p. 167.

The child knows that the set of children **includes** boys and girls, but he is unable to compare the number of boys to the number of children even to the extent of saying which is more.

Figure 7-4

Piaget concludes that the inclusion relation appears to be the stumbling block for children. For them, wholes are not logical classes. **Qualitatively** the child understands that one bead can be both brown and wooden, but **quantitatively** he cannot place the beads in two sets, such as brown and wooden, simultaneously. As soon as the child's attention is given to the part, the whole is forgotten. As beads are divided into sets of brown ones and white ones, the idea of the set of **all** beads is lost. Similarly, when the set or class of children is thought of as boys and girls, the idea of children is lost.

In the second stage of development the idea is grasped at the intuitive level or by trial and error. The child responds at first as if he were in stage 1 saying, for example, that there are more boys than children. Prompted by the question "Are the girls children?", he realizes his mistake and is able to correct it.

In stage 3 the discovery is spontaneous and immediate. The child understands the logic of the inclusion relation. If the set of children includes a set of boys and a set of girls, then there must be more children than either boys or girls. The problem is solved at the logical or intellectual level rather than by trial and error as in stage 2.

A logical class is a set of elements possessing a common property. The common property, or properties, in the example of the beads is that they are all wooden. Grouping the brown wooden beads and white wooden beads produces the class of brown and white wooden beads. This idea is known as **union of sets** in mathematics.

Piaget concludes that the real problem is that children at the first stage are still on the plane of perceptual intuition, which is immediate and irreversible. In moving their thoughts from the whole to the part, the whole is forgotten—from beads to brown beads and white beads, only the brown and white can be compared. The children are unable to reverse their thought to the whole again, that is, back to the class of beads, which includes both brown and white.

It is the achieving of reversibility of thought (from whole to parts to whole again) that constitutes a logical or intellectual action as contrasted to the perceptual or prelogical, which is based on sensory experience. At this age level of perception, the child bases his judgment on what he "sees" immediately as the beads are rearranged into a set of white beads and a set of brown beads.

Conclusion

Until this reversibility of thought is achieved, the logic of inclusion and addition of classes as operations cannot be learned. This transition from the prelogical level takes place at around seven years of age or when the child is usually in second grade. This means that many children are being introduced to addition of classes before they have the necessary reversibility of thought to learn it. We will discuss in the next section how the operation of "addition" of numbers develops as a logical operation in children at about the same time as addition of classes.

Piaget asks:

> Is not the additive composition of classes [brown, white, boys, etc.] the psychological counterpart of the additive composition of numbers, or to put it more shortly, is number not essential for the completion of the notion of class? It may in fact be, that it is not until the notions of invariance and conservation of numerical wholes are acquired, that the child is capable of regarding as permanent the relations of the part to the whole in the realm of classes. . . . Both class and number result from the same operational mechanism of grouping.[6]

---

[6] Ibid., p. 162.

Piaget concludes:

> In a word it seems clear at this stage [stages 1 and 2] that the child is still incapable of additive composition of classes, i.e., of grasping logical addition or subtraction. . . . He cannot handle successfully the relationship of inclusion. . . . These relationships are intuitive and dependent on actual perception, they cannot result in any stable composition and we therefore find on the logical plane the same fundamental phenomenon . . . : non-conservation of wholes.[7]

Addition of Number

From Class to Number

How can the idea of classes be transformed into numbers? The answer is not as simple as might be expected.

The understanding of 2 + 3 and 5 being the same was tested by Van Engen and Steffe[8] using classes or sets of candy. A set of 2 pieces and a set of 3 pieces were shown to each of 100 first graders.

The two piles were then joined and each child asked if he had a preference for the two piles or the combined pile. Forty-six children responded incorrectly, not recognizing the equality of 2 + 3 and 5. When the piles were increased to 4 + 5 and then joined, fifty-five children responded incorrectly.

Meaning of Addition

Addition of numbers does not mean to increase but to group, join, or rename a pair of numbers as a single number. The number idea is the same whether expressed as 3 + 2 or as 5. That the number 3 + 2 is the same as 5 is usually expressed as 3 + 2 = 5. The symbol =, known as the **equals relation**, means that 3 + 2 and 5 are names for the same number, hence the relation between them is equal.

Most of the activities in this chapter have involved two sets: boys and girls, brown and white, and so on. Addition is a binary operation—an operation on two elements or numbers. In considering the addition of three numbers, such as 3 + 4 + 5, addition is performed twice, first on one pair of numbers, and then on the resulting sum and the remaining number. For example, 3 + 4 = 7, and then 7 + 5 = 12.

[7] Ibid., p. 174.
[8] H. Van Engen and L. P. Steffe. *First Grade Children's Concept of Addition of Natural Numbers*. Madison, Wisc.: Research and Development Center for Learning and Re-Education, University of Wisconsin, 1966.

Addition is an operation that relates the parts to the whole or renames the whole in terms of its parts.

$$3 + 2 = 5 \qquad 5 = 3 + 2$$
$$1 + 4 = 5 \qquad 5 = 1 + 4$$
$$2 + 3 = 5 \qquad 5 = 2 + 3$$
$$4 + 1 = 5 \qquad 5 = 4 + 1$$

Psychologically, addition and its inverse, subtraction, are one operation, a reversible one.

According to Piaget,

> Addition is a reversible operation. There is therefore no more than a suggestion of it when, at the first stage, the child does not understand that a whole B divided into two parts A and A' is still the same whole ($B = A' + A$; $5 = 3 + 2$). The operation of addition comes into being when, on the one hand, the addenda are united in a whole ($3 + 2 = 5$), and on the other, this whole is regarded as invariant irrespective of the distribution of its parts ($5 = 3 + 2 = 1 + 4 = 2 + 3 = 4 + 1$).[9]

The Relation of the Parts to the Whole
in Addition of Numbers

Is the relation of the part to the whole (or the inclusion relation) the same problem to the child in the world of numbers as it is in the grouping of qualitative classes?

To find out when children learn that the whole remains invariant, regardless of the way its parts are rearranged, Piaget used the number 8 in the form of $4 + 4$ and $1 + 7$. The child is told that he can have 4 sweets at 11 o'clock and 4 at tea time. The next day he will be given the same number, but since he is less hungry in the morning he will be given 1 sweet at eleven and 7 at tea time.

I   II

Figure 7-5

[9] Piaget, op. cit., p. 189.

The child is asked if there is the same amount to eat on both days. At stage 1, lasting until six and one-half or seven years of age, he responds that there is more on the second day since there is "a big lot over there" (7). To be sure the question is understood, both sets in II are pointed out and the question is asked whether together they are the same as those in I. The answer is the same.[10]

The child at this stage cannot consider the two sets in I and in II simultaneously, but simply sees the biggest set (7 in II).

In the second stage of development the child does relate the two sets but only intuitively by trial and error or one-to-one matching or by counting. He may respond at first as if he were at stage 1, but he is not sure. If asked why, he may count or experiment by moving some of the counters from the set of 7 and placing them with the single counter. When he removes 3 from 7 and places them with the single counter, he sees that he gets the same display as in I.

Figure 7-6

He then concludes that I and II are the same.

At the third stage, the response is immediate. No experimenting or hesitating is necessary.

> Ter (aged 7): Will you eat the same amount on both days?—*Yes.*— Why?—*Because they're the same.*—How many each day?—*8.*—But there are 4 here in (4 + 4) and there's only 1 there in (1 + 7).—*Yes, but we've put the 3 here.*[11]

Figure 7-7

At this stage the child understands the number idea involved in renaming 4 + 4 as 1 + 7 without the need for qualitative reasoning (manipulating the counters). Each subset is seen in relation to the

---

[10] Ibid., p. 187.
[11] Ibid., p. 190.

other, and the whole and its parts, as far as addition is concerned, represents an operational system in which the whole remains invariant.

To really understand addition as an operation the child must be able to look at the addends such as 1 + 7 and realize that the number can also be expressed as 8. He must also be able to reverse the process and realize that 8 is also 1 + 7, 3 + 5, and so on. At stage 3, about seven years of age, the child is able to do this at the operational or mental level without counters.

Piaget continues:

> Additive composition comes late on the scene, in spite of appearances. A consideration of the facts usually observed in connection with the beginnings of counting might suggest, at first sight, that addition is understood as soon as the first sets of two, three or four objects to which a numeral is assigned are formed. We have shown that this is not so.[12]

Making Quantities Equal by Addition and Subtraction

Another important way of studying a child's understanding of the operation of addition and its inverse subtraction is to not begin with the same number, such as 8 sweets, each day. Instead, the objective is to see if the child can equalize two sets of counters such as a set of 8 and a set of 14 by using the operations of addition and its inverse, subtraction.

At the first stage the child is not aware that addition and subtraction can be used to compensate each other, that is, that we can add to one set by subtracting from the other.

At stage 1, given a set of 10 counters A, and a set of 16 counters A',

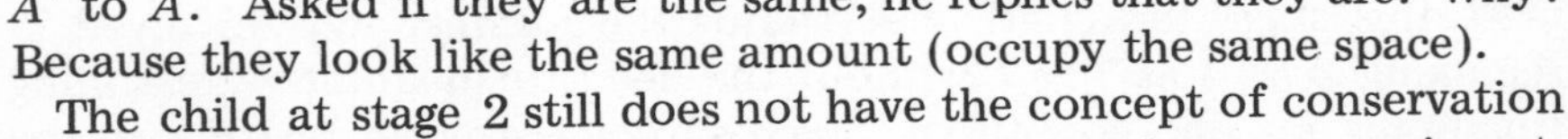

$$\circ \; \circ \; \circ \; \circ \; \circ \; \circ \; \circ \; \circ \; \circ \; \circ \qquad \circ \; \circ \; \circ \; \circ \; \circ \; \circ \; \circ \; \circ \; \circ \; \circ \; \circ \; \circ \; \circ \; \circ \; \circ \; \circ$$

$$A \qquad\qquad\qquad\qquad\qquad A'$$

Figure 7–8

a child of five and one-half arbitrarily moves some counters from A' to A. Asked if they are the same, he replies that they are. Why? Because they look like the same amount (occupy the same space).

The child at stage 2 still does not have the concept of conservation of number or of the invariant whole. By trial-and-error experiment, manipulating the counters, he solves the problem.

[12] Ibid., p. 198.

A six-year-old, given a set of 8 counters and a set of 12 counters, takes 2 from the set of 12, then 1 more, then another 1, and adds them to the set of 8.

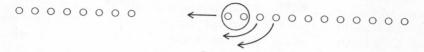

Figure 7-9

Thus the set of 8 becomes 12 and the set that was 12 becomes 8.
He then arranges the set of 12 into a rectangle pattern and the set of 8 into a square, but this does not help him.

Figure 7-10

He then arranges both sets in columns of twos and equalizes the two lengths by dividing the 4 left over in the longer column, one by one, between the two sets.

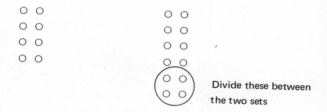

Divide these between
the two sets

Figure 7-11

This is a trial-and-error approach experimenting with geometric patterns and space occupied to determine more and less. Eventually he solves the problem using his ability to count, with the help of space occupied.   There is no additive composition at the number level. He does not realize that the combined number of the two sets is not affected if the same number is subtracted from the larger set and added to the smaller set. There is no conservation of the whole.

At stage 3 the child is not confused by the arrangement of the counters and can use one-to-one correspondence for equalization. He knows at this stage, for the first time, that if one set is larger, he must find the difference, which can then be divided equally. His is not an unplanned trial-and-error approach. He has a plan of action at the number level. Based on his plan, he knows immediately what to do with the counters. He matches the elements of the smaller set with the elements of the larger set and divides the remainder of the larger set between the two sets.

Given a set of 8 counters A, and a set of 14 counters A', a bright six-year-old puts the 8 counters in A in a row and matches them with 8 counters from A'. He then divides the 6 remaining counters between A and A'.

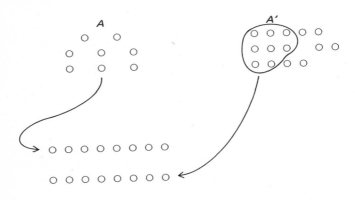

Figure 7-12

A seven-year-old uses a more sophisticated procedure. He makes a row of the 8 counters in A, counts them, then counts out the same number from A'. He doesn't bother to line up or match the two sets of 8. He then divides the remaining 6 without counting them between A and A'.

The Commutative Property of Addition

Children should discover in joining sets of objects such as 2 objects and 3 objects that the same number of objects is produced as when 3 objects and 2 objects are joined.

$$
\begin{array}{cccccc}
0\;0 & & 0\;0\;0 & = & 0\;0\;0\;0\;0 \\
2 & + & 3 & = & 5 \\
0\;0\;0 & & 0\;0 & & 0\;0\;0\;0\;0 \\
3 & + & 2 & = & 5
\end{array}
$$

Using an inductive procedure, that is, by trying other number pairs in opposite order, a generalization is arrived at that the **order** of adding whole numbers does not change the sum. This generalization or property of whole numbers and addition is called the **commutative** property. It is often stated algebraically for any whole numbers a and b as

$$a + b = b + a$$

This property is very useful in addition problems. To solve the problem $5 + 9 + 5$, for example, if the 9 and second 5 are commuted, the problem is then $5 + 5 + 9$, which can be solved as $10 + 9$, or 19. This property also makes it possible to "check" addition problems by adding in an opposite direction.

Readiness for Understanding the Commutative Property of Addition

A number of investigators have studied children's understanding of the commutative property by beginning with concrete materials. For example, "I am going to give my doll four apples and two oranges, so to be fair you give your doll the same amount of fruit. But your doll likes oranges better, so give her more oranges than apples."

Another approach was to use toy cars in two colors, for example seven red cars and four white cars. The cars are parked in a line, first the red cars (of different sizes) and then the white cars. A parking sign is put at the end of the row of cars. Then the cars are removed and the child asked to park the cars in a line again but to begin with the white cars. After the white cars and one red car are put down, the child is stopped and asked to predict if the other red cars will reach to the parking sign, not reach that far, or go beyond it.

Brown[13] reports that the commutative and associative properties are not abstracted until eight to nine years of age; yet such problems

---

[13] P. G. Brown. "Tests of Development in Children's Understanding of the Laws of Natural Numbers," M.E. Thesis, University of Manchester, 1969.

are found in many first-grade materials. Since reversibility of thought is present at around seven years of age, the answer may be somewhere between seven and eight years of age for the average child in "constructing" the commutative property.

The Associative Property of Addition

In adding any three whole numbers such as 3 + 2 + 4, would the sum be the same if the 3 and 2 are first added and then 4, as contrasted to adding the 3 to the sum of 2 and 4?

These groupings can be shown with parentheses as

$$(3 + 2) + 4 \overset{?}{=} 3 + (2 + 4)$$
$$5 \quad + 4 = 3 + \quad 6$$
$$9 = 9$$

Note that the order of the addends is the same: 3, 2, 4 for both groupings, so the commutative property is not involved.

Similar numerical examples would prove inductively that different groupings do not change the sum. This is called the **associative property of addition.** Stated algebraically, for any three whole numbers, a, b, and c,

$$a + (b + c) = (a + b) + c$$

Whenever three numbers are added, the associative property is involved, since there is a choice of association (the first two numbers or the second two numbers).

Readiness for Understanding
the Associative Property of Addition

Children should be shown three sets of objects and asked to predict if grouping them in different ways would produce the same amount. Brown's study cited in the preceding section on the commutative property would indicate that children are not ready for the associative property until about eight years of age.

Place Value and Addition

After children have learned the basic single-digit addition facts (0 + 0 to 9 + 9), they still have to learn the conventional algorism for adding numbers expressed with two or three digits.

For example,
$$
\begin{array}{r}
32 \\
+46 \\
\hline
\end{array}
$$

Using concrete materials such as popsickle sticks and tin cans labeled for sets of ten and sets of one, the children can represent 32 as 3 sets of ten and 2 sets of one.

Figure 7-13

The number 46 can be similarly represented in the cans to produce a sum of 7 tens and 8 ones.

The problem may then be solved in expanded notation without concrete materials as

$$
\begin{array}{r}
3 \text{ tens} + 2 \text{ ones} \\
+ 4 \text{ tens} + 6 \text{ ones} \\
\hline
7 \text{ tens} + 8 \text{ ones}
\end{array}
$$

And, finally, the problem is solved in conventional notation:

$$
\begin{array}{r}
32 \\
+46 \\
\hline
78
\end{array}
$$

For addition problems involving "carrying" or renaming, such as

$$
\begin{array}{r}
36 \\
+27 \\
\hline
\end{array}
$$

children should still begin at the concrete level. After the 6 sticks and 7 sticks are put in the "ones" can, the question is: Can the 13 ones be **renamed**? The desired answer, of course, is as 1 ten and

3 ones. The 1 ten is represented by wrapping 10 of the 13 ones with a rubber band and placing in the "tens" can to produce a sum of 6 tens and 3 ones.

After completing the problem at the concrete level, it can then be done without concrete materials in expanded notation as

$$
\begin{array}{r}
3 \text{ tens } + 6 \text{ ones} \\
+2 \text{ tens } + 7 \text{ ones} \\
\hline
5 \text{ tens } + 13 \text{ ones}
\end{array}
$$

or   5 tens + (1 ten + 3 ones)
or   (5 tens + 1 ten) + 3 ones
or   6 tens +   3 ones
or   63

The associative property is the basis for the renaming (carrying) process in addition.

In similar fashion, 10 tens can be renamed as 1 hundred. Children often have difficulty in renaming tens as hundreds even when they seem to understand renaming ones as tens. For this reason it is worthwhile to have concrete materials, such as a pocket chart, to work out addition problems expressed with three digits.

For example, to represent

$$
\begin{array}{r}
234 \\
+124 \\
\hline
\end{array}
$$

Hundreds	Tens	Ones
//	///	////
/	//	////
///	/////	////////

Figure 7-14

Subtraction of Numbers Expressed with Two and Three Digits

To subtract numbers expressed with two or three digits the procedure should be to begin at the concrete level as just outlined for addition, using tin cans or the pocket chart, for example. First, problems should be solved involving no "borrowing" or renaming. Then, for a problem such as

$$
\begin{array}{r}
42 \\
-18 \\
\hline
\end{array}
$$

one of the 4 tens is renamed as 10 ones and placed in the ones can. Then 8 ones can be subtracted from 12 ones and 1 ten subtracted from 3 tens to leave a difference of 2 tens and 4 ones.

Then, without concrete materials, in expanded notation,

$$
\begin{array}{r}
4^3\text{tens} + {}^1 2 \text{ ones} \\
- (1 \text{ ten} + 8 \text{ ones}) \\
\hline
2 \text{ tens} + 4 \text{ ones}
\end{array}
$$

and finally, in conventional notation,

$$
\begin{array}{r}
42 \\
-18 \\
\hline
24
\end{array}
$$

Subtraction is more difficult than addition at the concrete level in that the question is often asked whether the subtrahend or number to be subtracted should be shown on the pocket chart. If the problem is done in additive form, it is easier to visualize. For the problem $_{-18}^{42}$, one of the 4 tens is first renamed as 10 ones and added to the 2 ones. Then to verbalize the subtraction in additive form:

8 ones and ? ones is 12
1 ten and ? tens is 3 tens

Implications for Teaching Addition and Subtraction

Learning addition in the first grade is a rote or verbal activity for those who have not developed **reversibility of thought**. This includes most children until six and one-half to seven years of age. The Van Engen–Steffe study previously cited found that approximately half of 100 first graders tested did not even realize the equality of 3 + 2 and 5.

Children will begin to learn by trial and error based on experience with manipulative materials the reversibility of the equals relation. If 3 + 2 = 5, then 5 = 3 + 2. (If $A = B$, then $B = A$ is referred to in mathematics as the symmetric property of the equals relation.)

For example, give a child a set of five blocks and then ask him to separate the blocks into two sets. After he arranges the set of five blocks such as □□ □□□, he should be asked how many are in each set, then asked how many blocks will there be if they are joined. He then joins the two sets to check his answer. This joining of sets is a way of stressing the reversibility of the operation, from 5 = 3 + 2 to 3 + 2 = 5. Only after the reversibility concept develops in the child should addition be taught in a systematic manner.

Part of the same problem is the **inclusion relation**. At stages 1 and 2 children have great difficulty thinking simultaneously of the whole after it has been divided into parts. Children should have many experiences with qualitative grouping or logical addition of classes (e.g., beads as brown and white, children as boys and girls, and flowers as blue and white) as they prepare for addition.

If the child is unable to solve such a problem for a grouping of physical objects, then you can expect the same problem to occur as he attempts to solve a similar problem in the abstract world of number. The experiment with the candy confirms this prediction. At stages 1 and 2 the child does not realize that 1 + 7 is the same as 4 + 4.

Children should have many experiences with quantitative grouping or addition of numbers by using objects that are alike (such as blocks of the same color and shape) so that qualitative differences (color or shape) do not confuse the basic objective of number relationship. It is the numbers of the sets of blocks that are being compared or added, not blocks. Number is a property of each set of blocks.

Each addition family can be explored with manipulative materials, such as blocks. The "five" family might be explored by asking the child to arrange the set of five blocks into two sets in as many ways as possible. He should develop the following arrangements and be asked to name the number, such as 4 + 1, for each arrangement:

Expressed in block form

Expressed in symbol form

□ □ □ □   □

4 + 1

□   □ □ □ □

1 + 4

□ □   □ □ □

2 + 3

□ □ □   □ □

3 + 2

Figure 7-15

Addition exercises with symbols or numerals when introduced later should be in the form of 5 = □ + □ and also □ + □ = 5, to stress the reversibility and invariance of the number relationship. Such symbol manipulation should be developed systematically only after the conservation concept has been achieved as evidenced by mastery of such tests as described in this chapter. This may mean postponing addition facts using symbols until the second grade or after seven years of age for many youngsters.

The Commutative Property

Closely related to the ideas just discussed is the commutative property of addition. While it may seem easy to the adult, the study cited (see p. 123) indicates that it is difficult for the child of less than eight or nine years. Piaget concurs: "The genetic examination of commutativity (even for equalities such as 2 + 3 = 3 + 2) . . . clearly shows the belated character of the elaboration of such intuitions."[14]

The Relation of Subtraction to Addition

Subtraction is sometimes referred to as an operation distinct from addition. More often, however, subtraction is referred to as the inverse of addition. Conventionally, addition has been taught as a joining operation; for example, 3 + 2 or 3 joined with 2 produces 5. Subtraction as its inverse would be a separating action, 5 = 3 + ? or, with concrete materials, ○ ○ ○ ○ ○ = ○ ○ ○ + ?.

[14] Evert W. Beth and Jean Piaget. *Mathematical Epistemology and Psychology.* Dordrecht, Holland: D. Reidel Publishing Company, 1966, pp. 262-263.

Subtraction may be thought of as finding the missing addend when the sum and one addend are known. For example,

$$5 = 2 + \square \quad \text{or} \quad 2 + \square = 5$$

These are still subtraction problems in that the sum and one addend are shown. If they were addition problems the addends 2 and 3 would be shown and the children would be expected to name the sum.

As has been stressed throughout this chapter and book, children at the first two stages of development have great difficulty in thinking of three numbers simultaneously, for example the whole 5 and its subclasses, such as 3 and 2. The children should be asked how many blocks should be placed with the 3 blocks so they will be the same as the 5 blocks. But they need to arrive at stage 3, the operational thought level, before such activities will have any meaning. First-grade teachers have great difficulty teaching such symbolism as $3 + \square = 5$. Many children are simply not ready.

While $\bigcirc\,\bigcirc\,\bigcirc\,\bigcirc\,\bigcirc = \bigcirc\,\bigcirc + ?$ may be thought of as a subtraction problem, Piaget makes little mention of subtraction as an operation because it is inherent in the reversibility of the operational mechanism he describes as addition. If subtraction is stressed as a separate operation, it should still be taught at the same time as addition so that the reversibility of the concept is seen.

Regarding the necessity for manipulation of concrete materials at stage 2, Piaget thinks that experience is always necessary for intellectual development, and he fears that an "experience" such as seeing a demonstration performed or having something "explained" is not sufficient for a subject to disengage the structure or idea involved. More than this is required. The child must be active, must transform things, and must find the structure of his own actions on the objects.[15]

The child at stage 3 knows that the number of a set does not change as its elements are rearranged in some manner. He knows that $\bigcirc\,\bigcirc\,\bigcirc\,\bigcirc$ is the same in number as $\bigcirc\,\bigcirc\ \ \bigcirc\,\bigcirc$ or that 5 is the same as $3 + 2$. At stage 3, the child can hold before his mind the number 5 and also its parts, such as 3 and 2. He must have reached the stage of conservation or invariance of number. Nothing is lost when 5 is represented as $3 + 2$. When the child sees the whole 5 in terms of its parts, 3 and 2, 1 and 4, and so on, and can name the third number, either given two addends or the addend and sum (subtraction), and is not fooled by perception such as

---

[15] Frank Jennings. "Jean Piaget, Notes on Learning," *Saturday Review*, May 20, 1967, p. 81.

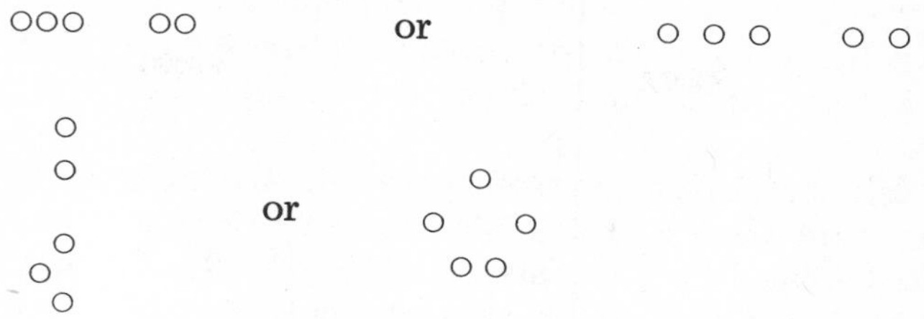

Figure 7-16

he is ready for systematic addition "facts" in abstract form.

Recording the Basic Addition and Subtraction Facts

The basic addition and subtraction facts should be developed by the children themselves and recorded in a table such as the following:

+	0	1	2	3	4	5	6	7	8	9
0	0	1	2	3	4	5	6	7	8	9
1	1	2	3	4	5	6	7	8	9	10
2	2	3	4	5	6	7	8	9	10	11
3	3	4	5	6	7	8	9	10	11	12
4	4	5	6	7	8	9	10	11	12	13
5	5	6	7	8	9	10	11	12	13	14
6	6	7	8	9	10	11	12	13	14	15
7	7	8	9	10	11	12	13	14	15	16
8	8	9	10	11	12	13	14	15	16	17
9	9	10	11	12	13	14	15	16	17	18

Such a table provides a convenient reference. The addends are placed across the top of the table and down the left side. The sum of 3 + 2 is found by first looking down to 3 on the left side. The child should put the index finger of his left hand on 3 and move it from left to right. At the same time he should place his right index finger on the 2 at the top of the table and then move this down. The two fingers should meet at 5.

To use the table for subtraction, such as for $3 + \square = 5$ or $5 - \square = 3$, look down the left side to the addend 3, then across in the 3 row to the sum 5, then up from 5 to the top of the table for the missing addend 2.

Such a tabular display provides a way of displaying both addition and subtraction facts and a reinforcement of the inverse or reversibility idea between addition and subtraction. This is in contrast to the old addition tables, which were learned separately from the subtraction tables with little if any reference to the important relationship between the two operations.

Addition and Subtraction of Numbers
Expressed with Two or More Digits

Procedures for introducing children to methods used for adding and subtracting numbers expressed with two or more digits were outlined in a preceding section. These procedures are usually developed during the second and third grades.

The primary implications of Piaget's work would be for the kinds of addition and subtraction activities that should precede and be prerequisite for such procedures.

8 Multiplication and Division

The construction of additive operations and that of multiplicative operations are bound together. It is wrong to think of additive structures as being established first. . . . These two structures develop through parallel stages, and in close mutual dependence [at about seven to eight years of age]. They constitute a single operational organization.[1]

In Chapter 7 a child's understanding of addition was investigated using as one experiment a set of wooden beads, some brown and some white.

Brown   White

Figure 8-1. Wooden beads.

It was found that children in the four-to-seven age group could not think of the whole (wooden) and the parts (brown and white) simultaneously. Once the wooden beads were divided into two subclasses, the child was only able to compare the parts or subclasses. The idea of the whole was lost. The child in this age range could not reverse

[1] Barbel Inhelder and Jean Piaget. *The Early Growth of Logic in the Child.* New York: W. W. Norton & Company, Inc., 1969, p. 195.

his thoughts by reasoning that since brown and white were wooden, they could be joined to produce more wooden than either brown or white. The same result was observed in considering a class of children in terms of its subclasses, boys and girls. If there were more boys than girls, the responses would be that there were more boys than children.

The ability to perform the operation of logical multiplication or intersection develops in children at approximately the same time as does logical addition or union of sets, and the stages are very similar.

Multiplicative Classification (Matrices)

This chapter came largely from *The Child's Conception of Number*, published in English in 1952, and *The Early Growth of Logic in the Child*, published in English in 1964. The latter is a most valuable addition to Piaget's earlier works on logic and number. It includes a chapter on what is commonly referred to in mathematics as the Cartesian product. This is a different meaning for the operation of multiplication than that developed in the latter part of this chapter. Both are important.

Consider, for example, a set of shapes (circles and squares) in two colors (red and blue). Multiplicative classification consists of classifying each element simultaneously in terms of two additive orders. The possible pairings as blue circle, blue square, red circle, and red square can be shown using a geometric form known as a matrix.

	blue, b	red, r
square, s	b,s	s,r
circle, c	c,b	c,r

Figure 8-2. Cartesian product shown by matrix.

Using a variety of tests and asking the children to put together the things that belong together, the ability to classify in two ways simultaneously was found to develop between the ages of seven and eight.[2]

---

[2] Ibid., p. 151.

More difficult tests, involving a third attribute such as size, necessitated a more complex operational thought level. The performance of the children was surprising in that the four- to five-year-old performed better than the six-to-seven age group until as many as six or seven elements are used. This is explained by the six- and seven-year-olds using a better intellectual procedure but a not yet perfected one. Even so, only approximately 60 per cent of the eight- to nine-year-olds were successful with three-attribute classification problems.[3]

One test involved a set of 16 pictures of rabbits, including four seated black rabbits, four seated white rabbits, four running black rabbits, and four running white rabbits. The child is first asked to put the rabbits together that "go well," or "belong," together. A box with four compartments is provided.

Figure 8–3. Classifying rabbits.

Then one of the partitions is removed to see if the classification can be only in terms of two sets of rabbits, such as running rabbits and seated rabbits. The child is then asked if it can be done another way (black rabbits and white rabbits). Finally, he is asked to place them again in the original four compartments so each set is alike in some way.

[3] Ibid., p. 155.

Children are first unable to classify by two attributes simultaneously, such as putting the **black running** rabbits in one compartment,
or they cannot complete the task—putting white running, black
seated, and white seated rabbits in the other compartments. Some
children will not be able to classify all the rabbits into two sets when
one of the partitions is removed. Finally, at stage 3, around eight
years of age, they have the necessary operational thought level to
perform these tasks immediately.

Simple Multiplication (or Intersection)

The complete cross classification or multiplication discussed in the
previous section involved the ability to classify simultaneously in
two or more sets based on common attributes or properties. **Simple
multiplication** (defined as logical multiplication in an older book,
Judgment and Reasoning in the Child) involves only two classes and
produces or generates a class common to both (intersection) and
two other classes, each consisting of the elements of one that do not
belong to the other. For example, in considering a class of red objects and a class of circular objects, the intersection will be the **red
circles**, the other two sets being **red not circles** and **circles not red**.
Piaget found simple intersection or simple multiplication more difficult for children than complete cross classification or multiplication
since it is only a partial operation.

As an experiment the child is shown a row of objects such as
different-colored leaves and a column of green objects. The space
where the row and column intersect is left empty, and the child is
asked to find something that fits with everything (a green leaf).

Contrary to what the reader and teacher might expect, at age nine
50 per cent of the children are still unable to classify simultaneously
an object as belonging in two sets.[4]   The question then arises of the
advisability of attempting to "teach" intersection in the primary
grades as is being done in many schools.

Development of the Equivalence Relation

The more conventional meaning of multiplication is considered in
this section.   To multiply, the child must understand one-to-one
correspondence or equivalence of two or more sets. Multiplication
is a multiequivalence or correspondence between sets.

[4] Ibid., p. 184.

The necessity for one-to-one correspondence or equivalence of sets was discussed in Chapter 5 as a basis for learning to count. The problem children have with conservation of number is seen in a display such as

Figure 8-4

The child would agree that there was one-to-one correspondence, but if one set of counters is spread apart

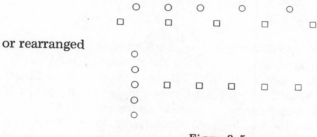

or rearranged

Figure 8-5

the idea of one-to-one correspondence is lost, and the two sets are no longer thought to be the same in number.

Since multiplication may involve more than two sets, the question arises as to whether one-to-one correspondence is more difficult when more than two sets are involved. It is interesting to find that equivalence of three sets is no more difficult for children to grasp than equivalence between two sets. The child considers the sets in pairs as separate problems.[5] Thus A is compared to B and then B compared to C to determine the equivalency involved.

To study children's ability to understand equivalency when more than two sets is involved, Piaget used a set of ten flowers X, a set of ten vases Y, and another set of ten flowers Z.

[5] Jean Piaget. *The Child's Conception of Number*. New York: Humanities Press, Inc., 1964, p. 208.

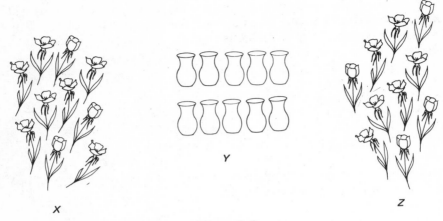

Figure 8-6

The child is asked to put a flower from set X in each vase Y. There is a flower for each vase, so $X = Y$. Then the flowers of set X are removed and placed in a bowl. The child is then asked to put a flower from set Z in each vase Y. There is a flower for each vase, so $Y = Z$. These flowers are then removed and placed in a separate bowl.

Can the child then use the logic of transitivity to conclude that since both sets of flowers matched or were equivalent to the set of vases that they are equivalent to each other? Symbolically, $X = Y$ and $Y = Z$; therefore, $X = Z$.

At the first stage, below five years of age, the child can put a flower in each vase or establish one-to-one correspondence of flowers to vases. After this has been done and the flowers of X and Y are in different bowls but one set is spaced out more in its bowl than the other, the child looks at the two sets of flowers and thinks there are more in the spaced-out set.

Figure 8-7

The idea of the number being the same, based on the one-to-one correspondence the child has just carried out, is no longer sufficient. Also the logic of $X = Y$ and $Y = Z$, hence $X = Z$, is not realized. Perception triumphs rather than logic, the child thinking there are more flowers in the spaced-out array. He has not reached the conservation stage of development.

At the second or transitional stage (ages five to six), the child is still swayed by perception, thinking there is more in the spaced-out set of flowers when placed in a separate bowl, even though he placed each set of flowers, one by one, in the set of vases. But if he is asked why there is more in the spaced-out set, he may count to find the number is the same and then change his mind. Or he may take the sets of flowers out of the bowls and line them up as a test of equivalence. He may even see the logic of $X = Y = Z$ if he is questioned along the lines of Hoeg, aged five years, eleven months:

> How do you know?—*I'd have to count.*—All right then, count. But wait a minute. Where were these flowers (X) before?—*In the vases.*—And those (Z)?—*In the vases as well.*—And was there exactly the right number?—*Yes. Oh! they're both the same!*—... Why are they the same?—*They were in the vases and the vases are the same as the flowers. But I'd like to count all the same* (he counted X, Y, Z). *It's 10 and 10 and 10. Yes, all three are the same.*[6]

Although at stage 2 the child is fooled by perception, he finds the correct answer by trial and error or proper questioning and believes it, but he may be fooled again by another problem in a somewhat different context.

At stage 3, the child is at the operational level and is no longer swayed by perception. He may also be found in the age range five to six, as is Cide, five years three months:

> *They're exactly the same, because I saw they were in the vases, I keep on thinking all the time that we're putting them back in the vases.*—But look at this bunch of big flowers (X) and the bunch of little flowers (Z), are they the same?—*Yes, they're the same. I think of those (X) and those (Z) and I count with the vases.*[7]

Cide is struggling with the reversibility necessary for operational thought, saying "I saw they were in the vases." The logic that if each set of flowers X and Z came from the vases, they could be put back in the vases and thus must be the same in number.

---

[6] Ibid., pp. 210–211.
[7] Ibid., p. 212.

From Equivalence of Sets to Multiplication of Numbers

We have now seen the ability of children to determine equivalence between three sets: two sets of ten flowers, X and Z, and a set of ten vases Y. At the third stage, or operational level, the children, after placing one set of ten flowers in the ten vases and removing them and then placing the other set of ten flowers in the ten vases and then removing those, knew that the two sets of flowers must be equal in number. Symbolically,[8] if

X (number of flowers) = Y (number of vases) = Z (number of the other set of flowers), then $X = Z$

To study a child's understanding of multiplication of numbers, Piaget began with the same three equivalent sets, two sets of ten flowers, X and Y, and one set of ten vases. The questioning, however, takes a different line.

After the child has put one set of flowers in the vases and removed them to a bowl and then done the same with the other flowers, he is asked: Now if I put all the flowers back in the vases, how many will go in each vase? Since there are twice as many flowers as vases, 2 flowers should go in each vase.[9]

At the first stage (ages five to six), the children are unsuccessful. Blu (aged five years six months) is asked:

> And now, if I want to put all the flowers back in these vases, how many shall I have to put in each one?—*You'll have to put one.*—Do you think they'll all go in?—(He tried it, but having reached the 5th or 6th he exclaimed): *Oh! we'll have to put more.*—(He put 2 and obtained the correct result, and then asked spontaneously): *Why did we have to put 2?* [10]

Blu does not see the relationship of 2 flowers for each vase. Not understanding the one-to-one correspondence or equivalence problem, he is no better able to think of a two-to-one correspondence. The one-to-one correspondence or "same number" idea is not understood except under very special conditions, such as when the flowers are "in" the vases. When one set of flowers is spread out, perception

---

[8] In the terminology of mathematics, if $X = Y$ we say the *relation* of X to Y is "equal." The idea of equal is called a relation. The equals relation has certain *properties*. One of the properties is discussed in this and the preceding section. The idea that if $X = Y$, and $Y = Z$, then $X = Z$ is called the *transitive* property of the equals relation.

[9] Piaget, op. cit., p. 214.

[10] Ibid.

overrules the conservation-of-number idea. Neither does he understand the transitivity of the equivalence: if $X = Y$ and $Y = Z$,
then $X = Z$.

Another problem is then framed using tubes or paper straws in
which the stem of only one flower will fit.

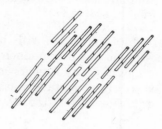

Figure 8-8

The idea is to see, if one flower is put in each tube or straw,
whether the child can discover that since there are 2 sets of flowers
he will need 2 times as many tubes as flowers in each set in order for
each flower to have a tube. Then when the number of flowers and
number of tubes are the same, if the flowers are removed from the
table, can the child determine how many tubes go with each vase?

A five-year-old is asked to place a flower in each tube. He puts
ten tubes opposite the vases. He is then asked if he has enough
tubes for all the flowers. The answer is yes. He is then asked to try
them and see. He then realizes he will need more tubes than vases,
saying that there will be a long line of tubes.[11] He does not realize
that the long line of tubes will be twice the number of vases.

Children at stage 1 are incapable of multiplicative composition.
They do not relate the two sets of flowers as 2 times the number of
vases. They do not understand that if the flowers in each set correspond or are equivalent to the number of vases that there are then 2
flowers for each vase. These children know there are "more"
flowers than vases, but the double relationship is not understood.
They simply estimate an answer.

At the second stage, the child has a more organized plan of attack,
but it is still trial and error.

> Uld (aged 5 years, 8 months): "If I put all these flowers ($X + Z$)
> in the vases (Y), how many will that make in each vase?—*2, 3 or*

[11] Ibid.

more.—Try it.—(He tried putting 2 and went on to the end of the row.) *That's just right.*

Now take just enough tubes for us to be able to put one flower in each.—(He put 1 tube in front of the 1st vase, 2 in front of the 2nd, 3rd and 4th, 1 in front of the 5th, 2 in front of the 6th and the 7th, 3 in front of the 8th and 9th, and 2 in front of the 10th. He then equalized them (2 in front of each vase).) [12]

Uld is moving toward multiplication with his educated guess of "2, 3 or more." If one-to-one correspondence does not work, then it must be 2 times or 3 times as many flowers as vases. To determine the equivalence of tubes to vases he starts out in haphazard fashion but then equalizes the equivalence relation between tubes and vases as 2 to 1.

These children are still unable to generalize $N + N$ as $2 \times N$, and $N + N + N$ as $3 \times N$, and so on.

At the third stage (ages six to seven) the child immediately understands the multiplicative relationship that exists as $2 \times N$ and can generalize the operation to other problems if more sets of ten flowers are considered, as $3 \times N, 4 \times N, \ldots$.

Gros, relatively young for this stage at five years ten months:

Gros was convinced that $X = Z$, if $X = Y$ and $Y = Z$. "If I put all the flowers $(X + Z)$ in these vases (Y), how many will there be in each?—*1 blue and 1 pink.* How many is that?—2.—And if I added these (a new set of 10), how many would there be in each vase?—3.—Why?—*I'd put one, one, one.* And now suppose we wanted to put them in these tubes that will only hold one flower? (He took $10 + 10 + 10$ tubes.)" [13]

In the various multicorrespondences of flowers to vases as 2 to 1, 3 to 1, 4 to 1, . . . , the operation being used by children at the operational level is seen as multiplication and not addition.

Division into Equal Parts

Multiplication and division are referred to as inverse operations. If $a \times b = c$, then $a = c \div b$.

However, it is the reversibility involved in multiplication and division (and in addition and subtraction) that is impossible for many

[12] Ibid., p. 216.
[13] Ibid., p. 218.

children below the operational level of approximately seven years of age.

Multiplication and division, because of their inverse relationship, must both be understood if either is to be understood. The two operations should be taught simultaneously once the child has achieved reversibility of thought. This logical construction is in accord with the psychological construction necessary—that of reversible thought.

Addition as an operation implies multiplication. This transition from addition to multiplication was studied by Piaget using the simple experiment of separating a whole into two equal parts. A child is given 18 counters and asked to give both himself and the interviewer the same amount. (A variation involves two dolls to which the child is asked to give the same amount.)

At the first stage, the child arbitrarily separates the counters into two groups. Even if he uses a one for me, one for you approach, when he has completed the division he does not use the logic of one-to-one correspondence as a basis for the same number in each set. Instead he evaluates the number of counters in each set by looking at the space or shape they occupy on the table. If one set is spaced out more, he thinks there is more in that set. He has not reached the stage of conservation or invariance of quantity.

At the second stage, the child, by trial and error, obtains a correct answer, sometimes after several false starts. A six-year-old divides and spaces out the 18 counters into the form of two squares.

O O O   O O O
O O O   O O O
O O O   O O O

Figure 8-9

But given 24 counters, he makes a square of 9 and a rectangle of 12.

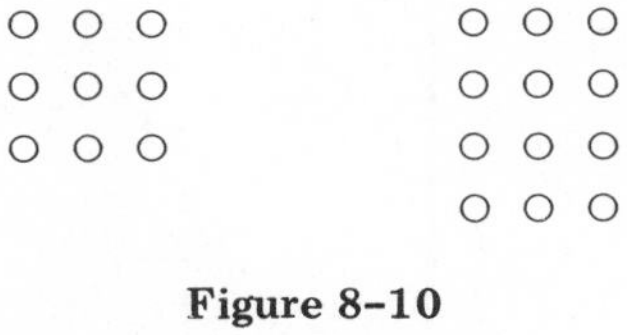

O O O   O O O
O O O   O O O
O O O   O O O
               O O O

Figure 8-10

The three left over he adds to the 9, making it also a rectangle.

Figure 8–11

The difference in the two figures confuses him and at first he no longer thinks the number is the same in the two sets. Then he moves 3 counters from the side of the figure at the left and places them at the bottom. Now that the rectangles look alike, he agrees that the number is the same.

Figure 8–12

At the third stage, the child distributes the set into two sets by taking the counters one or two at a time and placing them in each of the two sets until the division is complete. The spacing of the counters in each of the sets does not confuse him, if, for example, the counters in one set are spread out by the interviewer. The logic of the one-to-one correspondence triumphs over the perception of the space occupied. To test the reversibility of the child's thought, the interviewer asks, "What if I put the two piles together, will there be the same number as in the two piles?" The answer at this level is yes.

Piaget defines multiplication of numbers as an **equidistribution**. The example used in the preceding discussion was a equidistribution of 18 into 2 sets, or $18 \div 2 = 9$.

Symbolically, this is 2×9 or $m \times n$ (m sets of n terms, n being the same number for each set).

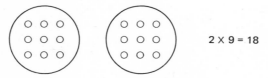

Figure 8–13

That addition implies multiplication is seen as

$$\begin{array}{lrcl}
\text{if} & 9 + 9 &=& 18 \\
\text{or} & n + n &=& 18 \\
\text{then} & 2n &=& 18
\end{array}$$

The problem of dividing the 18 counters into two sets, A and B, so that they are equal in number is accomplished by one-to-one correspondence or equivalence—that is, one for A, one for B, and so on. Two sets are said to be equivalent if for each element of A there is an element in B, and for each element in B there is an element in A. This one-to-one correspondence or equivalence of two or more sets is a **multiplicative equivalence**.

When the child has become aware of this one-to-one correspondence between the elements in two or more sets, he will sooner or later realize that there is an appropriate operation implicit that will give the total number of the sets involved. This we call multiplication. For example, the one-to-one correspondence or equivalence of the sets shown below determines that the number of each set is 6.

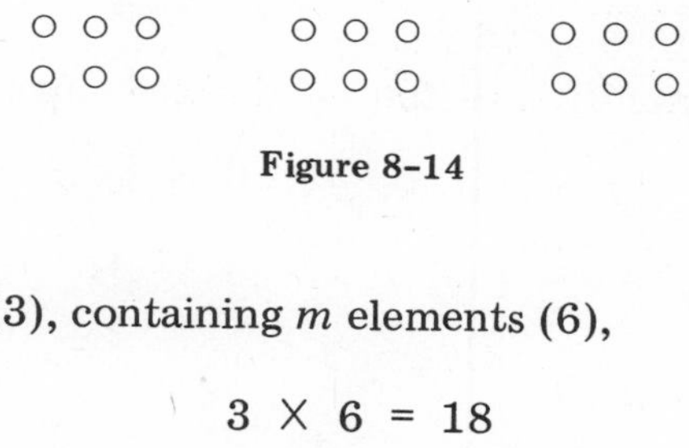

Figure 8–14

Thus, for n sets (3), containing m elements (6),

$$3 \times 6 = 18$$

Implications and Follow-up Activities

From a developmental standpoint children are able to learn multiplication at the same time that they are able to learn addition, approximately seven years of age. Yet in many schools multiplication is delayed. That children can multiply smaller numbers as readily as they add them may be due to the close relationship of multiplication to addition. For example, if $3 + 3 = 6$, then 2 threes is? If these premises are correct, multiplication at the abstract or symbol line should be introduced at approximately the same time as addition—approximately seven years of age for the typical child. The need for an individualized program of instruction is evident. Some children will be ready for addition and multiplication at six, others not until seven and one-half. If instruction cannot be individualized and understanding is important, it may be that addition and multiplication paper work, using the number symbols, should be deferred to the second grade. In other words, manipulative-type activities with concrete materials should be employed for the five- and six-year-old as a prelude to working with numerals only. It may be that in the typical graded school (grades kindergarten to third grade), where an individualized program is not possible, children should be grouped on the basis of the three stages described by Piaget.

How successful are the children in dividing a set of objects (such as counters) into two equivalent sets? A set of six objects divided into two equivalent sets makes how many in each set?

$$\circ \ \circ \ \circ \ \circ \ \circ \ \circ \quad = \quad \boxed{?} \ \boxed{?}$$

Figure 8-15

If this is done correctly, ask the child "How many is two sets of three"?

$$\circ \circ \circ \qquad \circ \circ \circ \quad = \quad ?$$

Figure 8-16

The symbolism and paper work should come only after the inverse relationship between multiplication and division is understood using concrete materials. Many such problems should be done at the concrete material level combining and separating sets of objects. Multiplication facts should involve the corresponding division facts as sets of objects are manipulated.

Does the child have the reversibility of thought that is characteristic of the third or "operational" thought level stage? The paper work should not begin until he does. If $4 \times 3 = 12$, then $4 \times \square = 12$ and $\square \times 3 = 12$. Also, $12 \div 3 = \square$ and $12 \div 4 = \square$.

Shown as a 4 × 3 array with counters,

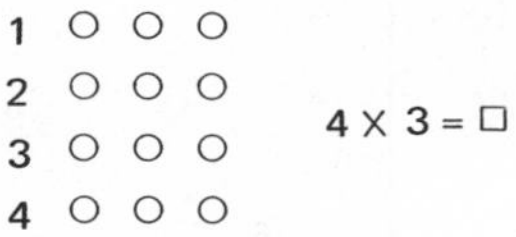

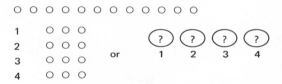

Figure 8-17

Similarly, for the equation 12 ÷ 4 = □, a set of 12 divided into 4 equivalent sets produces how many in each set?

○ ○ ○ ○ ○ ○ ○ ○ ○ ○ ○ ○

1   ○ ○ ○
2   ○ ○ ○   or   ⟨?⟩ ⟨?⟩ ⟨?⟩ ⟨?⟩
3   ○ ○ ○   1 2 3 4
4   ○ ○ ○

Figure 8-18

Partitive and Measurement Division

The teacher beginning to teach equations such as 6 ÷ 2 = □ should not verbalize as "6 divided by 2" or "2 goes into 6." Verbalizing a problem in such a way that the child can visualize what is meant is one of the most difficult problems for the beginning teacher. It is particularly true in division since expressions such as 6 ÷ 2 may have either of two meanings at the concrete level.

(1)   ○ ○ ○ ○ ○ ○ = ⟨?⟩ ⟨?⟩

Figure 8-19

This may be verbalized as "6 separated or divided equally into 2 sets makes how many in each set?" Three.

This is partitive division, the divisor representing number **of** sets.

The expression 6 ÷ 2 = □ can also be represented as

(2)   ○ ○ ○ ○ ○ ○ =   ○○   ○○   ○○

Figure 8-20

This may be verbalized as "6 divided into sets of 2 makes how many sets?" Three.

This is measurement division, in which the divisor represents the number in each set. The teacher should identify and verbalize whichever of the two meanings is being considered as sets of objects are separated. The configuration

Figure 8–21

can also be expressed as 6 ÷ 3, in which case it is verbalized as measurement division: 6 divided into sets of 3 makes how many sets? Two.

Similarly,

Figure 8–22

can also be expressed as 6 ÷ 3, in which case it is verbalized as "6 divided equally into 3 sets makes how many in each set." Two. This is partitive division—the divisor representing the number of sets rather than the number in each set, which is measurement division.[14]

Developing the Basic Multiplication Facts
(0 × 0 to 9 × 9)

In considering multiplication problems at the concrete level with children, a problem such as 3 × 2 = 6 might be displayed as

but not as

Figure 8–23

The expression 3 × 2 is 6 is 3 sets of 2.   Similarly, 4 × 2 = 8 is 4 sets of 2, and 5 × 2 is 5 sets of 2.   Each of these expressions is a

[14] For further discussion, see Richard W. Copeland, *Mathematics and the Elementary Teacher*. Philadelphia: W. B. Saunders Company, 1972, pp. 169–171, 279–280.

problem from the second multiplication table. Many teachers express the idea in reverse, that is, writing the table number first. While 5 × 2 does equal 2 × 5 at the abstract level, in beginning at the concrete level the number named first is the number **of** sets and the number named second is the number **in** each set. In normal English expression we do not say we want a 5-pound bag of sugar times 2, but instead we say we want two 5-pound bags. The expression 2 × 5 = 10 is also a sentence: 2 sets of 5 is 10.

Concrete materials are manipulated by children in order to develop an understanding of the basic addition and multiplication facts and corresponding subtraction and division facts. They will, of course, need to symbolize the work they do with concrete materials such as

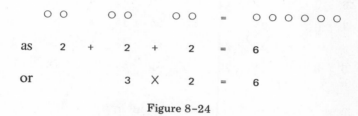

Figure 8–24

The studies of Piaget indicate that for many youngsters the symbol or abstract work might best be done in systematized fashion toward the latter part of the first grade or in the second grade since the necessary operational thought level does not occur in many children until around the age of seven. Some children have still not made the distinction between 3 + 2 and 3 × 2 at nine years of age.

When the child is able to work at the abstract level, he should organize his multiplication facts into a table, such as the one below, using manipulative materials only as necessary.

To develop the facts for the third multiplication table, for example, the child should work with sets of 3 objects as necessary to find out what 2 sets of 3 is, 3 sets of 3, 4 sets of 3, and so on.

A second procedure for studying multiplication facts is to consider a number in the ways it can be expressed as two single-digit factors. The number 12, for example, could be expressed as 6 × 2, 2 × 6, 3 × 4, and 4 × 3. This is similar to the number-family approach in teaching addition, that is, 5 being renamed as 4 + 1, 1 + 4, 3 + 2, and 2 + 3.

As the basic multiplication facts are developed they may be entered in a table.

X	0	1	2	3	4	5	6	7	8	9
0	0	0	0	0	0	0	0	0	0	0
1	0	1	2	3	4	5	6	7	8	9
2	0	2	4	6	8	10	12	14	16	18
3	0	3	6	9	12	15	18	21	24	27
4	0	4	8	12	16	20	24	28	32	36
5	0	5	10	15	20	25	30	35	40	45
6	0	6	12	18	24	30	36	42	48	54
7	0	7	14	21	28	35	42	49	56	63
8	0	8	16	24	32	40	48	56	64	72
9	0	9	18	27	36	45	54	63	72	81

These facts should be committed to memory with some kind of reinforcement activities.

For reinforcement there are a number of games which are fun and yet provide practice in recall of these basic facts. (See the list of commercial sources in Chapter 18. Most have a catalog describing games and activities which they market.)

Children will also need to understand the important ideas of place value and the commutative, associative, and distributive properties as they move toward the conventional procedures in solving multiplication and division problems for larger numbers.

Children discover that the **commutative** property holds for multiplication as well as addition. For example, 3 X 4 = 4 X 3. The **associative** property is also found to hold for multiplication. For example, 3 X (4 X 5) = (3 X 4) X 5.

Distributive Property
of Multiplication over Addition

After children have explored and understand the basic single-digit multiplication facts (from 0 X 0 to 9 X 9), they should explore procedures for multiplying numbers expressed with two or more digits.

The solution for a multiplication problem such as 3 X 23 can be developed at the concrete level using popsicle sticks, as 3 sets of 20 popsicle sticks and 3 sets of 3 popsicle sticks, or 60 + 9 sticks. Expressed symbolically,

$$3 \times 23 = 3 \times (20 + 3) = (3 \times 20) + (3 \times 3) = 60 + 9 = 69$$

This procedure uses a property called the **distributive property** of multiplication over addition. In a problem such as 4 X 321, the factor 4 can be "distributed" over the other factor 321 expressed as a series of addends:

$$4 \times 321 =$$
$$4(300 + 20 + 1) =$$
$$4(300) + 4(20) + 4(1) =$$

Then using the basic single-digit multiplication facts 4 X 3, 4 X 2, and 4 X 1 and the appropriate place value, the problem is expressed as

$$1,200 + 80 + 4$$

and then as

$$1,284$$

The same procedure will work no matter how large the numbers to be multiplied. If both factors are expressed with two or more digits, the distributive property is used at least twice. For example,

$$
\begin{array}{rl}
34 & \\
\times\ 12 & \\
\hline
68 & \quad 2(30 + 4) \\
340 & \quad 10(30 + 4) \\
\hline
\end{array}
$$

And this, of course, is the rationale for "dropping" over one place for the second partial product. It is not 1 set of 4 but 10 sets of 4 ones, which is 40 ones or 4 tens, so 4 goes in the tens column.

Verbalizing such a problem is difficult for the beginning teacher. If the problem is verbalized as follows, it is easy to develop with concrete materials.

34	
X12	

Think of the problem as 12 sets of 34 being solved as 10 sets of 34 and 2 sets of 34. Think of the 34 (ones) as 3 tens and 4 ones. Then

(1)   2 sets of 4 ones is ?   8 ones
(2)   2 sets of 3 tens is ?   6 tens
(3)   10 sets of 4 ones is ?   40 ones or 4 tens
(4)   10 sets of 3 tens is ?   30 ones or 3 hundreds

Verbalized in such fashion, it is not difficult to lay out the problem with concrete materials. Sets of ten can be represented with ten sticks wrapped with a rubber band. There are also convenient-to-use commercial materials made of wood or plastic to represent sets of hundreds, tens, and ones.

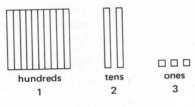

hundreds   tens   ones
1   2   3

Figure 8-25

Comparable procedures for developing the division algorism using concrete materials, as well as other examples of multiplication, are described in Chapter 18.

9

Fractions
and Proportions

It is a far cry from perceptual or sensori-motor part–whole relations to operational subdivision.[1] Conservation of a whole is an essential condition for operational subdivision.[2]

Fractions

Halves and Thirds

Although most of the Piaget activities are unique, the procedure used for investigating children's understanding of fractions was a conventional geometrical one. The child is shown a circular clay slab and two dolls. He is told that the clay is a cake and the dolls are going to eat it all up but that each must have the same amount. He is then given a wooden knife with which to cut the cake.

The experiment is then repeated with another cake and three dolls. A variation is to begin with three dolls rather than two to see if division in two parts first affects the approach to dividing into three parts.

For younger children who have trouble dividing with a knife, paper cutouts of circles, rectangles, and squares are provided. They are asked to cut these with scissors into two or three equal parts. The children may also be given a pencil and asked to mark where they plan to cut to make the division easier.

[1] Jean Piaget, Barbel Inhelder, and Alina Szeminska. *The Child's Conception of Geometry.* New York: Basic Books, Inc., 1966, p. 308.
[2] Ibid., p. 311.

Finally, after each division of a whole, the child is asked if the parts were stuck together again would we have as much as the whole cake, or more or less.

Stage 1. During stage 1, children up to four or four and one-half years find it very difficult to divide in halves. At first the child continues to divide, not stopping at two parts. There is no anticipating plan or schema. A little later he gives each doll the same amount but the pieces are small, leaving a large part undivided. Asked who the rest of the cake is for—"It's for nobody." Some of these children think the cake must be cut twice to produce two parts.

As far as dividing the different shapes is concerned, the rectangles seem easiest to divide, then comes the circle, and finally the square.

The most striking feature at stage 1 is the absence of any relation between the parts and the whole. The child does not consider his part as a nesting element in a larger whole. When a part is cut physically from the whole cake, it loses its quantitative relation to the whole cake. If the child has half, he cannot conclude that the other part is also half since this also involves relating the parts to the whole.

The problem of the relation of the part to the whole has already been discussed at length in Chapter 5. The child in considering nine roses and two daisies, even though he realizes they are flowers, responds that there are more roses than flowers. The same conceptual limitation is present in considering fractions.

Stage 2A, Four to Six Years. For regular and small-scale areas, halving is possible at four to four and one-half years of age. If the size of the original whole is increased, however, it postpones the ability to halve.[3]

The ability to divide into three equal parts is still not present. At stage 2A part of the cake may be divided into three portions and the remainder ignored. Asked what to do about that, one child says, "It's for the Mommy." Or the cake may be divided into a number of unequal portions and three of these taken out and given to the dolls. If the child has previously divided a cake in halves, he may begin dividing the cake into two pieces and then cutting one of the halves into two pieces so the third doll will have some.

---

[3] Ibid.

Using rectangular-shaped cakes provides a somewhat easier solution, but the basic problems are still the same. Trichotomy involves a part that is a third of its complement, whereas in dichotomy a part is equal to its complement.

Figure 9-1. John, 6, divides "cake" for two dolls.

Stages 2B and 3A, Six to Seven Years. Division into three equal parts is successfully performed usually at six to seven years of age. There is no longer a trial-and-error approach but an operational understanding, the concrete operational level. The problem is solved in gradual stages, with stage 2B solutions being transitional and stage 3 solutions immediate. Although in general this period occurs from six to seven years of age, brighter children reach it at four or five.[4]

Questions concerning conservation of the whole are also answered successfully at stage 3, the concrete operational level. Children now realize that the pieces together are the same amount as the whole cake, whereas earlier they thought the pieces were more or less than the original whole.

[4] Ibid., p. 320.

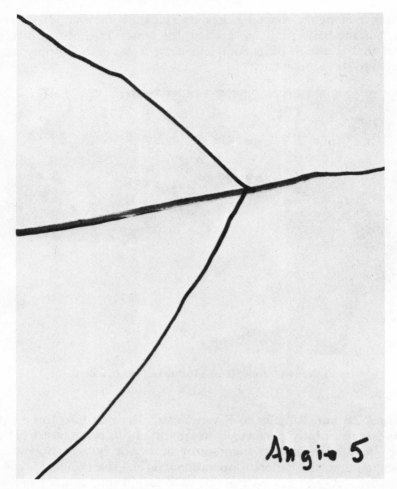

Figure 9-2. Five year old in dividing cake for three dolls draws two lines but then thinks there are not enough pieces so she adds another line.

Division into Five or Six Equal Parts

Although division into sixths can be accomplished with a combination of division into halves and thirds, there is a considerable time delay before this is achieved at stage 3B.

Children at stage 2A, five to six years of age, at first begin by cutting pieces and handing them out to the five or six dolls. They have no solution for the part of the cake that remains after this

Figure 9-3. John, 9, apparently late for stage 2, has difficulty dividing circular cake. By trial and error or moving lines he arrives at equal parts.

Figure 9-4. Class observes child preparing to divide cake for three dolls.

arbitrary division. Later, at stage 2B, there is a schema or plan, such as dividing the cake into two halves and then halving these. Finding he still has only four pieces, one child replies that there aren't enough. Another child divides each of the four pieces in half, obtaining eight pieces, and then gives six pieces to the six dolls.

At stage 3A, seven to nine years of age, children are successful using a trial-and-error approach, such as by arranging the six dolls around the cake and then dividing.

Finally, at stage 3B, around ten years of age, the child tackles the problem with some assurance, such as first trisecting the cake and then bisecting the three pieces.

Implications

Present school practice for timing the introduction of fractions seems to fit fairly well with the necessary developmental characteristics described by Piaget. Many six-year-olds will not, however, have the necessary concepts to understand halves and thirds. The usual teaching methods may be improved by allowing the child to formulate for himself the necessary operations rather than telling him how to divide in halves, thirds, or sixths with no assurance that such telling conveys understanding.

Before children can realize the necessary characteristics of fractions, that each part must be the same size or equal, they must first think of fractions as integral parts of the whole which can be separated and reassembled to form the same whole (conservation). This should occur on average sometime in the first year of school.

Piaget summarizes that children must be able to comply with seven conditions or characteristics of fractions before there can be an operational understanding.[5]

1. There can be no thought of a fraction unless there is a divisible whole. Children of about two years of age regard the whole as inviolable and refuse to cut it. They are stopped by its closed shape (or gestalt). At three, children will share and cut, the act of cutting makes the object lose its character of wholeness.

2. A fraction implies a determinate number of parts. Qualitatively sharing presupposes that the parts must correspond to the recipients (dolls). Yet younger children arbitrarily divide the cake in any way that suits their fancy.

5 Ibid., p. 309.

3. The third characteristic of a determinate fraction is that the subdivision is exhaustive. There is no remainder. Children who respect the first two conditions often use only a portion of the whole for the division or sharing.

4. There is a fixed relationship between the number of parts into which the whole is divided and the number of intersections (cuts). One cut produces two parts, but little children who cut off a small part think that one cut produces one part. Similarly, they think that two cuts produce two parts. Working at the topological rather than Euclidean level, they think that the number of boundary lines and number of areas correspond exactly.

5. The concept of an arithmetical fraction implies that all the parts are equal. Even if the interviewer insists that each doll must have the same, many children still leave part of the cake undivided.

6. When the concept of subdivision is operational, children realize that fractions have a dual character. They are part of the original whole (as a nesting series), and they are also wholes in their own right, which can be subdivided still further. The children who break off one piece after another show they have no understanding of a nesting series.

7. Since fractions relate to the whole from which they come, the whole remains invariant. "Conservation of a whole is an essential condition for operational subdivision."[6] As we have seen, this does not usually occur until six to seven years of age.

Exercise

Verify Piaget's results on children's concepts of fractions using activities similar to those described. (For further information, see Chapter 12, Piaget, Inhelder, and Szeminska, *The Child's Conception of Geometry*.)

Ratio and Proportion

Children's concepts of fractions as equal parts of a whole were considered in the first part of this chapter. The form $\frac{a}{b}$ is used to represent

[6] Ibid., p. 311.

the idea of a fractional number with a and b being integers and b not zero. The number a represents the part or parts and b the number of parts into which the whole has been divided.

The idea of a **ratio** can also be expressed as $\frac{a}{b}$, but a ratio is a comparison of two numbers. For example, in a class of 15 students, if 5 are boys and 10 girls, the fractional part of the class that is boys is $\frac{5}{15}$ or $\frac{1}{3}$. The ratio or comparison of boys to girls is 5 to 10 or 1 to 2, which may also be expressed in conventional fraction notation as $\frac{1}{2}$ but read as 1 to 2 or 1:2.

The idea of a **proportion** is that of two ratios that are equivalent. Proportions are extremely useful in solving many problems in the physical world. They will be used here to solve problems of speed and time, similar triangles, and probability.

The notation $\frac{a}{b} = \frac{c}{d}$ represents the idea of a proportion. Knowing the numbers represented by any three of these letters, the fourth is easy to find. For example, if we know that a train goes 60 miles in 1 hour, we have, as a ratio, 60 to 1. To find how far the train goes in 5 hours, the proportion can be set up as

$$\frac{distance_1}{time_1} = \frac{distance_2}{time_2}$$

$$\frac{60}{1} = \frac{x}{5}$$

Multiplying both members of the equation by 5, x is found to be 300.

It will be seen in the following discussion that children do not realize the equality of two equal ratios such as $\frac{2}{3}$ and $\frac{4}{6}$.

Speed and Time

We have found that the classical notion of speed as a relationship between the spatial interval [distance] and the temporal duration [time] appears very late in child development, about 9 or 10 years of age. By contrast, as early as the preoperational period, that is, even before the age of 6 years, there are intuitions of speed that are not based on this ratio.[7]

[7] Jean Piaget. *Genetic Epistemology*. New York: Columbia University Press, 1970, p. 62.

While there are "notions" of speed as a ratio of distance to time at nine to ten years of age, as reported in this quotation, the ability to quantify or measure speeds using the idea of a proportion develops some two years later at the formal operational level or not until the child is about ready to leave the elementary school. It is ironic that this research on speed and time, as reported in *The Child's Conception of Movement and Speed*, was not translated into English until 1970 and yet was published in French twenty-five years ago.

To study children's ability to use a proportion, a moving object was made to travel along a line as the child times its start and stop, for example, 2 seconds. The path of the moving object is then sketched and beside it the time of 2 seconds recorded. Then the experiment is repeated with another moving object traveling on a path parallel to the first one but taking a time of 4 seconds, for example. The child is then asked if the objects traveled at the same speed or if one went faster.

An operational understanding of speed as a mathematical ratio between time and distance appears at stage 3 *if* both objects, cars for example, are moved partially or wholly simultaneously. However, if the cars are moved in **succession**, one following the other as in the present experiment, old mistakes reappear.

An eight-year-old observing a car moving 4 centimeters in 4 seconds and another moving 5 centimeters in 4 seconds is asked if the trips took the same time. "Yes." Did they travel at the same speed? "Yes." Why? "Because one took bigger steps."

The same child is asked to compare two trips the same distance (4 centimeters) traveled by one car in 4 seconds and another in 3. Did one go faster? "Yes." Which one? "The one taking 4 seconds." Which one gets there in the shorter time? "The one that took 3 seconds." And which was going harder (faster)? "The one that took 4 seconds." Are these questions hard or easy? "Easy." [8]

If both distances and times are unequal for the moving objects, ratios as simple as 2 to 1 cannot be understood.[9]

Such children think the relation "more quickly" is equivalent to "more time."

Toward the end of stage 3, there is a gradual construction of proportion, and finally at stage 4, around twelve years of age, the stage of formal operations, there is a measurement of proportional ratios.

---

[8] Jean Piaget. *The Child's Conception of Movement and Speed*. New York: Ballantine Books, Inc., 1971, p. 227.
[9] Ibid., p. 226.

A twelve-year-old compares a trip of 8 centimeters in 6 seconds and a trip of 5 centimeters in 5 seconds. "It's the first one that goes faster because if the second one had gone the same distance it would have taken longer time. It went a shorter distance and even so it took 5 seconds." [10]

Children at the beginning of stage 4 can formulate ratios of 1 to 2, 1 to 3, and 1 to 4 but have difficulty in calculation of other ratios to compare speeds. Later they employ a systematic method, as in the case of Dis. Comparing trips of 16 centimeters in 6 seconds and 15 centimeters in 5 seconds, he measures them and reports that "You would have to divide 16 by 6 and 15 by 5." [11]

Proportions and Probability

> The notion of proportion appears at eleven or twelve in several different areas. . . . These areas are, among others, spatial proportions (similar figures), metrical speeds [speed and time] . . . [and] probabilities. . . .[12]

To estimate, for example, the probability that two balls of the same color will be drawn at random from a bag containing fifteen red balls, ten blue balls, eight green balls, and soon, the child must be capable of at least two operations. He must be able to use a combinational system in terms of all the possible combinations, and he must be able to understand proportions.[13] At the concrete operational level, the child cannot grasp the fact that probabilities like $\frac{3}{9}$ and $\frac{2}{6}$ are equivalent.[14]

Piaget, in a book on probability,[15] investigated children's understanding of proportion, since proportion is directly applied in granting the same probability to 2 of 4 as 3 of 6 cases. This work has unfortunately not been translated into English.

[10] Ibid., p. 242.
[11] Ibid.
[12] Jean Piaget and Barbel Inhelder. *The Psychology of the Child.* New York: Basic Books, Inc., 1969, p. 141.
[13] Ibid., p. 144.
[14] Ibid.
[15] Jean Piaget. *La Genèse de la notion de hazard.* Paris: Presses Universitaires de France, 1951.

Geometrical Proportions

It is one thing to perceive two figures as similar and quite another to be able to construct operationally a figure similar to an existing model but which does not yet itself exist.[16]

Children's understanding of proportion in the areas of speed and movement and probability was explored in preceding sections. A third investigation of children's understanding of proportion, a geometrical one, is the subject of this section. The data were drawn primarily from *The Child's Conception of Space* (Chapters 9 and 14), published in 1948 and following by two years Piaget's work on speed and movement. Children's understanding of proportion will be considered first in terms of similar triangles and then (in Chapter 15) in the ability to make a map.

Similar Triangles

Parallelism. Below the age of four, children cannot draw or recognize the shape of triangles from among other shapes. But an investigation of similarity can be begun with five-year-olds by showing them a triangle and a base line of another,

Figure 9–5

and asking them to draw a larger triangle using this line so the new triangle "looks like," "is the same as," "has the same shape as" the other.

Children in stage 2A, from five to six and one-half, can draw another triangle so that it circumscribes the model, but there is no concern for parallelism of sides or equality of angles. Children in stage 2B, from six and one-half to seven and one-half, begin to make the sides parallel but only for certain types of triangles (equilateral and isosceles).

At stage 3A, from seven to nine years, children discover and use the idea of parallelism to construct a triangle similar to any given model.

[16] Jean Piaget and Barbel Inhelder. *The Child's Conception of Space.* New York: W. W. Norton & Company, 1967, p. 321.

At stage 3B, nine and one-half to ten and one-half years, children begin a transition from qualitative (perceptual or visual) comparisons to dimension and proportion. They begin to think there is a proportional relationship involved. A child of nine and one-half, given as a model an equilateral triangle whose sides measure 3 centimeters and below which is a base line of 6 centimeters for a larger triangle, uses his ruler to draw the sides of the larger triangle parallel to the sides of the smaller and remarks, "Oh, you could measure it as well."[17] Given an isosceles triangle, base 3 centimeters and sides 6 centimeters, as a model, he immediately doubles his own measurements but then says, "It can't be; it's too high," but then checks to see that the sides are parallel, and is then satisfied.

Equality of Angles. To study children's ability to understand equality of angles as a basis for determining whether triangles are similar, they were presented with a number of triangular cutouts to be sorted into classes so they are alike. The child is allowed to handle the cutouts, such as putting one on another.

At stage 2A, five to six and one-half years, comparisons are global and similarities are not recognized. The child does not examine the angles carefully or superimpose one triangle on another. He says that two go together because they are both "fatter" or two are not the same shape because one is taller.

The inability at this level is worth stressing, Piaget points out, because it reveals that perceptual cues are insufficient for the recognition of similar figures (except for equilateral triangles, where errors cancel themselves).

"In the case of angles as such, length of sides, ratio of height to base and, we may now add, estimate of inclination, perception is invariably subject to constant errors." [18]

In stage 2B, around seven years, the child begins to notice different inclination of the sides (when the triangles are both the right way up), but the accuracy of his judgment of the angles is poor.

At stage 3A, seven and one-half to nine and one-half years, judgments are no longer purely perceptual or intuitive. There is a spontaneous superimposing of the cardboard figures, a procedure involving reversible actions and wholly operational in character. These children discover from this that angles can be equal independent of the length of the sides of the triangle. The equality of two

[17] Ibid., p. 339.
[18] Ibid., p. 344.

angles is described by the children as "pointed the same amount" or "slanted the same amount."

At stage 3B, nine and one-half to eleven years, the children's understanding is now stable and complete concerning the equality of angles as a basis for determining similarity. Asked if two triangles are the same shape, the replies are, "You've got to measure the corners (angles)." Do you have to measure all three angles? "No, only two, because the third is obviously equal."

Summarizing, the notion of parallel lines as a basis for discovering that triangles are similar is mastered at stage 3A. From this, the child goes on to find that their angles are also equal and finally arrives at the idea of proportionality.

Piaget also investigated children's understanding of the similarity of rectangles and found it a sorry contrast to that of triangles, because similarity of rectangles assumes some knowledge of dimensional proportions.[19]   He used rectangles as a basis for studying stage 4, finding that a full understanding of proportion in a quantitative or metric form involving measuring of sides and expressing as ratios does not develop until the formal operational level around twelve years of age, thus corroborating his other studies on the genesis of the concept of proportion.

The idea of proportion in terms of the ability to make a map is also found at stage 4. This idea is investigated in Chapter 15.

Implications

Not much attention is presently paid in elementary school mathematics to the ideas of speed and time, similar triangles, and probability.   Since the operational understanding is not present until around the age of twelve, it is probably just as well.

However, children are introduced to the idea of percentage in the sixth grade, using as a model the idea of a proportion, and many children may not be ready for it.

[19] Ibid., p. 338.

10 Time

It appeared that, at stages I and II [5 to 9 years of age] . . . the child is at a complete loss with both instruments [watches and sand glasses], at first (stage I) because he believes that their motions vary with the actions to be timed, and later (stage II) because he fails to synchronize these motions with those [the motions] to be compared [transitivity].[1] . . .

The fundamental postulate on which all time measurement is based is the existence of motions [measuring instrument and motion to be timed] that take the same time to recur under the same conditions.[2]

Sequencing of Events

Children's concepts of time are at first intuitive. Sensory impressions or perceptions are the basis for their conclusions. Later, logic rather than sensory data provides a basis for an operational understanding of time. Piaget refers to these levels of understanding as **intuitive time** and **operational time**.

To identify the operations involved, two flasks of the same capacity, one on top of the other, are used.

[1] Jean Piaget. *The Child's Conception of Time*. New York: Basic Books, Inc., 1969, p. 176.
[2] Ibid.

Figure 10-1

The top flask is filled with colored water and at regular intervals fixed quantities are allowed to flow from I to II.

The child is given six to eight pieces of paper, each with a picture of the empty flasks on them. He is asked to make a record of where the water is in each container after each flow.

After this has been done, the drawings are shuffled and the child asked to put them back in the order in which he drew them.

Then each sheet is cut horizontally to separate the drawing of the upper flask from the lower flask and again the sheets are shuffled. The child is then asked to find which drawing of flask I goes with a particular drawing of flask II.

To successfully complete this task, the child must arrange the drawings of flask I in correct order as well as the drawings of flask II. This, according to Piaget, is the essence to **time**—the coordination of at least two motions—a coseriation.

After this idea of ordering or **succession** is studied, the child is asked if it took the same time for the water to go from one marking on the flask to the next on each of the flasks. This is the idea of **duration** of time.

Psychologically speaking, the child, to become operational with respect to time, must be able to coordinate the two motions using the relations of **succession** or order and **duration**.

At stage 1, from five to seven years of age, the child is unable to arrange in correct order even the uncut drawings. He is unable to reconstruct the order of events in a single series, because he cannot fit them to unique points in directed time. To perform the task successfully, he would have to "watch" the experiment again (perception), picking out the correct drawings one at a time as he "saw" where the liquid was in the jar. Toward the end of stage 1, by trial and error, the child succeeds in ordering the uncut pictures.

At stage 2, from seven to eight years of age, the child can quickly arrange the uncut drawings, a single seriation, but is at first unable to

correlate two seriations, which is required for the uncut drawings,
Toward the end of stage 2, by trial and error, the child is successful
in matching the uncut drawings.

Trial and error is a perceptual technique. The child tries a drawing
to see if it "looks" right. If not, he tries another until he finds the
right one.

At stage 3, around nine years of age, the problem is solved immediately, not by trial and error, but due to an operational understanding
of succession and duration involving two motions.

Conclusion

Piaget asks himself the question why children eight to nine years of
age have no difficulty in making a double seriation of ten dolls, each
a different height, to ten sticks, each a different length, finding the
right stick for each doll (see p. 102). Yet these children cannot perform the flask experiment successfully.

Piaget concludes that arranging two series by height alone is quite
different from arranging not only by height but coordinating two
motions as well. "This inherent order of succession of two motions
is nothing other than time itself." [3]

Children will learn to tell time by observing the motion of the
clock hand as it measures some other motion, such as going to school.

Duration

To investigate children's understanding of duration of elapsed
time, the flasks are used again, but now the questions do not have
to do with order but with duration. The child watches the water
drop and then is asked, "Did it take as long for the water to rise
from here to here (II_1 to II_2) as it does to drop from here to here
(I_1 to I_2)?"

At stage 1, six to seven years of age, children think the time elapsed
is different. Why? "Because it takes longer to go from I_1 to I_2 (top
flask) than from II_1 to II_2 (bottom flask)." Why? "Because it (the
flask) is bigger on top and there's more water." Perceptual data are
the basis for the answer.

At stage 2, from six and one-half to nine years of age, children
have an intuitive idea that time and velocity are inversely proportional. (If I run home, it takes less time than walking.) Since the

[3] Ibid., p. 28.

liquid seems to run out faster from the top than it fills up the bottom, the child concludes that it takes more time in the bottom. This despite the fact that the liquid is turned on and off for both containers at the same time, synchronous duration, which is accomplished by a knob that connects the two flasks.

These children lack the operational thought necessary to realize the identity of time during which the liquid flows from I_1 to I_2 and from II_1 to II_2. They are still unable to coordinate durations with the order of events.

Quantitative time is both ordinal and cardinal. The order of events A, B, C, D (discussed in the preceding section) corresponds to the inclusion (colligation) of the partial duration time A to B, in the longer duration A to C, and in the still longer duration A to D.

At stage 3, eight and one-half or nine years of age, the child has the necessary operational "grouping" to construct a time scale embracing all moments and events. He realizes that while the liquid flows faster in one container than the other, the duration of flow or time is the same. He can synchronize the times of two different motions. This is the essence of time in which we synchronize the motion of the watch hand with whatever we are timing.

Physical Time

In the preceding sections children were asked to **reconstruct** two timed sequences in order to identify the operations involved, those of succession and (simultaneous) duration. In this section other reactions will be studied as children **observe** or perceive similar phenomena, rather than asking them to reconstruct what they have already seen.

To understand time, a child must be capable of fitting motions at different velocities into a single space–time framework. The interviewer places two dolls at a starting line and at a signal, such as rapping the table, both dolls are moved in hops with one hopping farther than the other. With a second rap on the table both dolls are stopped.

To investigate their idea of succession, the children are asked if the dolls started at the same time and stopped at the same time.

At stage 1, from five to seven years of age, children think the dolls did not stop at the same time, that one took longer because it went further. They thus confuse time with space. These children may not even think that the dolls began at the same time.

Similarly, questioned about duration, they think one took longer because it went further.

At stage 2, also five to seven, children may answer correctly the succession question, that the dolls started at the same time and yet miss the duration question saying one took more time because it went slower (or faster). Some stage 2 children answer the duration question correctly and miss the succession question, saying the dolls did not stop at the same time even though both took the same amount of time. Toward the end of stage 2, by trial and error and repeated questions, the children discover the correct answers.

At stage 3, ages seven to nine, responses are immediate and correct.

Transitivity

A child who is operational with respect to time relations is capable of "grouping," whereas a child working at the intuitive level cannot. The ability to group can be investigated with the transitive property.

$$
\begin{aligned}
\text{If} \quad & a = b \\
\text{and} \quad & b = c \\
\text{then} \quad & a = c
\end{aligned}
$$

Working at the qualitative level with three bottles of different shape but the same volume, if it takes the same time to fill A as B and the same time to fill C as B, then how do the times to fill A and C compare?

Not until around eight years of age can the child use the deductive logic of transitivity to solve the problem correctly. Before this, perceptual means are used. As the child looks at B and C, he can no longer retain the idea of the relation of A to B or A to C.

Measurement of Time

As expressed in the quotation at the beginning of this chapter, Piaget found children unable to use watches or sand glasses effectively until around nine years of age. At stage 1, children believe the speed or motion of the clock hand changes as the motion being timed changes, that is, goes faster or slower. At stage 2, he is still unable to synchronize the two motions, which, of course, is necessary for true measurement.

In effect, the fundamental postulate on which all time measurement is based is the existence of motions that take the same time to recur under the same conditions [isochronism].[4]

Children are then often unable to conserve the velocity of a clock hand, thinking its speed changes as it turns, going fast or slow, depending on what other motion is being timed. They fail to grasp the isochronism of watches.[5]

Isochronism and Conservation of Velocity in Clocks

To demonstrate that the conclusions drawn above are true, Piaget used as one experiment a sand glass with three gradation lines, each a different color, on the top part, representing $\frac{1}{4}$, $\frac{1}{2}$, and $\frac{3}{4}$. The bottom part is masked.

The child is asked to time the sand as it runs out by transferring marbles from one container to another or making marks on a piece of paper at regular intervals. Having done this, the child is asked to speed up his movement of the marbles as the experiment is repeated. He is then asked if it took more, less, or the same time for the sand to move from one gradation line to the next.

At stage 1, five to six years of age, the child thinks the sand runs more rapidly as he speeds up his own motion of making marks on paper or transferring marbles. Perception is the basis for his answers.

At stage 2, seven to eight years of age, the child realizes that the velocity of the sand does not change as the velocity of his own motion changes. He has the "necessary operational groupings and quantifications" to understand conservation of velocity.

However, although conservation of velocity is a necessary condition for understanding time, it is not a sufficient condition. Also necessary is an understanding of synchronous durations and of transitivity. The stage 2 child cannot apply the conservation of velocity concept to two moving bodies (synchronism), which is also necessary to tell time.

Synchronism

Measuring time means comparing at least two motions. Different clocks must "tell" the same time, but children do not understand this until stage 3, around nine years of age.

---

[4] Ibid., p. 176.
[5] Ibid., p. 177.

Figure 10-2. Susan, 6, cannot conserve time. She thinks it takes more time for the sand glass to empty when she moves the marbles slowly than when she moves them fast.

Figure 10-3. John, 9, can conserve time.

Figure 10-4. Misty, 7, watches the clock but thinks it takes more time for the second hand to move half way around (30 seconds) when she moves the objects slowly than when she moves them fast.

Figure 10-5. James, 9, can conserve time.

As an activity, the child may be asked to make marks on a piece of paper at regular intervals. These are timed with a stopwatch, which, for example, takes 30 seconds or makes half a rotation. The child is then asked to make marks on the paper again, and this time the timing is done with a sand glass. The children are then asked to compare the time taken by the clock hand and the sand.

Children until stage 3 lack the transitivity necessary to conclude that the sand glass and clock measured the same time (intervals of making marks on a piece of paper). They think that a job that takes 30 seconds by a stopwatch takes more or less time by the sand glass, because the clock hand moves faster than the sand in the sand glass.

Thus, and this is an important point, even though a child may realize that a clock hand moves at a uniform velocity, he may still be incapable of grasping the equality of time for two different clocks (conservation of time).

Construction of Time Units

Isochronism and synchronism as two necessary conditions for understanding time have just been described. The third and last necessary condition is dividing a time period or duration into number units which can be repeated and applied to other actions one may wish to measure, that is, true measurement in terms of a number.

As an experiment the child is asked to count up to 15 in unison with a metronome while looking at the hand of a stopwatch (which records 15 seconds in the same time). The stopwatch is then covered and the child is asked to count more quickly to 15 (the metronome is set to beat more quickly). He is then asked to predict how far the stopwatch hand went during the same period.

At stage 2, children are unable to synchronize the duration of the work done (counting to 15) with that of the clock hand, thinking the clock hand went farther, to 20 or 30 seconds, for example, because they counted quickly. Or they may say the clock takes more time because it goes more slowly.

Summary and Implications

Since concentrated work on telling time usually begins in the third grade, it fits fairly well with the stages of readiness as described by Piaget.

Some children, stage 3, will have understanding at eight to nine years of age. Others will still be at stage 2 at ten years of age and not ready for a true understanding of time.

As a summary for the busy classroom teacher, three activities[6] follow in outline form: (1) speed and time, (2) conservation and measurement of time, and (3) time in terms of age.

Speed and Time

Purpose of Activity
When should children learn to tell time? This is the purpose of this and the following activity.

Since time is measure by a constant speed of some measuring instrument such as a clock hand, we need to know what a child's conception of speed is.

Materials Needed
Two pieces of cardboard, folded to make tunnels, one tunnel longer than the other.

Two toy cars with strings attached to pull them through the tunnels.

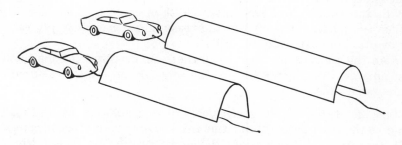

Figure 10-6

Procedure
The interviewer has the two cars placed at the same end of the two tunnels. He has the cars enter and exit from the tunnels at the same time. To do so he may need to make marks on the table so he knows how far each string must be pulled for the cars to exit at the same time.

[6] These activities are from Richard W. Copeland, *Diagnostic and Learning Activities in Mathematics for Children*. New York: The Macmillan Company, 1974.

The child is first asked if one tunnel is longer. The cars are then set in motion, entering and exiting from the two tunnels at the same time. The child is then asked if the two cars went at the same speed or if one went faster and why.

The tunnels are then removed and the paths under them marked with chalk. The experiment is repeated, the cars being moved along the chalk line while the child watches. The child is asked if one car went faster or if they went at the same speed.

The tunnels are then placed back over the chalk lines and the experiment repeated.

An alternative procedure is to use two circular tracks, one inside the other with the cars each making one revolution in the same time, the outside car, of course, having to go faster.

Levels of Performance

Stage 1. At stage 1, four to six years of age, the children agree that the cars went in and came out of the tunnels at the same time but think they went at the same speed because they came out at the same time. Their reasoning is based on the logic of order—out at the same time, hence same speed.

With the tunnels removed these children agree that the car in the longer tunnel went faster, but the reasoning is based simply on one car overtaking or passing the other.

When the tunnels are used again these children revert back to their first answer, that the speeds are the same because the cars come out at the same time.

Stage 2. From six to seven years of age, answers are at first the same as those of stage 1, but the child is able to correct his answers with repeated questions about the length of the tunnels and times of entry and exit.

Stage 3. Around seven years of age the child is operational. He is able to coordinate the idea of time, distance, and speed. If the cars entered and came out at the same time and one went a greater distance, then it must have gone faster.

Teaching Implications

Piaget finds the notion of speed a more primitive or fundamental one than the notion of time.[7] The notion of time involves a

---

[7] Jean Piaget. *Genetic Epistemology*. New York: Columbia University Press, 1970, p. 61.

co-ordination of speeds (the subject of the next activity). Thus the child can solve some questions concerning speed before he can those concerning time. He can say one car is going faster because it overtakes or passes another. He is using the logic of **temporal order** in a succession of events. First A is behind B, then even, then in front of B.

Thus there are primitive or intuitive notions of speed based on the idea of an order of events in time even at four to six years of age.

There is a second temporal notion which these children cannot understand, that of **duration** or elapsed time between two events, such as between entry and exit from the tunnel. Even though the child agrees that the cars enter and exit from the different-length tunnels at the same time, he thinks that the car was in the longer tunnel a longer time, as the next activity will demonstrate.

There is no primitive notion of time, and an intellectual construction by children is not made until nine or ten years of age.

Conservation and Measurement of Time

Purpose of Activity
To demonstrate that telling time requires an intellectual construction not usually found in children until nine or ten years of age. The preoperational child judges the amount of time based on how much was done or how fast it is done without the necessary condition of relating the two.

Materials Needed
Two dolls (the same size), three-minute timer and a stopwatch.

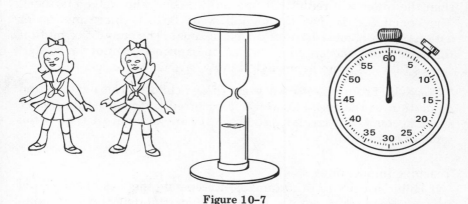

Figure 10-7

Procedure

The interviewer places the two dolls on a table side by side and says that they are going for a walk and the child should say when the dolls should "go" and when they should "stop." When the child says "go," the interviewer hops the dolls along the table, keeping them side by side. When the child says "stop," the interviewer asks him if the dolls started and stopped at the same time.

In the second procedure the dolls are started and stopped at the same time as before but the interviewer makes one doll take longer hops so that when it has stopped it has gone farther. The child is then asked again if the dolls started at the same time and stopped at the same time.

Levels of Performance

Stage 1. Below six to seven years of age, children think that the doll which went farther took more time.

To prove that it is not a case of perceptual illusion, the child is asked, "When one, A, stopped, was the other, B, still going?" and "When B stopped, was A still going?" "No."

Then again the question is asked, "Then did they stop at the same time?" The answer is again, "No."

These children cannot consider successfully the notion of simultaneity—two things happening **at the same time**—when the motions or speeds are different.

Stage 2. From six or seven to nine or ten years of age, children will agree that the dolls started and stopped at the same time, but the period in between—of **time interval** or **duration**—is still not the same. These children if asked if one doll walked for a longer time than the other will reply that one did (the one who walked farther). The conclusion is that if the doll went farther (more motion or action), then it must have taken more time. The amount of motion (distance) and the speed at which it happened cannot be related successfully. If more happened, it must have taken longer.

Stage 3. From nine to ten years of age children can relate action or motion to the speed at which it occurred and realize that greater speed accounts for greater distance while the amount of time is the same or conserved.

Teaching Implications

If children confuse or are unable to separate the idea of time from that of speed, they are not ready for understanding time. In comparing two clocks, one with a second hand, the preoperational child concludes that it takes more time for the second hand to go around once than for the minute hand to move one space because the second hand went farther.   Similarly, these children reason that it takes more rather than the same time for the minute hand to move around the clock than for the hour hand to move from 1 to 2, because the minute hand went farther.   These children think that going farther or doing more takes more time. Speed is not a factor. Thus to cook a 3-minute egg takes more time by a stopwatch than by a timer, because the watch goes faster (or farther).

Variations of this activity, to verify the results, may involve asking the child to make marks on a sheet of paper at regular intervals as they watch a 3-minute timer empty.   Then repeat the experiment asking the child to make the marks faster (or slower) while the timer empties again. The question is then asked, "Did the timer take the same time to empty or did it take longer the second or the first time and why?"

The same procedure can be used with a stopwatch, the child being asked to make marks at regular intervals on a sheet of paper as the second hand on the watch makes one rotation.

The 3-minute timer can also be compared to the stopwatch, the second hand on the watch making three rotations while the timer empties.   The child is asked if one took more time than the other. Using the stopwatch instead of making marks on paper, Piaget reports, " . . . does not help at all, because these children have no notion of the constancy of the speed of the measuring instrument." [8]

Thus, while the adult realizes that instruments used to tell time can move at different speeds (hour hand and minute hand) to measure the same time, the preoperational child cannot and will not until nine to ten years of age.

Piaget defines time as the coordination of movements or speeds (of the measuring instrument and whatever is being timed).[9] This the preoperational child cannot do. Psychologically, he cannot synchronize the durations (of time) of two moving bodies.

Concentrated work with learning to tell time then should begin at approximately nine to ten years of age when children reach the concrete operational level for intellectualizing the idea of time. Tasks such as those just described can be used to determine readiness.

Teachers can use the idea of time with younger children on a perceptual basis. For example, when the little hand points to 2 it is time

[8] Ibid., p. 72.
[9] Ibid., p. 59.

to go home or when the big hand points to 6 it is story time. But verbalizing explanations of what time really is in terms of clocks will not be meaningful.

Time in Terms of Age

Purpose of Activity
To determine children's conception of time in terms of age.

Materials Needed
None

Procedure
Ask the child of four to nine years of age if he has any brothers and sisters and what their names are. If he has no brothers or sisters, ask if he has a friend. Let us assume that the child being interviewed is five years old and that he has a younger brother, Joe.

"How old is Joe?" "Don't know."

"Who is older, you or Joe?" "Me."

"Why?" "Because I'm bigger."

"Who was born first?" "Don't know."

"How old were you when you were born?" "Two months."

"Who will be older when Joe starts to school?" "Don't know."

"Who will be older when you are grown up?" "Don't know."

"Is your Mother older than you?" "Yes."

"Is your Granny older than your Mother?" "No."

"Are they the same age?" "Yes."

"Does your Granny grow older every year?" "No, she stays the same."

"Who was born first, you or your mother?" "Me."

"How old was Granny when she was born?" "She was old right away."

Levels of Performance

Stage 1. Answers are similar to those in the interview above. The child does not grasp the idea of time as a continuum. His answers when he gives them might be classified as **primitive intuitions**.

He thinks aging stops when you are grown up so Mother and Granny are the same age. He often thinks he is older than his parents because he was here when he first saw them. He cannot reason that because Joe is younger he must have been born later.

Stage 2. From six to eight years of age one type of child can reason who was born first based on present ages, but as a young brother grows he will become "older than me (a girl) because he will be bigger." Age (time) is equated with size (space) and is not a continuum in its own right.

A second type of child in this stage cannot tell who was born first based on present ages, but realizes that the age differences remain the same as he grows older. As one child put it, "People grow bigger, and then for a long time they remain the same, and then quite suddenly they become old." [10]

These children have an intuitive or perceptual understanding of time. Toward the end of stage 2 with proper questioning, they arrive at the right answers on a trial-and-error basis.

Stage 3. After eight years of age children's answers are usually immediate and correct. Their answers are now on a logical rather than perceptual basis.

Children at this, the concrete operational level, understand

1. The idea of succession of events in time (in terms of order of births): "If I am older, I must have been born first."
2. The idea of **duration** or conservation of age differences; "If I am five years older, I will always be five years older."

Teaching Implications

Children's answers on questions of age are first based on size. Whoever is bigger is older. Thus time as measured by age is in turn measured by the spatial idea of size. Time (temporal succession) and space (spatial succession) are not separated as ideas and will not be until around eight years of age.

There are two particularly important implications. First, children hear parents talk about their ages, their "younger" brother, and so on, but the necessary logical or mental operations for understanding relative ages and time are not present until around the age of eight. Instruction in the conventional sense, by verbal explanation, will not convey true understanding but only a correct response at the verbal level. Thus, "Joe was born first. How do you know?" "Because you told me."

Second, if the young child of four to six years thinks he is older than his parents because he was there when he first saw them, then where is the logic of "Mother knows best"? Mother cannot give

[10] Piaget, *The Child's Conception of Time,* op. cit., p. 208.

as a reason that she knows best "because she is older and, there-fore, wiser." If the child, however, equates age with size, then Mother is older because she is larger. The logic then, of course, is larger → older → wiser.

Another problem is the egocentric nature of young children. It is difficult for them to look at a situation from other than their own point of view. In a family of three brothers, for example, the child often says there are only two brothers since brothers are a relation only to him.

Emotional insecurity may also affect the child's answers. Although he may be older now than a younger brother, he may not feel he will grow up to be a man as quickly.

Alternative Activity

An alternative and more objective activity to study children's con-cepts of age might be conducted as follows. Cut out six apple trees, each a different size. The child is told that these are pictures of the same apple tree, each a year apart, and the smallest is one year old. He is asked to arrange the trees in a row in order of age. He is then shown cutouts of five orange trees, each one year apart. The adult puts the smallest orange tree above the two-year-old apple tree, saying that when the apple tree was two years old a small orange tree was planted. The child is then asked to complete the row of orange trees (lining them up with the apple trees). Finally the child is asked: (1) Which tree is older in a particular year. Why? (2) By how many years is it older?

The developmental stages will be found to occur at approximately the same time as in the preceding activity. To avoid the factor of height as a determinant of age, the trees could be drawn the same size with one more piece of fruit shown each year.[11]

[11] For full discussion, see Piaget, *The Child's Conception of Time*, op. cit., pp. 218-228.

11 The Growth of Logical Thought

> There would seem to be two critical periods in the intellectual life of the child: the age 7–8 accompanied by a decline of egocentrism and the first appearance of the desire for verification or logical justification; and the age 11–12 when formal (deductive) thought first comes into being.[1]

Beginning activities in logical thought in the form of logical classification were considered (Chapter 5) as a prelude to number ideas. The ability to think logically develops gradually during the time the child is in elementary school. It is a developmental process, and even the best teaching methods must take the stages of development into account. Logical thinking is not something that can be taught at any time, if indeed it can be taught at all. As Elkind reports: "Much of our knowledge about reality comes to us not from without . . . but rather from within by the force of our own logic."[2]

Egocentrism of Thought

There are several limitations to a child's ability to think logically. One is egocentrism of thought. A young child may see a problem only from his own point of view and not trouble himself about being

[1] Jean Piaget. *Judgment and Reasoning in the Child.* New York: Humanities Press, Inc., 1928, p. 74.
[2] David Elkind. "Giant in the Nursery, Jean Piaget," *New York Times Magazine*, May 26, 1968, p. 54.

understood by another person. In so doing, his thought may be characterized as largely, if not entirely, egocentric. There is no apparent need to convince others of his ideas. He accepts rather than questions his own answers.

Introspection

Another limitation to a child's ability to think logically is his lack of consciousness of his own thoughts. As the teacher attempts to help a child solve a problem or find an error, she needs to know to what extent a child is capable of analyzing his own reasoning process. Can we assume that a youngster is conscious of his thoughts as expressed or is there some unconscious activity involved? As has been mentioned, a child does have an egocentric outlook that involves a certain degree of unconsciousness. A person who thinks only for himself and is not questioned or challenged has a greater tendency to believe or accept his own thoughts.

In a study of seven- to ten-year-olds Piaget was impressed by the fact that the children could not tell how they got an answer. He hypothesized that they were incapable of retracing the steps taken in the thought process or else they invented an artificial series of steps and became the dupe of illusions concerning their own thoughts.

> Weng (age 7): This table is 4 metres long. This one three times as long. How many metres long is it?—*12 metres.*—How did you do that?—*I added 2 and 2 and 2 and 2 always 2.*—Why 2?—*So as to make 12.*—Why did you take 2?—*So as not to take another number.*" "This window is 4 metres high. Another window half as high would be how many metres?—*2 metres.*—How did you do that?—*I took away the other 2's.*[3]
>
> Gath (age 7): You are 3 little boys and are given 9 apples. How many will you each have?—*3 each.*—How did you do that?—*I tried to think.*—What?—*I tried to think how much it would be. I tried to think in my head.*—What did you say in your head?—*I counted.*—What did you count in your head? ... Gath only gives answers like "*I guessed,*" "*I counted. ...*" "*I tried to see how much it was and I found 3.*"[4]

[3] Piaget, op. cit., p. 139.
[4] Ibid., p. 140.

From many such cases, Piaget concludes

> In no case is the child able to explain what he was looking for nor what he did to find his answer. . . . He starts from the result he has obtained as though he had known it in advance and then gives a more or less arbitrary method for finding it again.[5]

The reasoning process is not entirely conscious. Either the child remembers only a few terms of his reasoning and then combines them as best he can or he reverses the whole process starting with his answer and inventing the process back to the original premise or question.

When, then, is introspection possible? Piaget concludes that up to the age of seven introspection seems completely absent, but that from seven to twelve there is consistent effort on the part of thought to become more and more conscious of itself. The improvement in the ability to formulate definitions is one example of this development.

The implications of these ideas for the primary-grade teacher are important. From the standpoint of readiness the youngster less than seven years old may not be able to analyze his thought process. A child at this level then should probably not be given problems requiring a logical process of analysis. Teachers of seven-, eight-, and nine-year-olds are faced with a very rudimentary consciousness of thought and the logical thought process involved in solving problems in mathematics. They should plan their procedures with this in mind.

Transduction

Another limitation to childish reasoning is that of transduction. An eight-year-old observes a pebble being dropped in a glass of water and is then asked why the water rises. He responds, "It (the pebble) is heavy." He is shown another pebble and asked what will happen if it is dropped in the water and why. "The water will go up because it (the pebble) is heavy." Shown a smaller pebble and asked the same question, the response is, "No, because it is light." It would appear that the youngster is using a syllogistic argument, or deduction, by applying the generalization that heavy things cause the water to rise.

[5] Ibid., pp. 141–142.

The youngster is then questioned about a piece of wood. Would it make the water rise? "Yes, because it isn't heavy." The youngster illogically contradicts himself. He is not aware that he has done so. He simply has several things in his mind and he sees them as unrelated events.

The idea that to each object belongs a special explanation and consequently special relations that can only result in special reasoning is called **transduction**.   Transduction is a form of reasoning that proceeds from particular to particular without generalization or logical rigor.   Piaget concludes that children's reasoning does not move from the universal or generalization to particular or specific (deductive) nor from particular to universal (inductive).   In short, the child neither proceeds to or from a generalization but only from particular to particular. He is unable to generalize.

Definitions in Logical Thinking

If a child's reasoning process is not entirely at the conscious level, it follows that he would have great difficulty generalizing adequate definitions.   Binet and Simon report that up to and including the age of eight, children are incapable of defining. Terman would not include the eight-year-old.

A definition is characterized by Piaget as follows:

> From the psychological point of view, definition is the conscious realization of the use one makes of a word or a concept in a process of reasoning.[6]

But the child has difficulty examining his own thoughts (introspection).   Not really being aware of or conscious of his thoughts, he is unable to give a definition.   Asked to describe an object such as a "fork" or a "mother," the word may simply be repeated as "A fork is a fork."   If the object is defined at all, it is defined in terms of its use, such as "It's for . . . ."   A fork "is to eat with" and a mother "for cooking the dinner."

Asked what is rain, the reply of the five- to seven-year-old is again in terms of use, "It's for watering." Rain is not considered from the standpoint of its physical **cause**, such as rain is the result of_____.
Neither is rain considered from the standpoint of a **logic definition**,

[6] Ibid., p. 147.

that is, an answer that will define rain in terms of the way it is used in a sentence—for example, "Rain is water that falls from the sky." At this stage of precausality the mind projects itself into things and confuses it with them. The child cannot distinguish between concept and object.

At age seven to eight the child begins to distinguish thought from things and to be conscious of the reasoning process. He begins to use logical definitions such as "A mother is a lady with children." Such logical definitions, however, are not perfect or exhaustive until age eleven or twelve when general propositions can be considered such as "all mothers are ladies" or "all ladies are not mothers" and "all people with children are not mothers."

To determine a definition for "alive," children were asked to classify various objects as to whether they were alive or not and then asked why. Questions began with easy subjects like dog, fish, bird, and then became more difficult, such as river, cloud, car. Most of the responses were that an object was alive because "it moves." But when questioned about a car, cloud, or watch, the children became greatly complexed. Many could not say why an object is or is not alive or give a definition such as "it moves by itself." A few of the most intelligent may give such an answer.

Some children when questioned carefully give evidence that they do have the conception of self-movement as a definition but say only "it moves." Piaget concludes that such children are not yet fully conscious of their own thought and not until age eleven or twelve, or when the child is almost through the elementary school, can he be expected to give definitions that are complete.

The writer made a study of 100 eight-year-olds using the item "If you touched the sun, would the sun feel it?" Fifty-one responded that the sun would. Some would not accept the premise because "it is too hot," "too far away," "you would be dead," and so on. Only five responded that the sun would not feel being touched because the sun is not alive, reasoning logically that if it is not alive, then it has no feeling.

Since childish reasoning is quite different from that of the adult (i.e., less deductive and far less rigorous), it is challenging to the teacher to find out how a child thinks. Also, if a child feels no need to convince others, to what extent can his "reasons" be acceptable?

Language and Logical Thought

That there is little relation between verbal comprehension and operational thought can be seen in children who have a marked linguistic retardation but no trouble in intellectual operation, and also in children with operational retardation and no linguistic trouble.[7]

If linguistic competence is defined as comprehending the phonological and grammatical structure of a language and not its adequate use, it is present in the typical four-year-old. Language is not the limiting factor to operational thought.[8]

While words are usually not a shortcut to understanding, the language children use often does indicate their stage of logical thought. Very young children, when asked the meaning of a word, may simply point or gesture rather than verbalize. "Mother" is pointed out. Later "Mother" is defined in terms of purpose, such as "for cooking the dinner." Still later she is a "lady," and then a "lady with children." Perfect definitions from a logical standpoint cannot be expected below the age of eleven or twelve. Children do not reach the hypothetico-deductive level of abstract logical thought until around twelve years of age.

At the concrete operational level of thought (approximately seven to twelve years), children do begin to use words that express mathematical **relations** between two objects, such as "more" or "less," "taller" or "shorter," "heavier" or "lighter." This is in contrast to the preoperational level, where words expressing absolutes are often used. For example, in comparing two quantities, one larger than the other, the preoperational child may say there is "a lot" for one quantity and there is a "little" for the other.

Children's Understanding of Connectives in Logic

Conjunctions of Causality and Logical Relations

The study of how children think about logical relations was begun by Piaget by asking a group of children to complete or end an unfinished sentence so that it would be "true" or "make sense." The sentences were constructed so that the unfinished part would begin with conjunctions used in logic, such as because, therefore, since, then. For example,

> I took a bath because . . .
> The window was broken because . . .

---

[7] Hans G. Furth. *Piaget and Knowledge.* Englewood Cliffs, N.J.: Prentice-Hall, Inc., 1969, p. 129.
[8] Ibid., p. 114.

The girl fell off the horse because . . .
The fish stopped biting because . . .

Conjunctions such as "because" or "therefore" are used to denote causality and also to denote logical relations. The idea of **relations** is a fundamental and important one in both logic and mathematics because the relationships between ideas develop from logic.

The Conjunction "Because"

The conjunction "because" is a **relation of cause** and **effect** between two events or phenomena. "The boy fell off the bicycle (effect) **because** someone got in his way (cause)." The conjunction because also may represent a **relation** not of cause and effect but of **implication** or **logic**. "He must be going to work **because** he is carrying his lunch." This implication (that he is going to work) is not an observed event but an idea or judgment based on the fact that he is carrying his lunch.

It is the logic of **implication** in which we are particularly interested. In the area of arithmetic, children were asked by Piaget to complete the following sentence: "Half 9 is not 4 because . . . ."[9] This sentence might be completed correctly as "Half 9 is not 4 because 4 and 4 is 8." To explain why half 9 is not 4, we have to resort to a definition and a relation that is not a causal relation between two events. It is a logical relationship that is involved when we say "half 9 is not 4 because . . . ." If we arbitrarily define 4 + 4 as being 8, then half 8 is 4, and half 9 must be something else, since 8 and 9 are not the same. It is possible for a youngster to respond using "because" in its causal or psychological sense by saying "Half 9 is not 4 because he can't count," but this is avoiding the main point.

A third type of relation, a psychological one, that is intermediate to the two just described establishes a relation of cause and effect, not between two independent facts, but between an action and an intention. "I slapped Bill's face **because** he was laughing at me." This type of relation is important because children have a tendency to replace logical relations with psychological relations as in the example, "Half 9 is not 4 because he can't count."

In attempting to analyze the difficulties children have in establishing correct relations, it is necessary to identify the possible meanings that may be associated with a conjunction such as "because." These distinctions are also important in considering the often-used

[9] Piaget, op. cit., p. 27.

"why" of children. To each meaning of "because" there is a comparable meaning for "why."

causal (physical)	Why do boats float? (because . . .)
motivation	Why did you do that? (because . . .)
logical relation	Why is it a planet and not a star? (because . . .)

In a study of six-year-olds who used the relation "because" 134 times, Piaget found that 112 of these were motivational or psychological, 10 causal, and 12 logical. The preponderance of psychological relations involved such expressions as, "Look, he's laughing because . . . ," "René will be late because . . . ," "I want to make a stove because . . . ." [10]

The causal relation is comparatively rare, because, according to Piaget, there is little attempt on the part of the child to socialize his search for the causal explanation of external phenomena. Children do, however, feel the need for causal explanations. Approximately 20 per cent of their questions at age six were found to refer to physical cause. For example, "It is broken because it wasn't properly stuck." "She can't get in the nest because it's too small." [11]

In the logic of implication sense, the conjunction "because" was used only 12 times but this does constitute the beginning of proof. In the example, "No, it's a boat because it hasn't any wheels," the logical process is to begin with the premise that boats are objects without wheels. This object has no wheels, therefore, it's a boat.

Similarly, in the example "It's badly done (a staircase) because you don't make them that way," the premise is that good staircases are made a certain way—This staircase is not done that way. Therefore, it is poorly done.

"You can tell they are going to school because they are carrying their lunches." In this example the premise is that they carry lunches when they go to school and not when they go home. These children are carrying their lunches so (therefore) they must be going to school.

At what age then does the use of logical relations develop? At what age can children complete sentences which imply logical justification? Piaget investigated this question with 180 children in the age range seven to nine, using the two following propositions:

1. Paul says he saw a little cat swallowing a big dog. His friend says this is impossible because . . . .
2. Half 9 is not 4 because . . . .

[10] Ibid., p. 12.
[11] Ibid., p. 13.

	Age 7		Age 8		Age 9	
	Boys	Girls	Boys	Girls	Boys	Girls
Sentence 1	36 (47)*	38 (60)	50 (77)	54 (72)	88 (88)	61 (72)
Sentence 2	8 (41)	6 (44)	30 (57)	14 (46)	25 (62)	17 (48)
Together	21 (44)	22 (52)	40 (67)	34 (59)	56 (75)	39 (60)

Source: Jean Piaget, *Judgment and Reasoning in the Child*. New York: Humanities Press, Inc., 1928, p. 25.

*Percentage of correct responses, and, in parentheses, percentages of answers which were incomplete but which gave some evidence of logical justification.

The most inadequate responses gave psychological explanations such as "Half 9 is not 4 because he can't count" or "because it's silly," or "because it's wrong."

What reason can be given for a child's failure to deal adequately with logical justification? Piaget reports that it is not lack of knowledge but far simpler, and lies in the fact that because he thinks egocentrically, he does not realize the need for it.

> Children in so far as they are ego-centric believe that the other person always knows what they are thinking and their reason for doing so; in a word, they always believe themselves to be completely understood.[12]

Such a conclusion poses an important challenge to the teacher.

When a child does reason correctly, he cannot justify his reason because he is accustomed to taking the essential point for granted. Is the difficulty in dealing with logical justification by the child due to the inability to be conscious of his own reasoning process? Piaget asks:

> That "essential," that logical reason which always remains implicit because it is taken for granted—is the child conscious of it himself? Has he had clearly in mind . . . that "half 8 is 4 because 4 and 4 is 8"? It is obvious that he has not. The child has been conscious only of the particular cases to which his answer referred, and was unable to express the corresponding general laws.[13]

[12] Ibid., pp. 27–28.
[13] Ibid., p. 29.

For example, such responses as half 6 = 3 because "it has been divided" or half 6 = 3 because "half of six makes 3" are responses which simply repeat the original statement.   There were, however, a few correct answers, such as "Half 6 is 3 because 3 and 3 is 6."

If we accept the definition that 3 and 3 is 6 and that half of 3 and 3 is 3, **then** half of 6 is 3. Using the sentence structure "if . . . then . . . ," the "if" clause is the premise or definition. When the "if" clause is agreed on, the "then" clause must logically follow. Hence, **if** 3 and 3 is 6, **then** half 6 is 3.

The Conjunction "Therefore"

"Therefore" as a conjunction can be thought of as the **inverse** of "because."   The conjunction "because" relates cause to effect or reason to logical consequence.

It is raining **because** the grass is wet.
reason   logical consequence

The conjunction "therefore" relates effect to cause, or logical consequence to reason.

The grass is wet, **therefore** it is raining.
logical consequence   reason

Similarly, half 6 is 3 **because** 3 and 3 is 6.

3 and 3 is 6, **therefore** half 6 is 3.

The conjunction "therefore" implies more than the causal relationship of "because."   A deduction is necessary—The grass is wet, therefore (I deduce that) it is raining. "Therefore" is often used in formal proof.

Piaget concludes that logical justification is at a very imperfect stage up to the age of seven or eight, and there must be a long transitional period of learning before deduction can be properly handled.[14] It is usually not until the age of eleven or twelve that a youngster can consider a formal proof. The word "therefore" seldom appears in the child's vocabulary. When a child uses this word it is usually as a synonym for "because" or "and."

---

[14] Ibid., p. 32.

In a study of the use of the word "therefore" as a relation of implication or consequence, Piaget reports that

> Out of the 30 children between six and nine, whom we examined individually, not one proved capable of handling the word "therefore" in unambiguous manner nor of bringing out the particular relations which are indicated by the adult use of the term. In a word, the child possesses no special and unambiguous word for the relation of consequence.[15]

In fact, both "therefore" and "because" serve as synonyms for "and," since "and" may relate two independent events or ideas, and the child often views such ideas or events as being independent or unrelated. This difficulty of seeing relationships is sometimes called **juxtaposition**. It can be observed in a child's drawing of a human figure when arms, legs, or eyes are placed at any point rather than in proper relation to the other parts of the figure.

The Conjunction "Then"

The conjunction "then" is often used in proof, but it is also used for other purposes.

for time	What time will it be **then**?
for motivation	What would you like to do **then**?
and in logic or for logical consequence—the "if . . . , then" sequence	If the windows are frosty, **then** it must be cold.
or	If the fish are not biting, **then** they are not hungry.

The "If . . . , then . . ." is a basic connective sequence in logic. It is concerned with implication or deduction.

Even very young children often use the word "then" in its logical sense.[16]

A child of four and one-half asks: "Is that yours? No, then it is mine." (If it is not yours, then it is mine.)

A six-year-old: "If you lose one, then there is one left."

A seven-year-old: "He is small, then he is like me."

---

[15] Ibid., p. 34.
[16] Ibid., pp. 34–36.

Conjunction of Discordance

Conjunctions that **deny** relations of logical implication, causality, or sequence may be referred to as conjunctions of discordance. These include "although," "even though," "in spite of the fact," and "but." Piaget reports that such conjunctions are very little understood before the age of eleven or twelve.[17] The meaning is not differentiated from such conjunctions as "and" or "because" in completing sentences.

For example, a boy aged eight says:

"I have some big friends even though they are nice," meaning "and" they are nice.

"He fell out of the tree even though it does hurt," meaning "and" it hurts.

The same boy gives a correct response, however, for "Emile is playing in the street even though . . ." by completing it with the statement, "it is cold." [18]

Inductive and Deductive Reasoning

We know that water freezes. We measure the temperature at which this occurs. After a certain number of trials or experiments or readings, we conclude that water freezes at a certain temperature. A generalization such as "water freezes at 32° Fahrenheit," based on a limited number of observations, is subject to some doubt, however slight. When such a generalization includes more cases than have actually been observed, it is based on inference. This type of generalization from a number of specific cases is called an **inductive** inference. *We infer or conclude that what was true in the observed cases is true in all cases.*

In the elementary school use of the inductive rather than the deductive method is often better because induction is related to discovery. As children observe specific examples, they should be encouraged to look for patterns or generalizations. As we find that 4 + 2 is 6 and also that 2 + 4 = 6, apparently the order of adding addends does not change the sum. Trying several more examples, such as 1 + 5 and 5 + 1, we then may generalize inductively that the order of addends does not change the sum (the commutative property). Similarly, $\frac{1}{3} + \frac{1}{4} = \frac{7}{12}$. Can you look at $\frac{1}{3}$ and $\frac{1}{4}$ and think of a way to produce $\frac{7}{12}$? Adding the denominators of the addends 3 and

---

[17] Ibid., p. 38.
[18] Ibid., p. 44.

4 produces the numerator of the sum. Multiplying the denominators of the addends 3 and 4 produces the denominator of the sum. Would this work in adding other unit fractions? If so, we may make an inductive generalization.

Another way of arriving at a conclusion is called a **deductive** inference. It is not based on experiment or observation or "learned" through our senses in contact with the physical world as is the inductive inference. For example, we may say that (1) Bill Jones lives in Miami, and (2) all residents of Miami live in Florida, then (3) Bill Jones lives in Florida. There is no need for external evidence; the sole authority is orderly thinking. There is no question of probability. Deductive thinking is based on the consistency of the human mind and the system of logic employed. Once the hypothesis or premise is accepted as true, the conclusions are compelling. If we accept statements 1 and 2, we must accept 3.

But would a child accept or perform or understand such thinking or logic? Piaget describes the process of deductive reasoning as follows:

> ... to find the key which will enable one to pass from the personal, momentary point of view to another point of view without contradicting oneself. Henceforth the mind is constantly faced with the following problem: how to choose suitable definitions, concepts or premises, i.e., such that can be used from all possible points of view without contradicting either the results of immediate experience, or those of past experience or the experience of others. In other words, how to select notions that will have the maximum amount of reversibility and reciprocity .... [19]

In the example involving the relation between people who live in Miami and people who live in Florida, the child living in Miami must be able to use the logic of the inclusion relation (Chapter 5).

Since logic and mathematics are abstractions, they are not governed by the physical world. A theoretical problem can be chosen arbitrarily, such as "if there are 3 two-headed dogs in the yard, how many heads are there in the yard?" Piaget has this to say about such a hypothetical problem.

> Now, how will the mind be able to solve such problems consisting in the choice of definitions or relations, when these are not imposed upon it by reality itself? ... Definition is always the result of a choice and a decision, and reality occasions but does not compel this choice .... The individual adopts a certain rule as a hypothesis, to see whether by applying it he reaches a state of moral satisfaction,

[19] Ibid., p. 193.

and especially whether he can remain true to himself and avoid contradiction . . . . The question is resolved by a chain of reasoning which aims at discovering, not what will happen in the external world . . . but what will be the state of satisfaction or dissatisfaction of the will which has guided the thinking process.[20]

At what age can children use deductive logic or reasoning? Piaget began with the Binet-Simon test of five absurd statements, asking a group of 44 children (nine to twelve) to rearrange the following statements so that they are not silly.

1. A poor cyclist had his head smashed and died on the spot; he was taken to the hospital and it is feared that he will not recover.
2. I have three brothers: Paul, Ernest, and myself.
3. The body of a poor young girl was found yesterday, cut into 18 pieces. It is thought that she must have killed herself.
4. There was a railway accident yesterday, but it was not very serious. The number of deaths was only 48.
5. Someone said: If ever I kill myself from despair I won't choose a Friday, because Friday is a bad day and would bring me ill luck.

Of the 44 children, 33 had no difficulty with items 3 and 4. Only 13 solved item 5 correctly. The poor responses on this item seemed to be due mainly to the children's refusing to admit the premise, "If I ever kill myself," and to see that this is the main point. The importance of accepting the premise "If I ever kill myself" is ignored as evidenced by responses such as "it is silly to kill yourself."[21]

The writer tested 100 eight-year-olds using item 5. Twenty-nine would not accept the premise of "killing yourself." The largest percentage, 43, focused their attention on the premise of Friday's being a bad day, which they would not accept, thus missing the point. One child responded that Friday is a good day because you "have fun" on Friday. (Apparently Friday is a good day in school for children and teachers alike.) One child responded that "it is a good time to do it" (meaning to kill oneself on Friday). And another "If I ever kill myself, it will be when my husband dies."

Reasoning formally, that is, admitting an idea (premise) when it conflicts with reality and deducing what follows from it, is difficult before the age of eleven or twelve. If the premise is not in accord with the child's experience, he may not agree to it. Neither the premise of touching the sun or of killing oneself was accepted as a beginning point for discussion. However, the writer found that

[20] Ibid., pp. 193–194.
[21] Ibid., p. 64.

children would accept the premise of a two-headed dog (see pp. 198–201).

Although the results on item 4 did not vary greatly from those reported by Piaget, we found a sharp contradiction on the "brothers" item (item 2) and on the "dog" item. These items were taken from one of Piaget's earliest works, *Judgment and Reasoning in the Child*, which has been criticized because the testing was done largely at a verbal level.

Concerning item 2, Piaget found only one third of the children in his sample of nine- to twelve-year-olds able to correct the statement, "I have three brothers: Paul, Ernest, and myself." We found in testing 100 eight-year-olds that 40 responded correctly by saying there are only two brothers. Seventeen others substituted another name for "myself," such as "John," thus responding correctly. The second largest group, however, 35 in number, was concerned with the grammar of the statement, substituting the pronouns "I" or "me" in place of "myself," thus missing the mathematical or logical inconsistency. This test item for girls, incidentally, should be "I have three sisters: Sue, Mary, and myself."

In the illustrated examples of children's work shown here, item 1 was poorly constructed. The intent of the question was understanding the logic of "all," "some," "none." For the statement "Jean says—Part of my flowers are yellow. What is the color of my rose?" the desired response would be "yellow" or "not yellow." One youngster responded correctly, as shown in the following examples of children's work.

In reference to children being unwilling to accept a premise as a basis for logical thinking when it conflicts with their understanding of reality in the physical world, consider the dog item.

Premise: If there are 3 two-headed dogs in the yard, how many heads are there in the yard?

Piaget found that most children would not accept the premise of a two-headed dog, and responded to the question by saying that there is no such thing. However, we found that approximately two thirds of the 150 children ages nine and ten who we tested would accept the premise and gave the correct mathematical response of six. Only a few would not accept the premise, but there were many incorrect responses. One unique and humorous response was that there were "no heads in the yard, the heads are on the dogs." This response poses an interesting question in deductive logic, which involves the idea of the **enclosure** relation. If we accept the premise that the dogs are "in" or enclosed by the yard and that the heads are "on" the dogs, **then** the heads are "in" the yard.

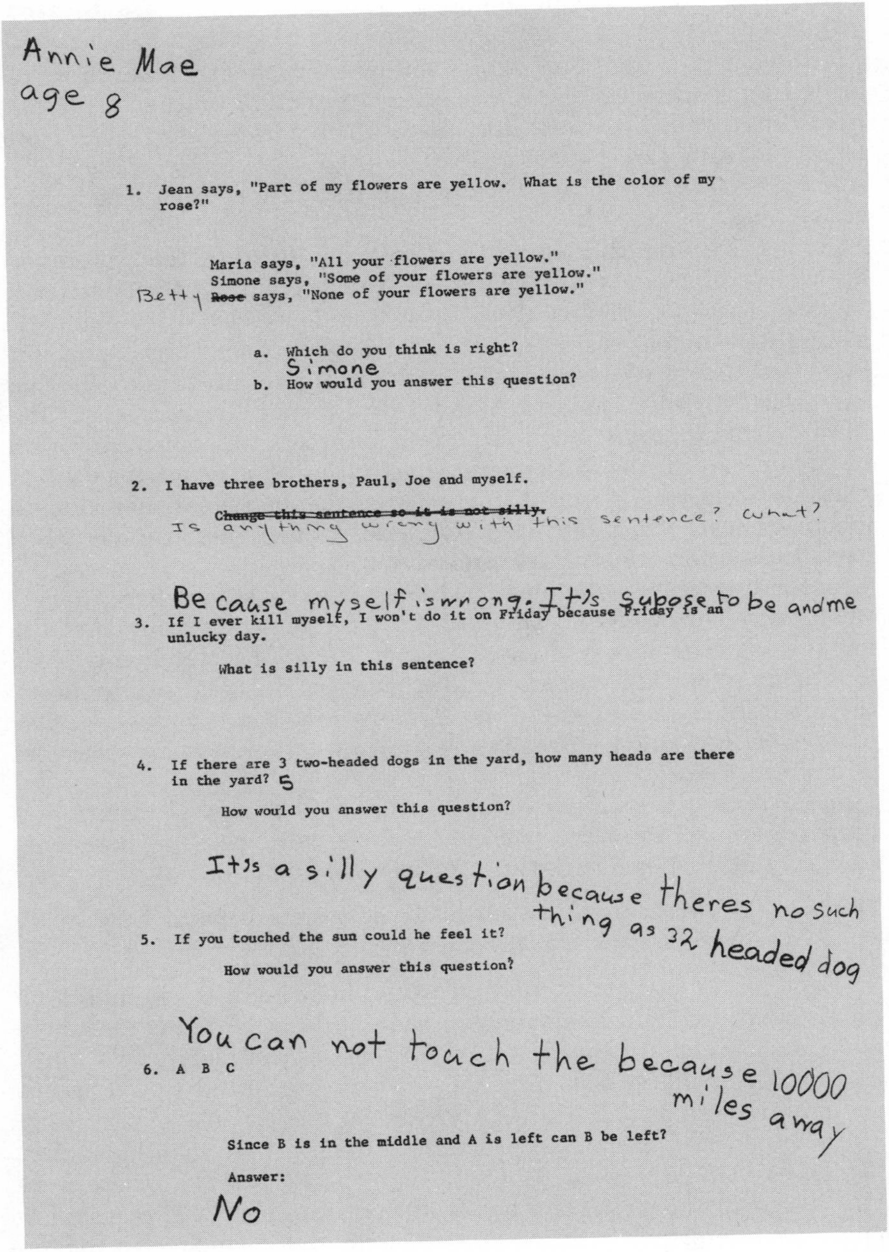

Annie Mae
age 8

1. Jean says, "Part of my flowers are yellow. What is the color of my rose?"

     Maria says, "All your flowers are yellow."
     Simone says, "Some of your flowers are yellow."
     Betty ~~Rose~~ says, "None of your flowers are yellow."

        a. Which do you think is right?
           Simone
        b. How would you answer this question?

2. I have three brothers, Paul, Joe and myself.

     ~~Change this sentence so it is not silly.~~
     Is anything wrong with this sentence? what?

     Because myself is wrong. It's supose to be and me

3. If I ever kill myself, I won't do it on Friday because Friday is an unlucky day.

        What is silly in this sentence?

4. If there are 3 two-headed dogs in the yard, how many heads are there in the yard? 5

        How would you answer this question?

     It's a silly question because theres no such thing as 32 headed dog

5. If you touched the sun could he feel it?

        How would you answer this question?

     You can not touch the because 10000 miles away

6. A B C

        Since B is in the middle and A is left can B be left?

        Answer:
        No

Figure 11-1

Mary   Grade-3

nof 8

1. Jean says, "Part of my flowers are yellow. What is the color of my
    rose?" red

    Maria says, "All your flowers are yellow."
    Simone says, "Some of your flowers are yellow." Simone
    Betty Rose says, "None of your flowers are yellow."

    a. Which do you think is right?

    b. How would you answer this question?

2. I have three brothers, Paul, Joe and myself.
    I have three brothers Paul, Joe and I.
    Change this sentence so it is not silly.
    Is there anything wrong with this sentence? What?

3. If I ever kill myself, I won't do it on Friday because Friday is an
    unlucky day.

    What is silly in this sentence?
    Be cause you have fun on friday

4. If there are 3 two-headed dogs in the yard, how many heads are there
    in the yard?

    How would you answer this question?
    There are six heads.

5. If you touched the sun could he feel it?

    How would you answer this question?
    No

6. A B C

    Since B is in the middle and A is left can B be left?
    Answer: No

Figure 11-2

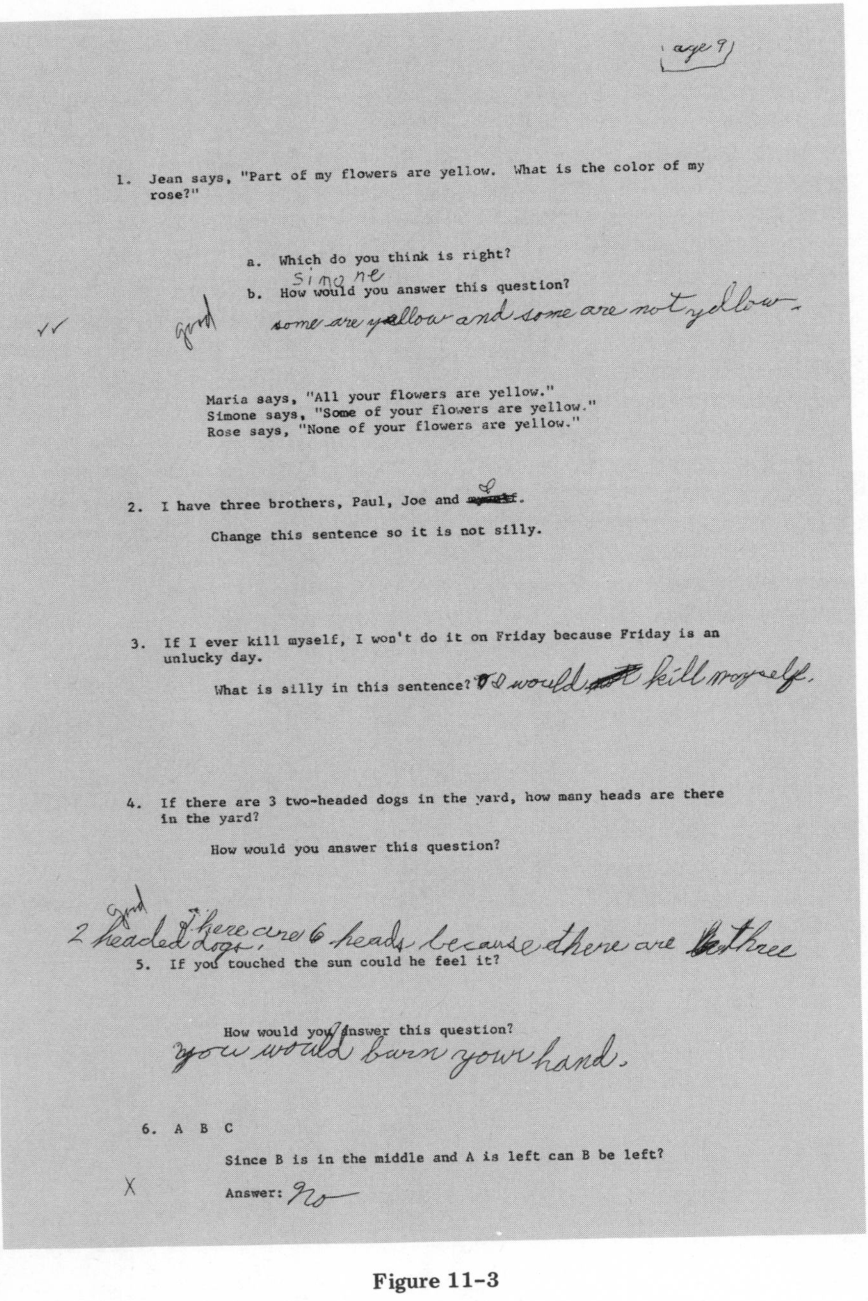

(page 9)

1. Jean says, "Part of my flowers are yellow.　What is the color of my rose?"

    a. Which do you think is right?

    b. How would you answer this question?
       Simone

    good　*some are yellow and some are not yellow.*

    Maria says, "All your flowers are yellow."
    Simone says, "Some of your flowers are yellow."
    Rose says, "None of your flowers are yellow."

2. I have three brothers, Paul, Joe and ~~myself~~.

    Change this sentence so it is not silly.

3. If I ever kill myself, I won't do it on Friday because Friday is an unlucky day.

    What is silly in this sentence? *If I would not kill myself.*

4. If there are 3 two-headed dogs in the yard, how many heads are there in the yard?

    How would you answer this question?

    2 headed dogs. *good* *There are 6 heads because there are three*

5. If you touched the sun could he feel it?

    How would you answer this question?
    you would burn your hand.

6. A B C

    Since B is in the middle and A is left can B be left?

    X　Answer: *No*

Figure 11–3

9

1. Jean says, "Part of my flowers are yellow. What is the color of my rose?"

   Maria says, "All your flowers are yellow."
   Simone says, "Some of your flowers are yellow."
   Rose says, "None of your flowers are yellow."

   a. Which do you think is right?
      Simone
   b. How would you answer this question?
      My rose is red.

2. I have three brothers, Paul, Joe and myself.

   Change this sentence so it is not silly.
   I have three brothers, Paul, Joe, and I.

3. If I ever kill myself, I ~~won't~~ do it on Friday because Friday is an unlucky day.

   What is silly in this sentence? *don't*

4. If there are 3 two-headed dogs in the yard, how many heads are there in the yard?

   How would you answer this question? *3 + 2 = 5*

5. If you touched the sun could he feel it?

   How would you answer this question?
   no one can touch the sun because it is too hot.

6. A B C

   Since B is in the middle and A is left can B be left?

   Answer:

Figure 11-4

The meaning of the word "in" should be checked with the boy who gave this response. He may have meant "in" the yard as "lying in" the yard. Also, he could have meant the dogs were "in" the yard with their heads over a fence of the yard. The idea of "in" or "enclosed" as a topological relation is considered in the geometry section (Chapter 12).

Figure 11-5

The enclosure relation and logic can be difficult for the adult. Consider the squirrel hunter. If he sees a squirrel on a tree and approaches the tree, the squirrel moves to the other side of the tree. The hunter moves around the tree but the squirrel moves also, staying on the opposite side from the hunter. Does the hunter go around the squirrel?

Reasoning formally:

If we accept the premise: that the squirrel is "on" the tree and that the hunter goes around the tree, **then** the hunter must go around the squirrel.

Figure 11-6

There may, however, be an argument about the definition of "around." These questions point up what formal deduction really is, that is, beginning not with a fact or judgment that we accept as true based on our experience or observation **but** with a statement that one simply accepts to see where it will lead.

Deduction even when it deals with reality as based on observation is formal to the extent that it claims to be rigorous. If water freezes at $32°F$ or less, will the lake be frozen if the temperature is $20°F$? If we accept the premise that water freezes at $32°F$ and that 20 is less than 30, then the lake will be frozen at $20°F$. The deductive logic involved is compelling if we accept the premise that water freezes at $32°F$ or less.

Examples of Inductive and Deductive Thinking

How to consider the commutative property using an inductive approach was considered in the last section. To consider the same idea using a deductive approach, we begin with a generalization or definition. For any whole numbers, a and b,

$$a + b = b + a$$

Then our authority in a specific case for making a statement such as $5 + 6 = 6 + 5$ is the definition. This is the high school- or college-level deductive-proof approach.

When we learn, as most of us must, from "experience," it is an inductive approach to life. After the same kind of thing happens to us several times or maybe only once, we make a generalization. After the generalization is formed and then used in specific cases, the procedure is deductive. While walking across campus, the writer overheard a girl tell a boy she could not have lunch with him. Pressed for a reason, she finally replies that she "got indigestion" when she had lunch with him. This was probably a generalization arrived at inductively; that is, she had had lunch with him several times and got indigestion each time.

If we accept the generalization or premise that "blonds have more fun" and Sue is a blond, then deductively the conclusion must be that Sue has more fun. The same idea approached inductively is to know some specific blonds such as Jane, Ruth, and Bill, who seem to have more fun, so the generalization is made that blonds have more fun.

Prejudice may begin as an inductive procedure and then change to deductive. Bill is redheaded and has a hot temper. The same is true of Joe and Helen. The inductive conclusion may be that all redheads are hot tempered. Once this generalization is arrived at, then deductively it is used to judge other redheads.

In the world of geometry, if we begin with a definition such as that a triangle is a three-sided figure and then identify specific examples, the approach is deductive. A better approach (inductive) in teaching children is to show them several triangles and ask them what the figures have in common and from this experience to form a definition or generalization.

Conjunction and Disjunction

The **conjunction** in logic, "and," has the same meaning as does intersection in set theory. The conjunction or intersection of a set of red blocks and a set of square blocks are those blocks both red and square. These should be in the intersection area.

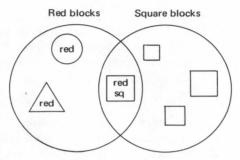

Figure 11–7

The **disjunction** in logic, "or," has the same meaning as union in set theory. The disjunction or union of the set of red blocks and the set of square blocks are all blocks red or square or both.

Although six-year-old children may solve conjunction and disjunction problems with blocks (see Chapter 3), Piaget claims that the child is incapable of either systematic use of conjunctions or disjunctions,[22] which if true has important implications for the elementary school teacher. Adult concepts are in a state of equilibrium because they are products of conjunctions or disjunctions, but the logic processes necessary for this mental equilibrium (equilibration) do not develop in children until approximately eleven or twelve years of age.

If life is defined by children as having the property of self-movement, what about the sun—does it have life or is it alive? No. Then

[22] Ibid., p. 159.

what do living things have that the sun does not? Blood. Then if life may be thought of as the conjunction of self-movement and having blood, the class or set of objects that have life may be defined as those having both blood *and* self-movement. The child, however, considers the two properties of having blood and self-movement separately. He says the sun is alive because it moves, forgetting that it has no blood. Conjunction does not take place in the child's thought.

Similarly, if an animal has long ears, it is a mule or a donkey; if it has a thick tail, it is either a horse or a mule; this animal has long ears and a thick tail. Which is it? Piaget concludes from a number of interviews that up to the age of eight two conditions (such as "thick tailed" and "long eared") cannot be held in the mind at the same time (that is, by 75 per cent of the youngsters).[23]

The thick-tailed class is (mule, donkey). The long-eared class is (horse, mule). Conjunction or intersection of these classes produces (mule).

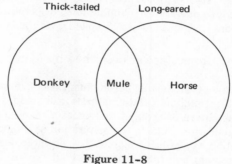

Thick-tailed   Long-eared

Donkey   Mule   Horse

Figure 11–8

Stages of Logic or Reasoning

The transition in childish reasoning may be classified in three stages. The first, **preoperational**, characterized by an inability to generalize (transduction), extends to age seven or eight. The second stage, from seven to twelve, the **concrete operational** stage, is characterized by fewer contradictions in thought and a move toward the ability to generalize. The child is becoming more aware of the relations that exist between separate events. This ability to generalize is still partially based on perception—or what the child observes in the physical world that can be tested by experiment. In the third stage,

[23] Ibid., p. 180.

formal operational, which occurs only after the age of eleven or twelve, the physical world of reality can be left and formal thought is freed from beliefs of the moment or experiments based on contact with the physical world. Instead a rule or hypothesis is adopted and applied in a chain of closely reasoned steps whose correctness is determined by the state of satisfaction or dissatisfaction of the will, which has guided the thinking process, and not by testing in the physical world. Piaget expands on these ideas as follows:

> We can say that during the first stage the reasoning mind does no more than to "imitate" reality as it is, without reaching any necessary implications; during the second stage the mind "operates upon" reality, creating partly reversible experiments and thus reaching the consciousness of implication between certain affirmations and certain results; finally, in the third stage, these operations necessitate each other in the sense that the child realizes that by asserting such and such a thing he is committing himself to aserting such and such another thing. He has at last attained to necessary implication between the various operations [conjunctions, disjunctions, negations, and implications] as such, and to a complete reversibility of thought.[24]

The formal operations stage as described by Maier:

> The last phase of intellectual development occurs between the ages of 11 and 15; childhood ends maturationally and youth begins. Moreover, the nature of thought undergoes a change, which Piaget, in a 1958 publication, links to the maturation of cerebral structures. Unlike the child, the youth becomes ". . . an individual who thinks beyond the present and forms theories about everything, delighting especially in considerations of that which is not." He acquires the capacity to think and to reason beyond his own realistic world and his own beliefs. In short, he enters into the world of ideas and into essences apart from the real world. Cognition begins to rely upon pure symbolism and the use of propositions rather than sole reality.[25]

Such a train of thought may begin with a definition or hypothesis arbitrarily chosen, as in the case of simple deductive proofs. The child uses the logic pattern—"if this" happens, "then that" will happen. He states propositions in terms of the variables he can identify.

---

[24] Ibid., pp. 194–195.
[25] Henry W. Maier. *Three Theories of Child Development*. New York: Harper & Row, Publishers, 1969, p. 146.

There are four basic ways that propositions in logic can be combined. In considering two variables, such as smell and color, in causing fish to bite:

by conjunction   it's smell *and* color
by disjunction   it's smell *or* color
by negation   it's neither smell nor color
by implication   if it's not color, then it must be smell

Each of the possibilities must be checked out and linked to its implications.

Implications for the Teacher

The main value of this chapter to the elementary school teacher may be (1) a realization of the stages through which children go before they are able to reason formally, (2) when these stages usually occur, and (3) the thought processes that occur during each stage. Many test items have been described to aid the teacher in determining her own pupils' stage of development. That reasoning formally is not accomplished until eleven or twelve years of age means that many children below this age are not ready for formal logic.

Formal Operations

Teachers of eleven- and twelve-year-olds need to be conscious of the fact that it is propositional-type thinking that they should foster as the child moves to the stage of abstraction involved in formal logic. Just telling a child to think does not give him the tools of conjunction, disjunction, negation, or implication that will help to process his thoughts. There is a structure to the logic process. Some fifth- and sixth-grade mathematics materials do have sections on logic as an introduction to formal or deductive logic.

The fifth- or sixth-grade (or middle-school) teacher interested in studying the structure of the **formal operations** thought processes of the child of eleven or twelve to fifteen or sixteen should read Piaget and Inhelder's book, *The Growth of Logical Thought from Childhood to Adolescence: An Essay on the Construction of Formal Operational Structure* (New York: Basic Books, Inc., Publishers, 1958). Unfortunately, the book is difficult to understand.

Less difficult information and examples of formal operations thought processes may be found in the proceedings of the third annual symposium of The Jean Piaget Society conducted at Temple

University in May 1973.[26]   Particularly helpful is the lecture by E. A. Lunzer.

Concrete Operations

Teachers of five- to eleven-year-olds will be working primarily with children at the concrete operational level. Logic can be begun but only as it relates to objects in the physical world. For example, in considering two sets of blocks, such as red blocks and squares, if the block is not red (negation), then it must be square (deduction). Such beginning activities in logic are described in Chapter 5.

In teaching mathematics, although it is considered to be a deductive science par excellence, it should not be so treated in the elementary school. To the mathematician, mathematics is an abstraction, a product of man's mind and not a part of the physical world, even if it can be used to describe phenomena in the physical world. Number itself is an abstraction. You do not see a number in the physical world. It is this abstractness that lends to mathematics, in part at least, its beauty as a science to be treated by deductive logic.

Children in the elementary school, however, are not ready to work at the abstract level with formal logic and proofs. They are very much a part of the physical world. Mathematics for them should be exploration and discovery—an inductive approach through the physical world with concrete objects. Children should be encouraged to discover patterns in mathematics, such as the commutative property based on specific observations in the physical world (an inductive approach).

The teacher of children from ages five to nine needs to be aware of the egocentric nature of the child. It is difficult for him to think from viewpoints other than his own. His limitations as described in the sections on "Introspection" and "Transduction" should be taken into account.

Fundamentally important is that much of our knowledge comes not from without but from within by the forces of our own logic. Knowledge is not a copy of reality but a reconstruction of it. It is reason or logic that allows the child to overcome sensory impressions. Since much of our knowledge does come from within, this means it does not come directly from the teacher. One basic responsibility of a teacher is to provide physical experiences and ask questions that may provoke the process of equilibration or logical operations within the mind of the child as a way of learning. In so doing it is hoped that there will be little "telling" or "explaining."

[26] Tapes available from The Jean Piaget Society, P.O. Box 493, Temple University, Philadelphia, Pa., 19122.

12 How a Child Begins to Think About Space

Study of the child's discovery of spatial relationships—what may be called the child's spontaneous geometry—is no less rewarding than the investigation of his number concepts. A child's order of development in geometry seems to reverse the order of historical discovery.[1]

Geometry is a mathematics concerned with position or location in space. There are many geometries, but those most closely related to children's experiences are topology, Euclidean geometry, projective geometry, and metric geometry or measurement.

In introducing geometry to children present practice is to begin with Euclidean geometry—figures such as line segments, triangles, squares, and circles. This is how geometry developed, historically speaking. It was the type of geometry studied by the Greeks 2000 years ago and has been until recently the basis for the geometry taught at the secondary level.

Geometry as presented in the primary grades mostly involves such activities as connecting points with line segments and recognizing and naming the resulting figures, such as triangles, squares, and rectangles.

---

[1] Jean Piaget. "How Children Form Mathematical Concepts," *Scientific American*, Nov. 1953, p. 75. Copyright © 1953 by Scientific American, Inc. All rights reserved.

Triangle   Square

Figure 12-1

Such activities involve Euclidean geometry, which includes a study of figures that might be referred to as "rigid" in shape. A triangle, for example, is considered to have rigid sides—they do not bend or stretch. In comparing it to another triangle, it may be moved, but its size and shape remain the same.

Geometry as now introduced to many children is structured on the assumption that a child's first conception of space is Euclidean, but Piaget maintains that this assumption is incorrect. Rather, the child's first concepts are topological. Topology as a branch of mathematics is relatively new, not being developed until the nineteenth century.

Topology

In the mathematics of topology, figures are not considered to be rigid or fixed in shape. They may be stretched or squeezed so that they assume a different shape; hence topology has the nickname "rubber geometry." Simple closed figures, such as squares, circles, and triangles, are equivalent topologically because they can be squeezed or transformed to form each other. Stretching a square may produce a rectangle.

Figure 12-2

The child's first impression of space or the world in which he lives is a very disorganized one. Figures come and go before him as in a moving tableau. He clutches for a feeding bottle and then doesn't know how to move it to get the nipple in his mouth. He grasps for something, but it is not where he puts his hands. His motions are random ones. If an object is hidden from view, such as under a blanket, he thinks it no longer exists.

As the child explores and develops, things begin to take shape and position for him; he sees the door open and that it is "separated" from the wall. His mother's face comes close and it changes in appearance as it moves near him. He sees the beads and toys on his crib as being "separate" from the crib and begins to play with them.

Shape to him is not a rigid thing. The shapes he sees are often changing ones. The door looks different as it is opened. His mother looks different as she moves closer. Her face (to him) changes in shape as it turns to right or left or up and down as it moves nearer or farther.

The actual fixed shape of the mother's face does not change, as the adult knows. It might be described as a circle or ellipse in Euclidean geometry, but the baby does not see it as a rigid shape.

In projective geometry, which involves perspective or how an object looks from different positions such as a side or front view, the mother's face looks different and is different as seen from different positions, such as from a baby's eyes. In projective geometry an object is considered not by itself but in relation to some other position in space. (This subject is studied further in Chapter 13.)

In topology, a circle can be squeezed to form an ellipse, triangle, square, and many other figures, all of which are equivalent topologically.

Figure 12-3

Such figures in mathematics are called simple closed curves. A simple closed curve is any drawing that begins and ends at the same point, with no other point being touched twice.

The triangle as first seen by the child is not as the adult sees it. The three-year-old asked to make a copy of a square or triangle may draw a circle, which is correct topologically. While a triangle is unique in Euclidean geometry, it is not in topology. Some topological problems are now appearing in the primary grades, but they are not the first experiences usually provided in geometry.

At the age of three a child often cannot distinguish between squares and triangles, drawing both as a simple closed curve like a circle, but he can distinguish between open and closed figures.

Figure 12-4. Open figures.

Figure 12-5. Closed figures.

Opened and closed figures are not equivalent topologically. The properties of **opened** or **closed** are topological properties, and the child recognizes this distinction. Stretching or squeezing (not tearing) will not transform an open to a closed figure. The child makes such a distinction before he can distinguish between such Euclidean simple closed curves as triangles and squares.

Since the child becomes conscious of topological relations before he becomes conscious of Euclidean relations such as congruence (same shape and size), he is at first unable to consider the idea of congruence. A triangle and a square are not congruent, but the three-year-old does not see this difference in Euclidean relationship.

Piaget summarizes, "Not until a considerable time after he has mastered the topological relationships does he develop notions of Euclidean and projective geometry." [2]

In this conclusion Piaget finds evidence for his logico-mathematical model theory of cognitive development. "Curiously enough, this psychological order [of development] is much closer to modern geometry's order of deductive or axiomatic construction than the historical order of discovery [of geometry] was. It offers another example of the kinship of psychological construction and the logical construction of science itself." [3]

To think of the distinction between topology and Euclidean geometry, consider a piece of string or rubber band placed in the form of a circle. Its shape could then be changed by squeezing or stretching to many other shapes, such as a triangle, square, or rectangle. In topology, each of these figures is **equivalent** to the others.

[2] Ibid.
[3] Ibid.

A figure 8, however, is not topologically equivalent to a circle. It would have to be "torn" or "separated" at its point of intersection in order to form a circle.

Figure 12-6. Not equivalent topologically.

A three-dimensional object such as a cube is considered to be topologically equivalent to a sphere. A cube of clay, for example, could be squeezed to form a sphere.

In fact, a topologist has been defined as a mathematician who can't tell the difference between a doughnut and a cup of coffee. By a process of squeezing and shaping, one could be transformed to the shape of the other.

Topology does not distinguish between circles and squares or between cubes and spheres, but it does distinguish between a sphere and torus (doughnut shape). A sphere could not be transformed to the shape of a doughnut without tearing.

Figure 12-7

Conservation

The idea of conservation of length or direction focuses on an important distinction between Euclidean geometry and topology. In Euclidean geometry, length as a property for a given line segment is rigid or conserved. In topology, length is meaningless. All line segments are equivalent. A line segment can be thought of as being stretched or made longer without disrupting the topological relations to be discussed in the next section. Similarly, the conservation of the **direction** of a line is a Euclidean principle. It may be wavy or straight without affecting the topological relations.

Relations in Topology

Family relations, such as "brother of" and "sister of," are good examples of "relation" to use with children. There are also relations in the mathematics of topology—those of **bounded** or **enclosed**, for example. A door is opened and the child sees it as bounded or enclosed by the wall and floor. There are a number of "relations" that can be classified as topological. The first and most elementary topological spatial relation that can be grasped by perception is that of **proximity** or "nearby-ness." The younger the child, the greater the importance of "nearness" of an object. He distinguishes between objects in terms of which is nearer and which farther away. In drawing a face he puts the eyes near the nose.

The second elementary topological spatial relation is that of **separation.** As a child grows older he is better able to "separate" or distinguish one object from another or the parts of an object one from another. He sees the door as being **separated** from the wall or a toy as separated from his crib. In his drawings of a face he separates the nose, mouth, and eyes. Before he can distinguish between the Euclidean figures of a triangle and square he can draw one figure inside another, such as a circle within a circle either touching or not touching, thus noting whether the circles are separated or not.

A third spatial relation is **order**—such as the order of beads on his crib or more importantly the order of a door opening, a light being turned on, a figure appearing, dinner time.

A fourth spatial relation is **enclosure** or surrounding. In the series ABC, B is between or enclosed by A and C in the horizontal dimension. In two dimensions an element such as a nose is surrounded or enclosed by a face. The nose is between the eyes and mouth. A window is enclosed by a wall. A smile is enclosed by a face. The child can draw a circle inside or enclosed by another, thus noting the enclosure relation that exists between the two circles. Although very young children may not be correct, even topologically, drawing an eye outside a head rather than inside or enclosed by the head, they will correct such errors before they can learn Euclidean relationships.

These ideas, all topological in type, are quite different from the Euclidean notions of rigid shape, distance, straight lines, and angles with which we confront children for first experiences in geometry, thus ignoring what psychology tells us of how the young child first learns about space.

Consider the properties relative to a specific geometric figure such as a line segment. Thinking of the line segment as a set of points, the topological relations between the points of **proximity, order,**

separation, and **continuity** remain the same whether the line segment is thought of as being stretched or curved. For example, considering only three points (A, B, and C) on the following figures,

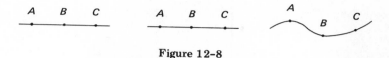

Figure 12-8

the "order" of A, B, and C is the same on each figure. B is enclosed by A and C on each figure. A and C are separated by B in each figure. Each figure is equivalent to the others topologically, since the topological relations are the same among the points A, B, and C.

Similarly, the following are topologically equivalent, since the topological relations among points A, B, and C are the same in each figure.

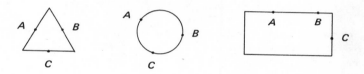

Figure 12-9

The human face that the baby sees is a flexible or topological structure, changing in size as it comes closer and in appearance as the head turns left or right or up or down. It is elliptical in shape at one moment and circular at another. In mathematical parlance, the **transformation** in appearance of the face is a study of homeomorphisms in topology. Shape appears to change, but a topological relation such as order among chin, nose, and mouth does not.

The following drawing is topologically correct in terms of the enclosure relation as far as the eyes are concerned. The eyes are "in" or enclosed by the head. However, the order relation of eyes, nose, and mouth is ignored in that the eyes are represented vertically in the middle figure. The order of head, trunk, legs is ignored in the left figure with just a suggestion of a body. The legs in the middle figure are not separated from the body. Hence even the topological relations of order and separation are not represented correctly at this stage of development.

Figure 12-10.   A teacher, child and teacher's aide.   Note placement of eyes in child, the center figure.

The Topological Relation of Order

The nearness of an object is the most fundamental way in which a youngster explores space.   This topological notion or relation of **proximity** is closely followed by the relation of **separation** of this object from other objects.   A third relation is that of **order** or sequence.

To study children's concepts of order, large beads, each of a different color, are placed on a rod and the children given a duplicate set of beads and asked to place them on another rod in the same way. The children were first tested to be sure they recognized the different colors.

red   blue   orange   white

Figure 12-11

Two- and three-year-olds are unable to understand the request. Four- to five-year-olds understand the notion of order if they can check it constantly by having the model rod directly opposite their own. If the model rod is not placed beside their own or the model rod is bent in the form of a circle, they can no longer make a copy. Neither can they place the beads on the rod in an opposite order, because they have not yet achieved the intellectual level of "reversibility" of thought.

These inadequacies or difficulties in coordinating the horizontal order relations of left and right or the vertical order relations of up and down or circular order involve basic motor coordination difficulties.   Piaget concludes that motor activity in the form of skilled movements (in this experiment with beads and rods) is vital to the development of intuitive thought and the mental construction of space.[4]   From a mathematical standpoint, the idea of left and right (horizontal dimension) or up and down (vertical dimension) involves a coordinate system that you may remember from graphing in algebra or analytical geometry.   This mathematics of dimensions between fixed points in space is the mathematics of Euclidean space.

Between the ages of six and seven, children arrive at a point where they can resolve order difficulties.   When shown a model, they can copy and reconstruct it in either order, left to right or right to left or in a circular form.   There is now reversibility of thought, characteristic of an intellectual activity, as contrasted to purely sensory-motor activity.

In a variation of the colored-bead experiment, laundry items, such as different-colored dresses, are hung on a washing line and their order considered.   The six- to seven-year-old child, using paper cutouts from a stack given him, is asked to make a copy using another washing line.   He is then asked to put his on in the opposite way, starting with the last one to see if he can reverse the order.   Asked what the laundry would look like if he did the opposite of what he had just done, he replies that it would be like the original.

Varying the experiment by asking if the laundry was stacked vertically, the child predicts correctly the middle and bottom articles for both directions.

[4] Jean Piaget and Barbel Inhelder. *The Child's Conception of Space.* New York: Humanities Press, Inc., 1963, p. 97.

Figure 12-12. A six year old orders clothes on a clothesline.

Shown a necklace in a circle, the child is asked to show what it would look like if in a straight line.

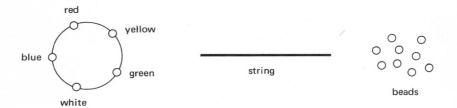

Figure 12-13

Whereas this causes no great difficulty, if the beads are arranged in a figure 8 pattern,

Figure 12-14

the child is misled at first by the intertwining in making a straight-line copy. He checks his copy by unwinding the figure 8 model and comparing it to his copy.[5]

The Topological Relation
of Surrounding or Enclosure

We have considered the elementary topological relations of proximity, separation, and order. Another important topological relation is that of **surrounding** or **enclosure**. In considering the line segment below, the relation of point B to points A and C is "between." Considering only one dimension (horizontal), B may be said to be "surrounded" or enclosed by A and C.

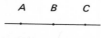

Figure 12-15

The relation "between" is a special case of the relation "surrounding." Similarly, if a point is located within a closed figure,

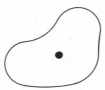

Figure 12-16

[5] Ibid., pp. 101–102.

the point is surrounded or enclosed by the figure. This relation of surrounding involves a two-dimensional figure. Considering a seed within an orange, a three-dimensional surrounding idea is involved.

Topologically, if the orange is squeezed, its shape changes and the seed may move, but the topological relation of surrounding of orange to seed does not change.

Knots

There is in topology a study of the theory of knots. Topological relations can be studied using a piece of string and making simple knots. The relation of surrounding or enclosure can be considered in a simple loop knot. If a loop is placed in the string,

Figure 12-17

and then one end of the string is passed through the loop, a surrounding (intertwining or enclosure) realtion exists.

Figure 12-18

Without this "surrounding" relation, there is no knot.

To study children's grasp of the relation of surrounding and ability to tie a knot, Piaget used a piece of string, first asking the children if they could tie a knot. If not, they were shown and then asked to reproduce the procedure. If this failed, a piece of string half red and half blue was used and the process explained as a story, such as "the red goes underneath, then on top, then inside."

Up to the age of four or five the children were unable to tie a knot even after seeing one tied. An example of this stage:

> Col (3; 10). "Can you tie a knot?" (A piece of string is placed in front of him.)—*Yes*. (He merely brings the two ends together.) No further explanation enables him to improve on this, so a knot is tied while he watches. This is left slack. "What is that there?" Now pass this bead through there—(He passes the bead through the loop.)—Now move the bead along the string—(He moves the threaded bead all the way along the string.) Despite this lesson he cannot copy the knot but can only bring the ends of the string together.

Mer (3; 11) does not stop when he has brought the ends of the string together but goes on to remark, *You can go into the little hole like this*, and thereupon passes one end through the half-loop formed by the curved part of the string. The ends are then pulled and Mer is amazed to see the "knot" disappear and the string come untied. He is then shown that the string "must be crossed." This is demonstrated for him but he cannot repeat it for himself.[6]

The idea of a loop, overlapping and passing the end of the string through the loop, cannot yet be mastered.

In the second stage (four to six years of age) the child can without help copy a simple knot he can see, but if the knot is loosened or tightened he no longer recognizes it as the same knot. This loosening or tightening does not change the topological relations that exist, but the youngster is not yet aware of it. Neither can he in many cases tell a true knot from a false knot (where there is overlapping but no intertwining or surrounding relation that would produce a knot if the string were drawn tight).

A five-year-old ties a knot without any model.

"How did you manage it?"—*I pass it through a hole, then after that I make a knot.* He is shown an overhand knot very loose and all parts clearly visible. *No, it isn't a knot*—"Pull it"—*Oh, it is*—"And this (a half loop without a knot)?"—*No it's not a knot because it doesn't pass through the hole*—"And this (loose knot)?"—*No, neither is that*—"Run your finger along the string. Let's suppose it's a pipe and an ant starts crawling along it. He can't get out until he reaches the other end. Which way will he go?" (on reaching the crossover point he blunders and slips from one section to the other)—And by slipping this bead along the string (it is moved a few centimetres and he has to continue on his own)?—(He fails again)—And this (a taut knot), is it a knot?"—*Yes, that's on top and that's underneath.*[7]

Another five-year-old is shown a taut knot and asked to draw it.

Figure 12-19

[6] Ibid., p. 108.
[7] Ibid., p. 113.

He draws a straight line and for the knot, a circular shape filled in.

Figure 12-20

Given a piece of string he is able to make a copy of the taut knot. He is then shown the same knot as a loose knot. Although he can make a copy of it, he thinks it is a different knot but is unable to explain why.[8]

When one part of the string passes beneath another (a three-dimensional idea), the child loses track of "the real order of succession, the true proximity of neighboring parts [of the string]."[9] Instead the child passes over into another part of the knot that is not adjacent to the first. Thus, although he can reproduce a knot, he fails to note the three-dimensional aspect necessary for surrounding and attempts to make a knot on the table top (a flat surface or two-dimensional space).

The relation of proximity of points on the string and the relation order of position of points on the string does not change as the knot is loosened or tightened. The knot does not change topologically speaking as it is loosened or tightened. It is the same knot, and the relations of order, proximity, and surrounding do not change.

The child fails to recognize this because, according to Piaget, the underlying ideas are still far too perceptual in character and have not yet achieved a sufficient degree of flexibility. The child's ideas are still tied to static configurations.

The idea that the configuration of a knot tied loosely or tightly is the same topologically is characterized in mathematical parlance by saying they are **homeomorphic** or topologically **equivalent**. Topology is a study of such homeomorphisms—changes in configuration or transformation.

At the third or operational stage (toward the age of seven) the child recognizes the correspondence between the taut and loose knot. He can also distinguish between the true and false knot and predict whether a knot will be produced as the string is tightened or whether the apparent or false knot will "pull out" so that the string is straight with no knot when tightened.

At this level, when a knot is loosened or tightened, the child recognizes that the topological relation of "surrounding" does not vary as do the Euclidean ideas of "size" of loop (circle or eclipse) or

[8] Ibid., p. 114.
[9] Ibid., p. 118.

"length" or "width" of knot. The topological relations of proximity, order, and separation of points along the string do not change, even though the Euclidean shape of loops does. The adjacent parts of the string remain adjacent. The parts near or separated remain near or separated; the surroundings reappear unchanged as the knot is loosened or tightened.

The Relations of Continuity and Infinity

The relation of **continuity** is a drawing together of the topological relations—proximity, order, separation, and surrounding.

A point as a position in space and a line as a set of points is now seen in some first-grade materials. The idea of a line or line segment as a set of points infinite in number is a difficult concept, as we will see. Just what notion a child has of these concepts is interesting to observe. His ideas are quite different from those usually introduced in geometry—arbitrarily defining a line as a set of points. The notion of continuity does not depend to any great extent on what the child learns in school, according to Piaget, but must wait the appropriate stage of development, which, for this concept, is relatively late. The child does see some examples of this idea as, for example, when he watches a lump of sugar in water dissolve first into grains, then into a cloud, and finally disappear.

The idea of continuity can be investigated by thinking of a line segment or a square as it becomes smaller and smaller. Not only conscious actions but the process of abstract thought will be studied as it begins to develop between the ages of seven and twelve and finally develops into formal thought at ages eleven and twelve.

Asked to draw the smallest possible line segment or square that he can think of, the child at the first stage does not grant the existence of what cannot be seen. He can only make a limited number of subdivisions. In considering a line segment being divided, he may not be able to consider half of a half. The smallest line segment he can think of will be a visible line segment, and the smallest square a visible square and not a point.

A five-year-old manages to draw three squares in an order of decreasing size and then draws a fourth larger than the third.

Figure 12-21

He is unable to continue what he started out to do, to draw a very small square, even when he has a correct start of squares in decreasing sizes. He has the same problem in drawing sizes in a larger order.[10]

A seven-year-old is asked to draw the smallest possible line. He draws one 2 millimeters long. Asked if there are any points in the line, he replies that there are not. Asked how many little lines he would need to make a line 2 centimeters long, he says "ten" as an estimate. Asked how many points could be placed between two points 2 centimeters apart, he guesses "one hundred." Starting to fill in the gap with points, he puts in 23. Is 100 right then? The reply is then "no," because the points would be too close together. Asked if this would not be right then, he says "No, because when you are making points it isn't a line."[11]

From age seven or eight to eleven or twelve the child passes through a second stage, in which he admits the possibility of a larger number of subdivisions but does not regard them as infinite in number. He does not generalize beyond the finite or visible size.

An eight-year-old draws the smallest possible square at his first attempt. Asked what it is, he describes it as a point. He also describes the smallest possible line segment as a point. But asked if it is like the point made by the smallest square, he replies that it is not because that is a square point while the other is a little dash.[12]

Thus this child does not conceive of a point as having no dimensions (of length and width). The youngster in considering the relations between points on a line has mastered the topological concepts of proximity, separation, order, and enclosure. He recognizes that there are spaces between points which are themselves filled with points close to, yet separate from, the other points. The four relationships of proximity, separation, order, and enclosure, however, cannot be brought together in a single whole in the absence of the idea of unlimited subdivision and enclosure, which appears at the next and last stage of development.

It is most interesting that not until a youngster is eleven or twelve or almost ready to leave the elementary school can he grasp the idea of unlimited in number. And yet we arbitrarily introduce the line as a set of points in the primary grades. Until this stage the youngster cannot perform the abstract operation of thought that allows the subdivision or separation of the whole indefinitely, thus visualizing the line as an infinite set of hypothetical points.

---

[10] Ibid., p. 130.
[11] Ibid., p. 132.
[12] Ibid., p. 139.

Here is a ten-year-old approaching this last stage of development:

Alf (10; 2). [For] The smallest square. He makes a tiny point. "When you cut a line, what is left in the end?"—*A point*—"Can you cut it in your mind?"—*Yes, it will get smaller and smaller and in the end there won't be any left*— . . . "How many points are there in the square (3 cm side)?"—*Thousands*—"And in this table?"—*Billions*— "How far could you go on counting them?"—*I think I could go on forever*—"And would a grown-up come to the end of the number?"— *No, never, because no-one has ever come to the end.*[13]

Finally, as a clear example of this last stage of development, a youngster almost twelve years old:

Bet (11; 7). "How many points could be drawn along this line?"— *You can't say. You can't count them. You could make points that get smaller and smaller* (cf. the decreasing enclosures)—"How many are there in this circle?"—*It's impossible to tell*—"But roughly; 10,000, 100,000, 1,000,000?"—*It's impossible to tell, there are so many you just can't say*—"Make a drawing showing what the smallest possible line looks like"—*But it can't be done because it could always be made smaller still.*[14]

It is at this level that thought becomes hypothetical and deductive, freeing itself from the concrete level of sensory experience or perception. A line is seen as an infinite set of points. The concept of continuity, constituting as it does a synthesis of the topological concepts of proximity, separation, order, and enclosure, "rounds off the development of the topological concepts on which rest the child's idea of space."[15]

Since the idea of infinite is not understood to any great extent until eleven or twelve years of age by most children, it is obvious that introducing a line segment, a triangle, or other geometric figures as "sets of points" in the primary grades is to teach without meaning. This is not to say that some children cannot consider the concept earlier where instruction is on an individual basis. But the foregoing discussion does give the teacher a good idea of the type of performance that can be expected. Also the interview techniques quoted provide an excellent guide for procedures to determine each child's stage of development as far as continuity or infinity is concerned.

[13] Ibid., p. 146.
[14] Ibid., pp. 146–147.
[15] Ibid., p. 149.

Implications

The discoveries of Piaget that children's first geometric concepts are topological rather than Euclidean would thus call for the first type of geometric activities in the nursery, kindergarten, and grade 1 to be topological in character. These activities should be based on the topological relations just discussed—those of proximity, separation, enclosure, and order.

Children should be questioned on the topological relationships that exist between various objects. Many sample activities, together with appropriate interview techniques, have been described in this chapter.

Can children reproduce a circle inside or enclosed by another circle, thus noting the enclosure relation? Can they draw a circle inside another but touching at one point, thus noting the proximity relationship between the circles? Can they differentiate these figures from circles in other configurations, such as intersecting at two points or not intersecting at all?

Shown a picture of a yard with a house "inside" the yard and a dog "outside" the yard. Can the child note the distinction in the topological relations among dog, fence, house, and yard? Asked to draw a picture like it, does the child draw the house as enclosed by the yard and the dog as not enclosed by the yard? Is the dog separated by the fence from the yard?

In order to determine his understanding or proximity or nearbyness, consider the following illustration.

Figure 12-22

Is the house really near the school or is it near the church? Is the tree near the house? Or near the barn? Concerning separation, is the barn separated from the silo?

Concerning the enclosure relation, is the cow in the pasture or outside? Is the house in the yard? Is the car in the street, the boat in the river? Children may be asked to draw a mother or father or boy or girl and asked questions about the drawing. Are the eyes in the right place? The arms? The legs?

In drawing a house are the proximities correct? Are the chimney, windows, and door approximately where they should be? All of these activities are topological in character and good mathematics.

Art and Mathematics

The close relationship of mathematics to the artwork of children is obvious, and teachers can determine the topological abilities of children as they observe their artwork.

The human figure is a good example to use in seeing how it is represented or drawn by children. How are the arms and legs drawn and how are they attached to the body? At first the arms and legs are just sticks attached to the head.

Figure 12-23   Figure 12-24

Drawings of human figure by four year olds.

Later the legs are attached to the body and not to the head. Thus the "proximity" of legs to body and head is correct. The "order" of legs, body, head is also correct. Later, fingers will be added to the arms and feet to the legs.

Figure 12-25

Again the "order" is correctly shown: feet, legs, body, head, hat. And each of these elements is shown as separate from the others. The legs are shown as enclosed by the feet and body. Greater differentiation will be possible later. Hands will be placed between the fingers and arms, thus noting the topological relation of order: fingers, hand, arm. Hands are enclosed or between fingers and arms.

As children begin to draw faces, again the topological distinctions can be noted. The very young child may even be incorrect topologically putting a mouth or eye outside the head. Thus the head does not enclose the eye as it should. Later, eyes may be placed inside the head but vertically rather than horizontally, as shown earlier in the chapter. In studying children's drawings, is the **order** of mouth, nose, eyes correct rather than eyes between nose and mouth, for example? Are the elements nose, mouth, and eyes **separated** from each other? As ears and hat are drawn, are they attached to the head or are they drawn separated from the head?

By the time the average child is six to seven years of age, these topological relationships should be resolved. The teacher of four-, five-, and six-year-olds should observe these developments, asking questions such as: "Is that where the hat (or nose) should be?" "Is your picture like this drawing?" "Is the dog in the right place?" "Is the door on the house in the right place?" "Did you put your toys back in their place?"

The questions are asked, not answered. The art teacher as well as the mathematics teacher is interested in creativity. The child's interest in drawing should not be squelched for accuracy of representation. The uncomplimentary name "broad" might be appropriate

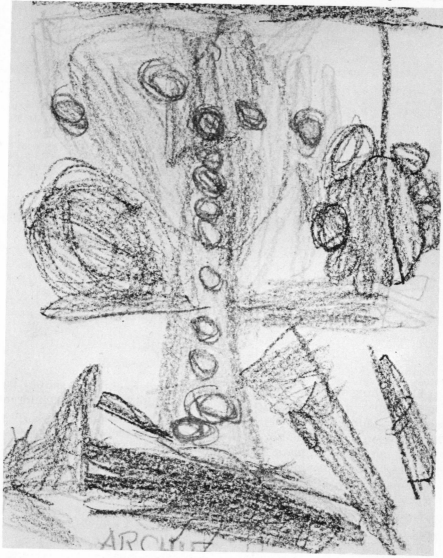

Figure 12-26. A retarded youngster's concept of his teacher. Legs separated from body and ear rings drawn large because of his interest in them.

for a drawing of her teachers (see next page) by a child of five and one-half. The "order" of legs, body, arms is ignored since the arms are attached to the legs.

Figure 12-27

Concerning the topological relation of order, children should be given many opportunities to use it. What is the order of the children as they stand in line? Who follows Jim? Who is first, who last, who in between Joe and Tom? At lunch period, is the order of the elements napkin, fork, plate, knife, spoon correct? Can you name them in reverse order starting with the spoon?

In playing with blocks, can the children order them in a certain way? Can they represent a given order of colored blocks given a set of duplicate blocks? In a row, in a circle, in a square? Can they reproduce a linear order such as 1 red, 2 blues, 1 red, 2 blues, and so on? Can they also reverse the order of the colored blocks? Such activities provide good mathematical experiences at the concrete level and will contribute to the development of operational thought.

The present practice in the primary grades of teaching that geometric ideas (lines, triangles, squares, etc.) are sets of points should be reexamined. The smallest line to many children is a line segment, not a point. As to the concept of how many points or line segments there are in a line, the necessary drawing together of the topological relations of proximity, order, separation, and surrounding to form that of "continuity" (which allows the consideration of unlimited or infinite) is not developed in children until eleven to twelve years of age.

If Piaget is correct, it is a purely rote exercise to talk of lines as sets of points in the primary grades. In so doing the new math becomes as rote as the old math. Children begin to parrot definitions for rays, line segments, triangles, and so on. They are not ready for such concepts. Logically, space can be considered in terms of sets of points, as can lines and rays, but not psychologically before eleven to twelve years of age.

Figure 12-28. Drawing by four year old interested in earrings.

13 From Topology to Euclidean Geometry

Motor activity [is] of enormous importance for the understanding of spatial thinking.[1]

Pictorial Space

Since mathematics is a deductive science based on logical reasoning, there has been a tendency by some elementary school textbook writers trained in mathematics to present mathematical ideas to children at an intellectual or deductive logic level. Thus in geometry the beginning is often a treatment of Euclidean ideas such as distance, length, angles, lines, triangles, and squares as if they were "real elements" in space when, in fact, they often are not for young children.

The child may observe a "distance" or a "straight line" or a "square" and yet be unable to translate these ideas into a mental representation. His ability to construct a mental representation is studied in the way he draws a picture to represent an object that he has seen but is no longer visible. These drawings give evidence of a topological notion of space rather than an Euclidean one.

In figures on pages 216 and 227, for example, eyes are correctly placed, topologically, "in" the head but incorrectly as far as Euclidean geometry is concerned, because they are vertical rather than horizontal. Similarly, the hair is "on" the head but on the side rather than top.

---

[1] Jean Piaget and Barbel Inhelder. *The Child's Conception of Space.* New York: Humanities Press, Inc., 1963, p. 13.

In the accompanying drawing of a horse and rider, a four and one-half-year-old draws the man in the shape of a large head to which is attached four strokes, representing two arms and two legs.

Figure 13-1. A 4-1/2 year old, who is the son of an artist, represents a horse and rider.

The topological idea or relation of proximity is observed to the extent that the rider is "on" the horse, and the idea of separation in the way the legs and arms are represented as separate from the face and body. But the idea of order (the synthesis of proximity and separation) is not observed in locating the arms and legs of the rider. Neither is the body shown as separated from the head.

The topological idea of enclosure is correct in that the face encloses or surrounds the eyes and mouth. Children that do not have the topological concept of enclosure may draw an eye outside the head. Euclidean and perspective relations are lacking in the location and length of the horse's legs and yet there is the quality of "motion" which may have been all this young artist was concerned about.

At this stage Euclidean and projective or perspective ideas are beginning to emerge, but they are still overshadowed by topological relationships.   For example, **proximities** are correct, such as in locating arms and legs approximately where they should be representing an arm not as a stick but separated into fingers, hand, and arm.

At this stage Euclidean ideas of line, angle, circle, square, and other simple figures appear. Not until the age of eight or nine do drawings usually reflect perspective, proportion, and distance. This last stage, perspective and projective geometry, is studied in Chapter 17.

Drawing Basic Euclidean Shapes

Piaget investigated the ability of children to represent basic Euclidean shapes by asking them to draw 21 shapes.

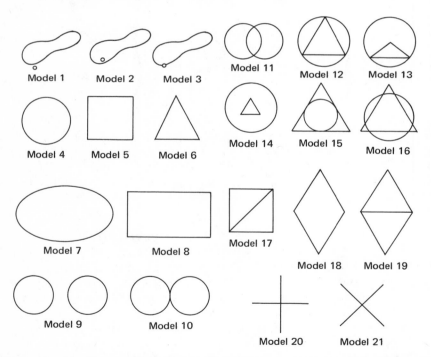

Figure 13-2.   From: Jean Piaget, *The Child's Conception of Space,* p. 54. (Courtesy: Humanities Press, New York, N.Y.)

Below stage 1 no purpose or aim can be observed in the scribbles. This usually occurred below age three. During stage 1 (usually occurring in the third year) two levels are observed. At the lower level the scribbles vary, depending on whether the figures are open (e.g., X) or closed (e.g., O). At the upper level the drawings begin to take a more definite form. Circles, squares, and triangles are all represented in the same way by an irregular closed curve. Since these figures are equivalent topologically, the child is correct topologically. However, the Euclidean relationships of length of sides, angles, size, and number of sides are completely ignored.

Stage 2 begins at about the age of four and extends to the age of five to six. The lower level is represented by a progressive differentiation of Euclidean shapes. Curved shapes begin to be differentiated from straight-sided ones, but there may be no differentiation between the polygons (straight-sided figures such as triangles, squares, and pentagons).

A higher level of stage 2 is marked by a differentiation based on the number of angles. (Binet and Terman report that the ability to copy a square is a test for a mental age of four.) Dimensions are noted, differentiating the circle from the ellipse. Finally, at the highest level of this stage, circumscribed figures such as

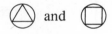

Figure 13-3

are drawn correctly. Between six and seven years of age the rhombus is mastered (at age six, according to Binet, and in the United States at seven, according to Terman).[2]

At stage 3 (six to seven) all the figures, including the composite ones, can be reproduced.

Implications

In the foregoing discussion the important stages of geometrical and psychological development through which children are going during the age range three to seven are pointed out. Appropriate activities for nursery, kindergarten, and first grade are not the same. Geometrically the emphasis at the nursery level should be topological.

[2] Ibid., p. 68.

Figure 13-4

At the kindergarten and first-grade levels the transition from topology to Euclidean geometry can be made. The stages of development described will give the teacher a good idea of the type of performance that can be expected at each age.

Figure 13-5. Five, six, and seven year olds' reproduction of drawings that were on blackboard (except for man for which they were given no model).

Perception and Thought

Our experience might tell us that our knowledge and concept of space have developed through our sensory experiences of "touching" and "seeing" objects in our physical world and somehow fitting these objects into a meaningful whole on the basis of these sensory perceptions. This is the assumption on which many mathematicians and teachers have based their instructional procedures.

Piaget found that this assumption or conclusion was erroneous, that in fact the evolution of spatial ideas proceeds at two different levels—the level of perception (as learned through the sense of touch and seeing) and the level of thought or imagination. The second does not follow logically from the first as one might think, but each develops along its own path; so at some point there must be a reconciliation of these separate developments. As an example, a child is shown two sticks and asked if they are the same length or if one is longer.

Figure 13-6

He agrees that they are the same length on the basis of perception by observing that their ends line up or are matched. One stick is then moved and he is asked if the sticks are still the same length.

Figure 13-7

He now says one is longer based on perception, because its end is farther away. He has not reached the stage of conservation of length, an intellectual idea that conflicts with what perception tells him.

The understanding of just how one does learn about space becomes more difficult because of the conflict between intellect and perception. We will consider first the conception of space developed through perception by our senses.

Space on a Perceptual Basis

A child's concepts of space develop on two levels. One is the perceptual level, the level of learning based on sensory impressions received through touching, feeling objects, and "seeing" or visual impressions. The psychologist describes this as the sensory-motor level.

Even at this level the adult may be tempted to assume that the visual impressions received by the child are translated into the same result as those received by an adult and that "perceptual fields" have the same basic structure from the simplest to the most highly developed. If this structure has a geometrical character right from the start, there should be immediate recognition by children of such Euclidean properties as size and shape. Thus a baby might be expected to recognize the shape of an object independent of perspective and its size without regard to distance. From the beginning then there would be a perception of relationships in space. If this were true, instruction could begin on the basis of the laws of spatial configuration of Euclidean geometry (as is presently being done).

Piaget found that these hypotheses are not true, that "shape" is not constant or fixed as perceived by the young child and that in fact great differences still exist between the eight-year-old and the adult as regards size constancy. The seven- or eight-month-old, for example, has no idea of the permanence of objects; figure appear and disappear as in a tableau. He does not think of reversing a feeding bottle presented to him backward.

The child only a few months old lacks coordination between vision and grasping. Thus space is not a coordinated whole—what he sees he is unable to readily find by touch. Thus solid objects seem not to be fixed in position or to have a permanent size and shape.

The problem of shape and size may also involve the observer as in perspective (projective geometry). To the observer, railroad tracks appear to come closer together in the distance, and if the observer is involved, this is the way the tracks should be drawn.

In Euclidean geometry, the tracks remain as they actually are in space, that is, parallel.

Learning Euclidean Shapes

If a youngster is given a triangle and asked to describe it, he may handle it feeling its straight edges and corners. His knowledge of the triangle that develops from seeing it and touching it or by sensory

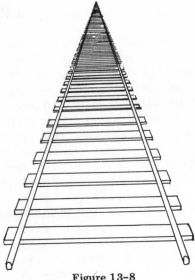

Figure 13-8

impressions is **perception**. Perception is knowledge of objects result-ing from direct contact with them. But does being shown a triangle register a mental image for the child? Does he recognize the straight-ness of the sides, the number of the sides, the size or length of the sides? These are Euclidean properties.

The child's ability to use these properties in order to abstract the idea of a triangle and recognize others as belonging to the class of triangles involves **representation**. It is not a photographic process. At what age can a youngster represent or reconstruct an idea of a Euclidean figure, noting straightness, number of sides, length, and so on? What are the difficulties involved?

To study children's ability to abstract a geometric idea or "con-struct an image" based on a sensory experience (perception) in the age range two to seven, Piaget used a familiar experiment. A child is placed on one side of a screen and allowed to touch and handle an object on the other side of the screen. Younger children are then asked to point out the object from a collection of objects or pictures shown to him. Older children are asked to draw the object. Younger children were first given familiar objects, such as a spoon or ball; older ones were given cardboard cutouts of geometrical figures.

In the following photograph, this procedure was used as a game with a demonstration class in Ft. Pierce, Florida. The class included a boy who had not spoken in his regular classroom situation for three months. The teacher had so warned the demonstration teacher. The boy could not resist reacting to the game situation even though classed as dumb by his classmates.

Figure 13-9. A game situation enjoyed by children. For diagnostic work individual interview technique should be used.

Three stages of development can be observed. In the first stage, extending to six years four months, familiar objects such as a spoon are recognized but not geometric Euclidean figures such as a triangle. In the second stage, a transitional one, six to seven years of age, some figures are recognized and others are not. Curvilinear shapes such as circles and ellipses can be differentiated from rectilinear shapes, but discrimination within each of these classes cannot be made. For example, a square is not differentiated from a rectangle, parallelogram, or rhombus. In the third stage, a synthesis of complex forms is achieved. Exploration is more methodical in nature.

Stage 1. In examining each stage in more detail, it was found that there are two levels in stage 1. In the lower level familiar objects such as a spoon are recognized, but basic geometric shapes are not. In the upper level some shapes are recognized. The most interesting thing is that the shapes recognized are not Euclidean but topological.

For example, the circle and square are not differentiated because both are closed forms, but open forms are distinguished from closed forms. Thus the sequence of development of recognition of geometric forms is (1) familiar objects, (2) topological shapes, and (3) Euclidean shapes.

The child distinguishes between open and closed forms before he can distinguish between two forms both of which are closed or open. Thus his concepts are topological.

Exploration by young children at stage 1 in handling the objects is passive. The child simply grasps the object with both hands, possibly thrusting a finger through the hole if there is one. Neither straight lines nor angles are yet identified.

A three-year-old recognizes a ball, a pencil, a key, and scissors, but does not recognize a spoon. He is also unable to identify a cardboard circle, ellipse, or half-circle from other figures.

Another three-year-old

> . . . recognizes objects in the same way—takes hold of them, passing them from hand to hand. Takes hold of a triangle but makes no attempt to explore it. "Have you any idea which one it is?—*No*— Keep trying—(He seizes it in both hands and turns it over.) Can you draw it?—*Yes*—(scribbles). (Given several models to choose from) Is this it? (square)—*Yes*—Or is it this one? (rhombus)—*No*—Look at them; which is it?—*This one* (square)." [3]

Thus this child is unable to differentiate a triangle from a square or circle. Neither can he differentiate a square from a circle or ellipse. Another child, three and one-half, is shown a circle and a square but draws or represents both as ellipses.[4]

Thus the Euclidean distinction of a circle and square is not made. The figures are not different at this age for many children. And topologically, of course, the circle and square are not different.

The shape of an object is abstracted by the action the child performs on it with his hands, such as tracing its contour, surrounding it (cupping hands), or separating it (putting finger through a hole). These perceptions of the boundaries of an object, noting whether it is opened or closed or separated, involve the mathematical relations of topology rather than Euclid.

Piaget concludes that these fundamental relationships have for a long time escaped the attention of geometry (and geometry teachers), noting that geometry began with the practical problems of measure-

---

[3] Ibid., p. 22.
[4] Ibid., p. 26.

ment of Euclidean figures (such as rectangular fields) in the days of the Egyptians and that the tendency is to begin instruction or learning this way today.

Stage 2.   Discrimination at the stage 1 level is global (or general) in character with little if any attention to detail. But basic topological shapes such as a doughnut are identified and the hole in it noted. In stage 2, with greater attention to detail, Euclidean shapes begin to be recognized. The ability to draw shows signs of progress. Exploration is more active because the child is no longer satisfied to simply grasp or feel the object.   But exploration is still haphazard, with little attempt to follow the contour of an object in systematic fashion. The child does pick up enough clues to differentiate between a curve and straight edge, between a circle and a square, for example.

At stage 2, Lam, a five-year-old, is able to differentiate the square from a circle but is unable to differentiate between the rectilinear shapes (rectangle, square, cross, rhombus).   The rectilinear shapes are all drawn as squares.[5]

Another five-year-old, given a star, recognizes the points but is unable to differentiate it in a picture containing a star, hexagon, pentagon, and cross because they all have points.[6]

Another five-year-old is able to identify a rhombus from other shapes, describing it as "leaning," but at first he refuses to try to draw it. Later he draws it successfully.[7]

A seven-year-old turns the cardboard figures around in his hands in a clockwise direction, exclaiming, "I've got the hang of it. I turn them and feel them."[8]   He describes a rhombus as like an egg but pointed.

Stage 3.   Piaget defines an operation as an action that can return to its starting point or one that possesses "reversibility." By the age of seven or eight this reversibility has been achieved. The youngster during his investigation begins at a certain point as a point of reference and returns to that point in a systematic fashion.   He has a general plan as contrasted to the first two stages, where each movement was a separate action not connected into a meaningful whole. The youngster at this stage carefully explores the figure with his fingers, returning to the same reference point so as to coordinate the whole figure. The simple shapes are easily recognized.

[5] Ibid., p. 29.
[6] Ibid., p. 32.
[7] Ibid., p. 35.
[8] Ibid.

An eight-year-old, for example, draws crosses and half-crosses correctly. To draw a six-pointed star, he explores the six arms with his fingers, returning systematically to the center of the model to coordinate the sensory impressions of the whole.[9]

Teaching Euclidean Shapes

Can the child then learn the idea of shapes (such as a triangle) by perception, that is, by seeing one and being told its name? Or is it necessary for him to physically explore the object, handling it, tracing its outline with his fingers, and through these "acts" structure the idea of a triangle?

This is a subtle distinction. Do we learn from the object directly or is it from the **actions** of our fingers as they move through space tracing the outline of an object that we coordinate and abstract the idea of shape?

Piaget asks the fundamental question—How does one abstract (develop a mental image of) a geometric shape? Is perception (looking at a shape) sufficient? These experiments indicate that perception or seeing is not enough. There must be a physical action of the child on the object. In these experiments the action or operation necessary is the **movement** of the fingers and hands as they trace the outline of the object from which shape is abstracted. Piaget concludes:

> Our findings with regard to the part played by movement help to clarify what we have already learnt from the study of our experimental data. We may now go so far as to say that in each of the three stages yet covered, the children are able to recognize, and especially to represent, only those shapes which they can actually reconstruct through their own actions. Hence, the *"abstraction" of shape is achieved on the basis of co-ordination of the child's actions and not, or at least not entirely, from the object direct* [that is, by just looking at it].[10]

Note that the random action of tracing the outline of an object is not enough. It must be a coordinated one; that is, the child must have a point of reference on the figure to which he can return (reversibility) to check the various relationships that exist in the figure. This does not occur until stage 3.

---

[9] Ibid., p. 36.
[10] Ibid., p. 43.

Piaget summarizes:

> Thus during Stage 1 the only shapes which are recognized and drawn are closed, rounded shapes and those based on simple topological relations such as open-ness or closure, proximity and separation, surrounding, etc. . . .
>
> With Stage II, we encounter the beginning of recognition of Euclidean shapes, based on the distinction between straight and curved lines, angles of different sizes, parallels, and especially on relations between equal or unequal sides of a figure. . . .
>
> Lastly, at Stage III, the connection between [geometric] shapes and co-ordinated [physical] actions [of exploring the object by handling it] becomes clearly apparent in that the child returns to a fixed point of reference [in tracing the figure] which is necessary to their conceptualization for recognition and representation. . . .[11]

Implications

We have discussed the order of psychological development in learning or abstracting basic Euclidean shapes. Geometric activities should be selected for children on the basis of their development. Since topological development is first, activities of this sort should come first (differentiating open from closed shapes for example). Then to help children in abstracting familiar Euclidean shapes, have them begin with familiar objects such as pencil, fork, or ball. When they can do this, they should begin work on such basic Euclidean shapes as triangles, squares, and circles, first distinguishing curved figures from straight-edged figures.

Later, differentiation should be made between more closely related shapes, such as quadrilaterals:

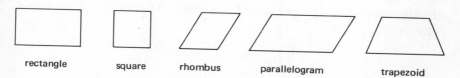

rectangle   square   rhombus   parallelogram   trapezoid

Figure 13-10. Quadrilaterals—all but trapezoid are also parallelograms.

[11] Ibid.

Also, differences in the various polygons should be studied:

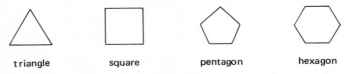

Figure 13-11

The method of teaching should be one that allows for the physical exploration of the various shapes (for example, by handling cardboard or wooden cutouts). Piaget remarks that "motor activity [is] of enormous importance for the understanding of spatial thinking."[12] The teacher can test understanding by having the child pick a given shape, which he handles but does not see, from a collection of shapes. He is then asked to identify this shape from a set of objects shown to him. The child may also be asked to draw the object to test his ability to abstract the given shape. Representation, such as by drawing, is more difficult than recognition.

The children in nursery school, kindergarten, and first grade should have many experiences with handling models of geometric objects, tracing outlines with their fingers and hands, and drawing them, if they are to construct an adequate mental representation of the objects. Showing and telling is not enough. Just to "see" and be "told" is not to abstract and understand. The child must form his own mental constructs based on his own physical action on the objects.

Children like to discuss models of these shapes that they see in the physical world, such as a cardboard box, stop sign, railroad crossing sign, or table top. They should be asked to find how many sides, edges and corners these objects have. Following these activities geometric names can be given to the various shapes such as the side of a box is like a rectangle. These names for geometric shapes grow out of experiencing the properties of the object in terms of sides, edges, corners, and so on.

[12] Ibid., p. 13.

14 Measurement in One Dimension

It is not difficult to see how the facts brought to light in the
present study of the psychogenesis of metrical notions may
someday be given a practical application in teaching.[1]

The extent to which teaching procedures do not take into account
a child's notions of measuring length or linear measurement will be
considered in this chapter.

Measuring as an activity or operation involves physical objects and
is a very concrete type of activity. Possibly because it is concrete,
involving, for example, rulers of various types, children enjoy it.
How children learn to measure is an interesting study. It has its roots
in perceptual activity, but the concepts are not completely developed
until sometime between the age of eight and eleven. We will also see
that measurement notions develop in relation to the basic concept
of conservation.

Just what are the stages through which children go as they develop
an understanding of the geometry of measurement? Contrary to
what might be expected, the necessary concepts are not fully developed until approximately eleven years of age, at which time the
children are usually in the fifth grade. Prior to this time, there may
be a considerable amount of learning of a perceptual sort, since
"measuring" is a very concrete type of activity. Being able to
observe or perceive a particular phenomenon is not sufficient.

[1] Jean Piaget, Barbel Inhelder, and Alina Szeminska. *The Child's Conception
of Geometry*. New York: Basic Books, Inc., 1960, p. vii.

Recognizing a straight line and being able to reproduce one are different problems, the second being more difficult (Chapter 17).

> The study of how children come to measure is particularly interesting because the operations involved in measurement are so concrete that they have their roots in perceptual activity (visual estimates of size, etc.) and at the same time so complex that they are not fully elaborated until sometime between the ages of 8 and 11.[2]

The concept of conservation, already discussed at such great length, is also fundamental to the development of measurement concepts. We find students in the methods classes unable to believe that children of less than seven think the length of a stick changes as it is moved—that is, until they see it for themselves.

One of the basic difficulties for children in the earlier stages of development is that when they go somewhere they consider only the end point or destination. The points in between do not matter. Thus paths, whether crooked or straight, are the same length if they end at the same distance from the observer. This can be demonstrated by showing the child two paths, such as

Figure 14-1

and asking whether an ant would have to walk as far on one path as on the other. If the end points of the paths are the same distance from the child, then to him the paths are the same length. These children do not visualize a path in terms of an ordered system of points and intervals. Piaget concludes that such children do not consider change of position as action in space, but seem to leave space altogether at their starting point and come back to it at the end point.

Measurement seems simple enough to the adult on the basis of his experience if someone provides him with a measuring instrument calibrated in appropriate units. But much is taken as self-evident. Using a measuring instrument involves **changing its position** the appropriate number of times to measure some object. Also, to measure,

[2] Ibid.

the child must develop the concept of conservation of length. The length of an object such as a measuring instrument does not change as it is moved.

First Attempts at Measurement

How does a child then approach a problem situation that requires measurement? Piaget investigated the question by using a tower of blocks of various shapes. The child is asked to make a tower "the same as mine" or "as tall as mine." The child is asked to build the tower on another table, which is lower, so as to avoid visual transposition (attempt to place them together visually). A screen may be used to separate the two towers but the child may go and look at the model.

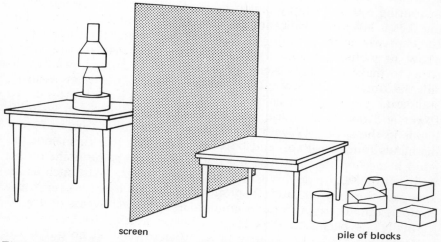

screen

pile of blocks

Figure 14–2. Attempting to build a tower the same height on a lower table with different sized blocks.

Stage 1. At stage 1 the method of measurement is only that of visual comparison. Nothing is moved except the line of vision. The child makes a visual estimate. He makes no attempt to use a measuring instrument, such as a stick, even if given one and asked if it might help.

A four-year-old looks at the model tower, then carefully makes a tower of his own without looking at the model. After he has finished his tower, he looks back at the model, is dissatisfied, and so builds his all over again. He does the same thing a third time. Asked if his tower is the same height, he replies that it is. Given a stick and asked if it will help to measure, he simply places it on top of his tower as a decoration.[3]

Stage 2. At stage 2 measuring instruments are used but incorrectly. At this level the youngster still lacks a coordinated idea of space. He needs such a coordinate system or framework for comparing the two towers. If he places a stick such that its ends rest on top of the two towers, he has no reference system to use in order to interpret the result. He does not have the use of Euclidean concepts of parallel, vertical, horizontal, and angle.

The youngest children build a tower until, judging visually by stepping back and sighting, their tops "look" level. The fact that the bases of the towers are not at the same level is not taken into account. At a slightly more advanced level the child takes the measuring rod and simply lays it across the top of the towers, thinking if it is level the towers are the same height. Later he realizes that the bases are not at the same level, and if the rules of the game would allow, he would move his tower to the same table as the other tower so as to make a better visual comparison. Not being allowed to do this, he finally looks around for another object to use as a measuring standard. He may first use his hands, placing one at the top of his tower and one at the base, and then, while attempting to keep his hands in the same relative position, move to the other tower to see if his hands touch it at top and bottom. Realizing that this is not too good a method, he may use his body, lining up some point on his body with the top of his tower and some other point, such as his knee, at the bottom and then moving to the other tower for a comparison. These procedures are used at around six years of age.

Finally, he begins to look for another measuring tool more convenient than his body. It may be another tower that he builds the same height as his own, which he is allowed to move. This step involves the logic of mathematical relationship.

The second tower he builds, B, is equal in height to the first one he built, A. If B is also equal in height to the tower he is attempting to measure, C, when he moves it to the table on which C is located, this must mean that A and C are equal in height. This idea is referred to in mathematics as the transitive property of the equals relation. If $A = B$ and $B = C$, then $A = C$.

---

[3] Ibid., p. 34.

Ano (aged five) is not yet ready to use the transitive idea.

> He finishes his tower and goes to look at the model: "Are they the same height?—*Yes.*—Are you sure?—*Yes, I'm sure because I've looked.*—Do you never make a mistake when you look?—*No.;* . . . (he hesitates)—Could you measure?—*No, I don't know how to.*— What else could you do?—*We could take it down and put it up again here* (by the side of the model)—Can you measure with your hands?—*No, I don't know how to,*" etc.[4]

Also at stage 2 but at a higher level, Lou (almost seven) uses a common term as a unit of measure, his hands, thus arriving at the transitive property of the equals relation. He is following the logic that if the distance between his hands, B, is equal to the height of both towers, they must be the same height.

> Lou (;6): *"They're the same.—How do you know?—I've seen.— How can you be sure?—I could take away the screen so as to see better.—What else?—*(He puts one hand to the top of the tower and the other to the base and walks away; but finding that his hands have moved he begins all over again.)—Aren't you liable to go wrong that way?—*No.*—What about this (a stick which is too short)?—(He stands it against his tower and tries to move it horizontally while maintaining it in an upright position, ignoring the difference in base levels.)[5]

Piaget summarizes:

> The analysis of the way in which children come to discover the use of a middle term [measuring instrument] is sometimes complicated by the experiences they have had. Many subjects, while still belonging to stage II, have learned how to measure; others have seen adults measuring. In these and similar cases, it is easy to distinguish between external and internal factors, because the child assimilates whatever he is shown to his own schemata of representation and only remembers what he understands (that is, apart from mere parrot-wise verbal reproduction). Thus he discovers the need for an independent common measure only when, towards the end of substage IIB, he senses the difficulty of transferring sizes by spreading his fingers and arms.[6]

Thus, after using a third tower as a measuring standard, the child finds that a rod would be more convenient, first choosing one the

[4] Ibid., p. 42.
[5] Ibid., p. 46.
[6] Ibid., p. 51.

same length as the tower to be measured, then choosing one that is longer and marking on it the height of the tower. Finally, at stage 3 he comes to true measurement by choosing a shorter rod and applying it the appropriate number of times along the tower being measured.

Stage 3. At stage 3 measurement is intellectual or operational. Children can now use any long object as a common term of measuring instrument. It no longer has to have the same length as either of the objects being compared and does not have to look like the object being measured.

This last development involves two new operations in logic. The first operation is the arbitrary **division** of the object to be measured into subunits the same length as the measuring rod, realizing that the whole is the sum of its parts. The second operation, **displacement** or **substitution**, allows him to apply or substitute one part (the measuring rod) upon another (the object being measured) an appropriate number of times, thereby building a system of units.

> Chri (8;3) says: "*You have to take their measurement*—How?— (He uses a long stick to measure height and width.)—What about using this (small brick)?—*That's easy.* (He turns it over and over on its 4 equal sides, measuring his own tower by rotating it 13 times. When measuring the model, he simply moves the brick stepwise from base to top, and marks off 13 unit lengths.)" [7]

Piaget concludes that measurement is a synthesis of the operations of **subdivision** into parts and of **substitution** of a part upon others. The ability to measure develops later than the number concept (which is a synthesis of the inclusion of categories and of serial order) because it is more difficult to divide a continuous whole, such as an object being measured, into interchangeable subunits than it is to count a set of objects that are separate and discrete from each other, such as beads or blocks.[8]

Measurement is then first and foremost a **change of position**, whether it is movement of the eye or a measuring instrument. This change of position must also be related to a coordinated reference system in space such as horizontal and vertical axes.

Also fundamental to and a prerequisite for understanding measurement is the conservation or invariance of distance and length. For how can a child measure if he thinks the ruler changes in length as it is moved?

[7] Ibid., pp. 62–63.
[8] Jean Piaget. "How Children Form Mathematical Concepts," *Scientific American*, Nov. 1953, p. 78.

Conservation of Distance and Length

The Distance Relation Between Objects

The concepts of distance and length are not the same psychologically, according to Piaget, and must therefore be treated separately. "Distance" is used to refer to the linear separation of objects or empty space. Length refers to a property of objects themselves.

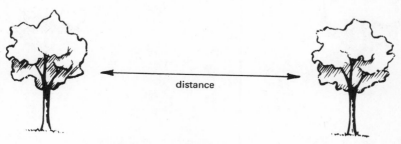

Figure 14-3. Distance as linear separation.

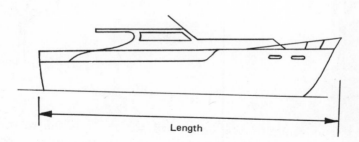

Figure 14-4. Length as property of an object.

The understanding of distance allows children to make the transition from a topological notion of space to the Euclidean notion. "Distance" as a relation between two objects involves measurement and the coordinated reference system of Euclidean space.

Is the "notion" of distance understood by perception? Similarly, can distance be represented by a child? Is the mental construct of distance conserved when other objects interfere? For example, in considering points A and C and the distance between them, is this distance conserved when another point is placed between them?

To investigate these ideas, Piaget used models of two trees placed 50 centimeters apart. Children were asked to say whether they were near or far apart, avoiding use of the term *distance*. A cardboard screen was then placed between the trees and the question asked again.

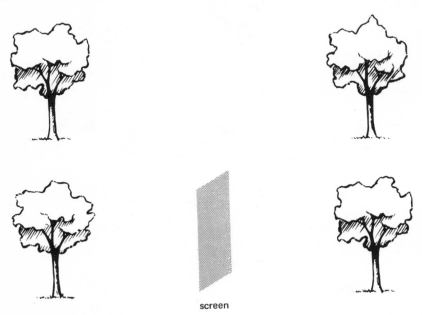

screen

Figure 14-5

The introduction of the cardboard screen ends the relation between the two trees for the child less than four to five years of age. He cannot consider the two intervals as a single whole, and, in considering only the part of the whole with which he began, reports the distance as less (stage 1). During stage 2, the child sees the overall distance between the trees but thinks the screen takes up some of the space so the distance must be less. At stage 3 children understand that the distance does not change between the trees.

Children arrive at stage 3 or the operational level when intervals no longer refer to the distance between objects but to the sites or positions of the objects in space. These sites or positions or points are part of the stationary or fixed spatial field of Euclidean geometry. The sites or positions are organized in the mind of the child using reference or coordinate axes in this spatial "field."

Piaget concludes:

> It is clear that the development of notions of distance is independent of any measuring behavior. When that development is complete, distances can be measured, but no measurement is possible until the subject has convinced himself of three points:
>   1. A distance AB is not altered by the interposition of additional objects S_1, S_2, etc.

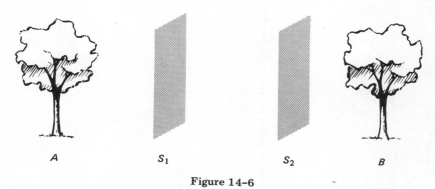

A $\qquad\qquad$ S_1 $\qquad\qquad$ S_2 $\qquad\qquad$ B

Figure 14-6

>   2. An order AB may be reversed, giving BA, without disturbing the identity of the distance.
>   3. If S lies between A and B, then $AS < AB$. An understanding of these three points must antecede Euclidean metrics, because these deal only with identities and relations between part and whole while measurement deals with relations between one part and another, e.g., AS and SB.[9]

The second point above involves a basic and important mathematical idea, the **symmetric property**. In considering a distance from A to B, is it the same as the distance from B to A? A has the same relation to B in terms of distance as B does to A. The distance relation is then said to be symmetric. But many children will not think the distance is the same if one object is put in a higher position, such as on a table. They think it is farther "up" than "down."

Change of Position and Conservation of Length

It is taken for granted by the adult that there is no change in the length of a ruler as it is moved along an object being measured. But do children "conserve" the length of an object when it is moved or

---

[9] Piaget, Inhelder, and Szeminska, op. cit., p. 85.

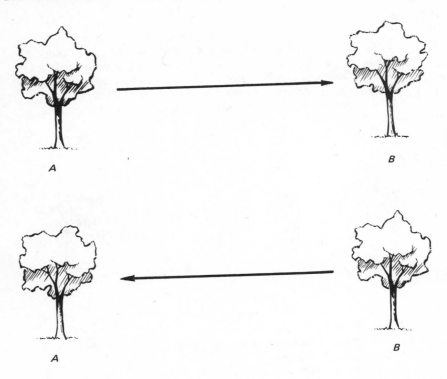

Figure 14-7. *BA* is the same distance as *AB*.

do they think the length of an object changes as it is moved? Also, as the ruler is moved to a new position, do children think that the space from which the ruler has been moved remains constant? If children do not conserve the notion of length and distance, then how can they measure?

To investigate these questions Piaget used two straight sticks 5 centimeters long. The children are asked if the sticks are the same length and then one stick is moved forward (away from the other stick). The children are then asked again if the sticks are the same length.

At the stage 1 level children think the stick that has been moved is longer, since they look only at its extremity or end point, which is now farther away. They do not consider the other end point of the stick moved, but, of course, it has also moved, in that length is constant.

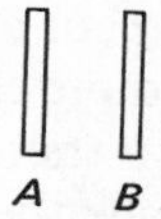

Figure 14-8. Which is longer or are they the same? "The same."

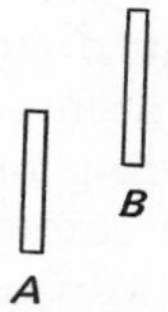

Figure 14-9. Now is one longer or are they still the same? "*B* is longer."

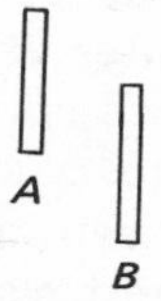

Figure 14-10. And now? "*A* is longer."

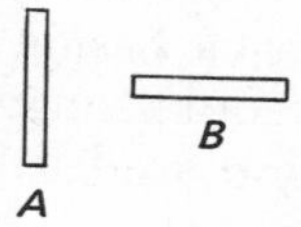

Figure 14-11. And now? "*A* is longer."

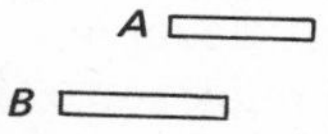

A ⬜ ⬜

B ⬜ ⬜

Figure 14-12. And now? "*B* is longer."

Children at this level consider both end points of the stick simultaneously and the interval between or length of the stick. As the stick is moved some children watch its end point only. Others simply equate movement with longer. If a stick is moved, it "grows" longer. These children think that objects can grow or contract when moved forward or backward. Thus they are not ready to measure. They do not conserve Euclidean length of an object as rigid when the object is moved. Mathematically, these children are still working at the more primitive topological level, which allows an object to be stretched rather than having to remain rigid as in Euclidean geometry.

It is amusing to watch mothers of six- to seven-year-olds. They are unable to accept the fact that their children make such responses because the answer is so obvious to them. They think they can "teach" the idea, which they cannot, since the child has not reached the stage of development where length as an idea in space is conserved. At this level responses will be inconsistent, sometimes right, sometimes wrong. Some children will say A is longer, others will say B.

Thus **change of position** of an object such as a ruler leads to non-conservation of length for children at this level and so they are not yet ready to measure. Measuring necessitates the construction (in the mind) of an independent reference system in space in which objects can be moved to new positions, but the length of each position of the object in space does not change. It is necessary to be conscious of a reference system in space composed of stationary sites occupied by the ruler or object as it is moved. These children cannot take into account stationary sites as distinct from moving objects. They think only of the object as contrasted to the space or position occupied by the object, and this of course does not change. In fact, the moving object is not even seen in terms of the relation of its two end points but only one end point, usually that farthest away.

At stage 2, through processes that might be called trial and error, children begin to realize that the sticks are the same length. They may move the moved stick back beside the other and see that they are the same and respond "It looks longer but it's the same after all." But they are still not sure and are easily confused as the sticks are moved to various positions.

At stage 3, children have the concept that the sites or positions in space occupied by the sticks are the same length. Moving an object does not change the space it occupies. The conservation of length of an object as it is moved in relation to these sites in Euclidean space becomes logically necessary.

> Cal (7;7): *They're still the same, they can't grow!* With various arrangements: *They're always the same length and they'll always stay the same.* The experimenter persists in showing possible modifications, until, like Leibnitz, Cal invokes both the principle of sufficient reason and the wisdom of the Almighty: "Because God doesn't want to make them shorter. He could if He would but He doesn't want to! [10]

This youngster has mastered the concept of conservation. He knows that the objects can be placed side by side and lined up end to end so

---

[10] Ibid., pp. 101–102.

that manipulating them does not change their length relationship. Piaget concludes that the discovery of logical relationships is a pre-requisite to geometrical concepts, as it is in the formation of number concepts.[11]

Thus the necessary concepts of change of position, conservation, and an external reference system as a prelude to measurement do not appear for many children until age seven to eight or until sometime during the second or third grade of school. Yet many teachers attempt to teach measurement before this time.

Subdivision and Conservation

As described in the preceding section, measurement is a synthesis of the operations of **change of position** (as the measuring instrument or ruler is moved along the object being measured) and **subdivision** (of the object being measured into units the same length as the ruler).

The preceding study illustrated the difficulty children have with conservation of length of an object as it is moved. As an object is moved away children less than seven years old usually think it be-comes longer. It is obvious that measurement has no meaning if the measuring instrument is thought to change length as it is moved along an object to be measured.

In measurement it is also necessary to consider the object being measured as being subdivided into smaller units the same length as the ruler. Can children then conserve the length of these subunits, or do they somehow change length, too?

To investigate the conservation of length of subunits, Piaget used two rows of match sticks placed side by side and the same length.

Figure 14-13

Then one row is altered by placing one or more of the match sticks at an angle to the others so that the row is no longer straight.

[11] Piaget, op. cit., p. 78.

Figure 14-14

The children are then asked if the two are the same length using such questions as would an ant have to travel as far on one as on the other? If children attempted to count the matches in each row, a match in one row was broken in two so that the number of sticks would not be the same.

A similar and more important experiment was conducted using two strips of paper the same length.

Figure 14-15

One strip was then cut into two and then three segments and the segments arranged at various angles in relation to each other.

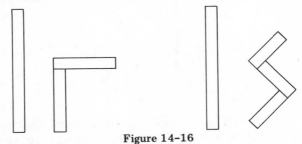

Figure 14-16

The children were asked if the strips were still the same length.

At stage 1 children do not conserve length. The straight row is thought to be longer because only the extremities or end points are considered. Such children are still thinking at the topological level.

A five- to six-year-old considers the following display:

Figure 14–17. Are they the same length? "Yes."

Figure 14–18. And now? "*A* is longer."

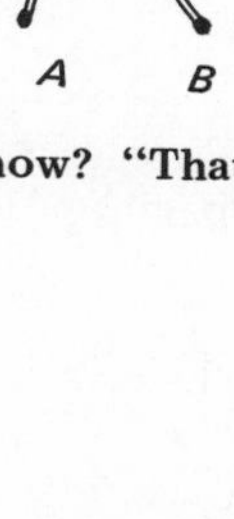

A   B

Figure 14–19. And now? "That one (meaning *A*)."

Show me the roads which the two ants would go along.—(He runs his finger along them.)—Are the roads the same length?—*No. Here it's longer.*—(One match added to the more contracted shape:) How many matches are there? Can you count them?—*One, two . . . six.*—And these?—*One . . . five.*—Good.   Then are they both the same length or not—*Yes.*—Why?—(Points to extremities.) [12]

The difference in position of extremities overrides the number concept to the extent that the row containing five matches is thought to be longer than the figure with six matches.

At stage 2 children oscillate between conservation and near conservation as they respond to questions.

At stage 3 children have attained the concept of conservation of length of subunits and cannot be fooled by altering the shape of one row.   They recognize that appearances tend to fool them.   Shown paper strips placed at angles,

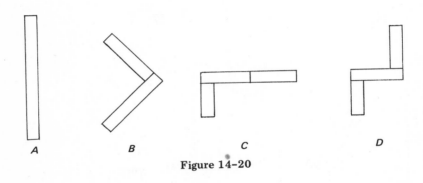

A   *B*   *C*   *D*

Figure 14-20

they respond that one "looks" longer but is "not longer."   Why? "Because they were the same size to start with. They stay the same." Piaget concludes:

The idea of necessary conservation [in order to measure], which entails the complete coordination of operations of subdivision and order or change in position, is accomplished at stage III. This stage was found to have been reached by one in ten in the age range 6–7, by half of those 7–7½, and three-quarters of those 7½–8½ years old. [13]

[12] Piaget, Inhelder, Szeminska, op. cit., p. 107.
[13] Ibid., p. 114.

Measurement of Length

Attempts at actual measurement are now investigated by using two strips of paper pasted on a piece of cardboard with each strip made up of segments at various angles.

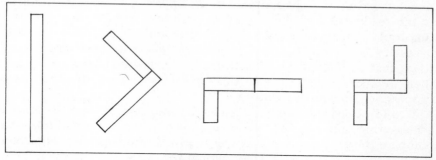

Figure 14-21

The children are asked if the strips are the same length and then asked to verify their answer using a movable strip of paper. The child may be helped by asking him to use the paper strip as "steps" of a little man walking along one of the strips of paper; this is not a spontaneous approach to measurement, but one based on suggestion by the experimenter.

Children at stage 1 are unable to use the suggestion of the experimenter effectively. They are at the nonconservation level, the main reason being the lack of differentiation between subdivision of the strip of paper being measured and the change of position of the strip being used as a ruler as it is used to measure. These two concepts are not complementary as they must be to measure. The children have not constructed a **single** spatial framework that involves the space occupied by the objects as well as the objects.

For example, Dor (six years four months) is asked to compare two figures that are equal in length, one being broken by a right, the other by an acute angle.

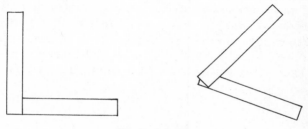

Figure 14-22

He is shown how to measure, using a strip of paper as a unit measure. He moves the strip he uses as a measure, counting as he goes. He finds an answer, 6, after measuring one strip and replies that it's bigger without even measuring the other.[14]

At stage 2 children are moving from nonconservation to conservation but have not fully arrived. In the experiment they are required to use ready-made rulers to see how well they can use these intellectual tools. They are beginning to understand the mathematical idea necessary in comparing two lengths by using a third length as a ruler; that is, if the ruler is the same length as each of the two strips, then the two strips are also the same length (again the transitive property of the equals relation).

A child of six and one-half at stage 2 is beginning to see the role of a measuring unit. He is given a card 3 centimeters long and asked to compare the lengths of two strips of paper. He begins by aimlessly sliding the 3-centimeter ruler along the strips to be measured. Prompted by the question, "Can you tell that way?" he replies "no." Asked "What can you do then?" he replies "count." He then measures, finding one strip 5 units long and the other 6 and replies that the strip 6 units long is longer, thus showing an understanding of transitivity.

He is then shown the outline shape of a staircase with some long segments and others short, and another shaped like the teeth of a saw. He measures the second shape, B, with the 6-centimeter card finds that his card is too long for the short segments in A. He ignores this difficulty, puts in measuring marks, and arbitrarily says or guesses that the objects are the same length. Asked if he is sure, he replies, "quite sure," even though he is wrong.[15]

At stage 3 with the coordination between **subdivision** and **change of position** the measuring conservation is achieved.

The youngster now knows that the length of the unit used as a measuring instrument does not change as it is moved (change of position) and neither do the subunits of the object he is measuring as he subdivides it with his ruler in order to measure. Piaget concludes that the necessary intellectual concepts for measurement (subdivision and change of position) are now fused and operational (usable). The child can now perform systematic measurement with understanding.

An eight-year-old shown two figures, both in the form of acute angles, replies immediately that B is bigger. Asked if he is sure, he measures each strip with a ruler and shows how much longer B is than A.

[14] Ibid., p. 119.
[15] Ibid., p. 124.

Shown two staircase designs, each containing both 3 and 6 centimeter segments, he measures correctly using both the 3 and 6-centimeter rulers to complete the task.[16]

Subdividing a Line Segment

In the preceding section the children were aided in choosing the length of the measuring unit. The shorter segments offered appropriate measuring units so that the measuring unit was to some extent arbitrarily imposed on them. This was done in order to more easily study the development of the concept of conservation of length. Conservation is an essential condition for measurement.

In this section, the child is not provided a measuring unit of the appropriate length in order to see how he will solve the problem of selecting such a unit.

Piaget used two line segments the same length. The line segments were represented by pieces of string or wire, 30 centimeters long, tied to two nails. A bead is placed on each string to represent a car.

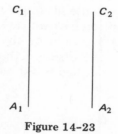

Figure 14-23

The interviewer refers to the car on A_1C_1 as his and the car on A_2C_2 as belonging to the child. The interviewer moves his car to a position B_1 from A_1 and asks the child to make his car travel the same length or just as far.

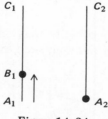

Figure 14-24

[16] Ibid., p. 126.

This experiment is then varied to test the reversibility of the child's thinking. His car is placed at C_2 and again he is asked to make his car go just as far as the interviewer's.

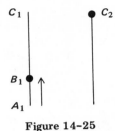

Figure 14-25

A second experiment is then conducted with the line segments the same length and still parallel but without the end points being lined up.

The child is given an unmarked ruler longer than the distance the car is moved to see if he can use his finger to represent $A_1 C_1$ on the ruler so as to correctly position his own car on $A_2 C_2$.

A third experiment is a variation of the second, but the child is given a ruler shorter than the distance the car is moved. For this experiment the string is lengthened to 50 centimeters.

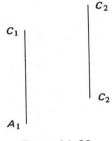

Figure 14-26

Variations of these experiments may involve strings of different lengths and also strings not parallel, such as

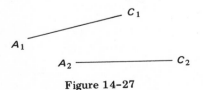

Figure 14-27

Children at the first stage of development are unable to conceive of the length of a journey as an interval or distance between two points, but consider only the end of the journey or the position to which the car has been moved. This is readily seen in the second part of the first experiment when the interviewer moves his car from A_1 to B_1 and asks the child to move his car from C_2 the same distance (which of course is in an opposite direction).

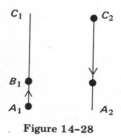

Figure 14-28

The child simply uses a visual method, placing his car in approximately the same position on his string as is the car on the other string, thus looking only at the final position as the determining factor. He makes no attempt to use a ruler, even if asked if it will help.

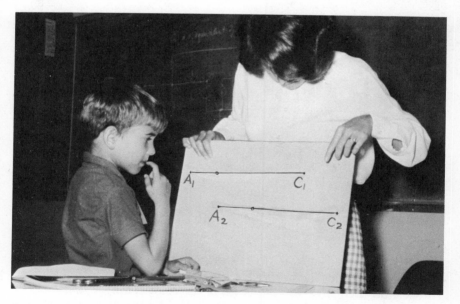

Figure 14-29. Allen has made his car go "as far" from A^2 as student teacher's car from A^1.

At stage 2 children use a trial-and-error approach, solving some problems correctly and others incorrectly. For example, a seven-year-old solves the first experiment using a ruler, and thus sees distance as an interval to be measured; but when he gets to the second experiment, that is, when the end points of the line segments are not lined up, he may have great difficulty.

At stage 2 measurement with a ruler is still a secondary way to solve the problem. The child uses it as a check on his visual estimate or as a check on an approximate measurement made using his fingers or hands as measuring instruments. His approach is an intuitive one. He has not developed a generalized intellectual procedure for solving measurement problems as is the case in stage 3.

At stage 3 the child has developed an intellectual and generalized procedure for solving measurement problems. His is not a trial-and-error approach. He is able to appraise the problem and set out immediately on a correct procedure to solve it. He is at the operational or reasoning level of thinking.

Figure 14-30. Allen has tried to make his car go as far in a reverse direction (from C_2).

In stage 3, however, there is an intermediate point of development. There is no difficulty for the child if the ruler is longer than the distance to be measured; but if it is shorter, he uses other objects to complete the measurement, such as his hand. After this intermediate point of development the child is able to think of the ruler as a unit and to move it along the distance to be measured, counting the number of movements and marking on the ruler any remainder that may exist.

Implications

Concerning linear measurement by the child, it appears that the necessary conservation concepts are achieved on the average at age seven and one-half. Measurement in its operational form (with immediate insight rather than by trial and error) is not achieved until eight or eight and one-half years of age.

This study indicates then that if systematic measurement is to be "taught" it should not be presented before the latter part of what is usually the third grade. Even then, for most children it will have to be an experimental or trial-and-error readiness-type experience. The necessary concepts, as usual, develop from within rather than without for operational understanding.   You cannot tell children how to measure; they should be provided with materials similar to those just described and be allowed to experiment and try to solve measurement problems for themselves. The teacher should play the role of questioner in moving toward the objective desired, in this case, measurement.   The necessary concepts will develop (1) when the child is old enough (eight to eight and one-half, according to Piaget), and (2) when he is allowed to operate on (experiment with, manipulate) objects used in measurement. Both conditions are necessary for the operational thought necessary to perform measurement.

First, before attempting systematic measurement, the child must be able to conserve the idea of length of an object. Simple experiments to determine this developmental level have been described. To measure the length of one object by comparing it with another marks the beginnings of measurement. Until "length" of an object can be conserved as an idea, measurement is meaningless. Second, the child must understand the concept of **subdivision** since the object to be measured must be subdivided into subunits the same length as the measuring instrument or ruler.   He then moves the measuring unit along the object being measured, marking off or subdividing the object into units the same length as the measuring unit or ruler. The length of these subunits must also be conserved for meaningful measurement.   Third, the child must realize that a distance between two objects is conserved when other objects are placed between them.

The relation of the development of the ability to measure and the ability to understand number is an interesting one.   The arithmetic unit called "one" and written 1, is the initial building block in understanding numbers.   Each succeeding counting number is "1" more.   In contrast, the concept of a "measuring" unit involves the arbitrary subdivision of "one" continuous whole (the object measured).   The achievement of this type of operational thinking or the ability to measure comes later than does the first understanding of number.   Similar difficulties are encountered in attempting to measure time and fractional parts (Chapters 9 and 10).

15 Structuring Space in Terms of Vertical and Horizontal Axes

> It is precisely the development of abstract operations [at age 11–13] which enables the child to understand maps and coordinate axes in his school work . . . a combination of individually worked out and formally learned concepts.[1]

Topology is a branch of mathematics concerned with an object as a thing in itself and the relationships that exist between the elements or parts of the object (Chapter 13). Projective geometry involves perspective or the appearance of an object from different positions or points of view, such as an end or side view (Chapter 17).

Euclidean geometry is concerned with the relations or coordination between different objects in space. Are they the same length, height, distance? Is one larger, smaller, or are they the same size? Are they vertical or parallel;

One Euclidean relation between objects is their position relative to each other. The adult in order to study a set of objects and the relative position of each object to each other object in space uses a vertical and a horizontal axis as a frame of reference. Objects are located in relation to these axes, such as "above" and "to the right." Locating objects relative to each other involves both an angular and distance measurement or two distance measurements if horizontal and vertical axes are used as a frame of reference.

---

[1] Jean Piaget and Barbel Inhelder. *The Child's Conception of Space.* New York: Humanities Press, Inc., 1963, p. 445.

Figure 15-1

That such problems are not easy to solve may be recalled by the adult when he attempts to find his car in a parking lot or attempts to find his way about in a strange city. The person "good" at directions retains the idea of a north–south line or axis and an east–west line as he changes directions in driving.

A Child's Frame of Reference

Horizontal and Vertical

At what age does the child develop the imaginary or abstract idea of horizontal and vertical axes as a frame of reference for locating the relative positions of objects in space? To make a map or reproduce a layout, for example, necessitates this understanding of a frame of reference in which to properly position the objects relative to each other.

To investigate the idea of the child's concept of "horizontal," as a basis for performing such tasks, Piaget used a bottle partially filled with colored water. Younger children were asked to indicate on an empty bottle what the position of the liquid would be if the bottle containing the liquid was tilted.

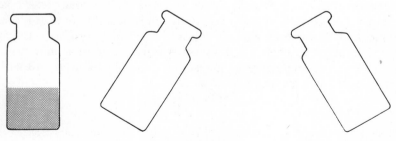

Figure 15-2

Older children were given drawings of bottles and asked to draw the surface of the liquid when the bottle containing the liquid was tilted.

At four or five years of age there is no understanding of the horizontal plane. These children in attempting to represent the surface of the water when the glass is tilted do so with scribbles.

In the second stage of development the line representing the surface is drawn parallel to the bottom of the bottle or, as in the case of Tina, age six, the water is thought to divide, half-parallel to the base and half-parallel to the side.

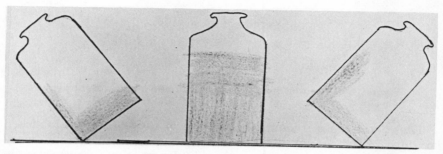

Figure 15-3. Tina, age six, approaching stage 2, uses side and bottom of jar as reference system.

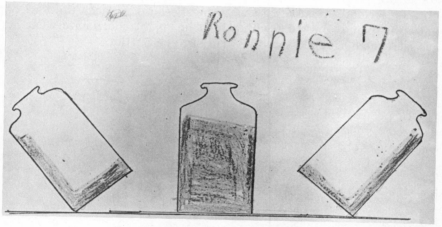

Figure 15-4. Ronnie, age seven, stage 2.

These children are using a reference system, the line of the bottom or side of the glass, and are able to approximate the idea of a straight line. The idea of stable horizontal and vertical axes is still not known to them, however.

Figure 15-5. Approaching stage 3 as indicated by drawing at right.

Thus a reference system, the bottom of the bottle, is established at stage 2 even though it is a mobile one rather than the stationary abstract horizontal one.   According to Piaget, these discoveries are not sufficient for building a frame of reference in space, but they do constitute preparation for it.   The child is still unable to position objects correctly relative to each other because he lacks the idea of lines and planes in space with which he might coordinate what he has seen (such as liquid that moves about in a bottle).

Figure 15-6.   Advanced 6 year old approaching stage 3.

To investigate the idea of "vertical," a plumb line is suspended in the bottle with a weight on the end. The children are asked to draw the position of the line if the bottle were tilted.

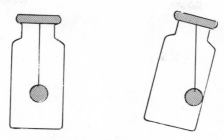

Figure 15-7

At stage 2 the plumb line suspended in the bottle is thought to tilt with the bottle instead of remaining vertical. The child retains the parallel relation of the side of the bottle and the plumb line. Even when the experiment is performed before the eyes of the children, when they are asked to draw how the plumb line looked when the bottle was tilted, they cannot do it. They do not yet have at their disposal the abstract idea of vertical.

A study of the idea of vertical can also be made in observing children's drawings. Five-, six-, and seven-year-olds draw trees on a mountain perpendicular to the side of the mountain. Chimneys are drawn perpendicular to the side of the roof. (See illustration next page.)

Piaget concludes that children at this level are unable to develop an abstract reference system (such as a horizontal axis and a vertical axis) in order to correctly position objects relative to each other. They do not yet have such ideas as stationary lines and planes in space with which to coordinate what they see.

At stage 3 the child establishes the idea of horizontal and vertical as a constant reference system in space. However, this is accomplished only after repeated experiments. The abstract idea of a horizontal and vertical axis is not completely organized or operational until about nine years of age, and for some children it will be as late as eleven or twelve years of age.

This type of operational or abstract thought begins at about nine years of age for most children, but it may occur in more advanced children at six and one-half to seven years of age.

In the case of the most advanced children like Cue and Tis who are on the verge of abstract thought, we find that their system of co-ordinates has become virtually conventional or hypothetico-

(a)

(b)

Figure 15-8

deductive. "I say that the base is horizontal" Tis decrees, "and I draw the water in relation to the base," after which he proceeds to arrange the whole affair according to a set of parallels and perpendiculars, whether the paper [on which he is drawing] lies straight or askew.[2]

General Systems of Reference

The physical world provides a natural frame of reference in the form of horizontal and vertical. Horizontal is represented by the floor or ground and vertical by the many vertical objects, such as the side of a wall, a tree, a mast of a ship, a flagpole. Will a child make use of such a vertical and horizontal system when it is needed? Children beginning school seldom do.

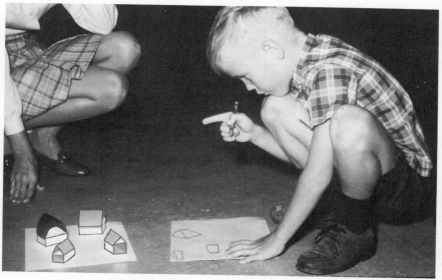

Figure 15-9. Reproducing a layout. White base for model should be larger.

To study a child's ability to locate several objects correctly in relation to each other Piaget used a set of blocks arranged in arbitrary fashion and asked the children to make another pattern like it with another set of blocks. After first attempts the child is given paper strips or sticks to serve as a set of axes or a reference system and asked if they will help in positioning the objects correctly.

[2] Ibid., p. 411.

(a)

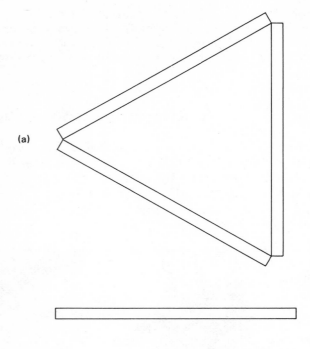

(b)

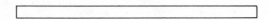

(c)

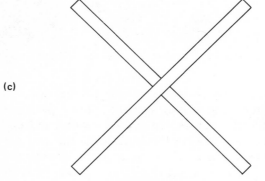

Figure 15–10

As might be expected, some of the children fail to see the value of the strips of paper as a reference system even when their possibilities are pointed out. At stage 3 the children begin to make use of the strips of paper as a reference system.

Various procedures to solve the problem are used. One nine-year-old places the paper strips in the form of an X on the model and does the same on his copy. He is able to locate the blocks in the appropriate general area, one of the four quadrants made by the paper strips, but the relative distance between the objects is incorrect. He is unable to correct his error.

Another begins to copy the model by eye and then encloses it with three strips of paper. He does the same for his copy. After trying this he places the strips parallel, to use as a reference system, and finally in the form of an X, commenting that that makes it easier.[3]

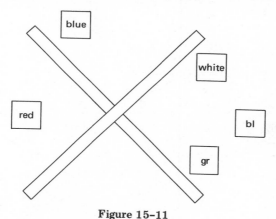

Figure 15-11

The child at stage 3 makes definite progress in constructing a system of reference, but he is still unable to coordinate relative distances and true positions of objects in an over-all way.

Piaget concludes that only after the age of eleven to twelve, during the stage of formal operations of thought, is the child able to establish true conventional reference systems that enable him to compare distances and positions simultaneously.[4]

Thus it is only toward completion of elementary school and entrance to junior high school that youngsters are ready for the type of experience necessary for map making, for example. In fact, map

[3] Ibid., p. 414.
[4] Ibid.

making involves fractions in the form of proportions or drawing to scale. This requires a fourth stage of development, as will be described in the next section.

Making a Map

Locating a Single Object

Just how does a child proceed from simple topological notions to those involving projective and Euclidean concepts necessary for the reproduction of a simple map? For younger children Piaget used two model villages with identical layouts containing a road, several houses, a hill, and a river.

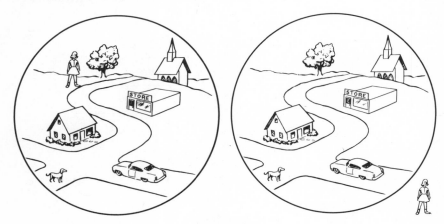

Figure 15-12

A doll is placed in each of 15 positions on one model and the child is asked to place another doll in corresponding positions on the second model. The second model is then rotated 180° in relation to the first so that the child does not use his own position as a point of reference and the experiment is repeated. A third variation is to place a screen between the two models. The child may look at either but is not allowed to see both models at the same time.[5]

At stage 1, about four years of age, only the topological concepts of proximity or enclosure are used. The doll is placed "near" the

[5] Ibid., p. 421.

house, but the proximity relation of the doll to other features such as the river is ignored. Similarly, if a copy is to be made of a doll "in" the river, the doll is placed in the river but it may be at the wrong end of the river, on the wrong side, and not located correctly with respect to the other features such as hill and house.

The child is correct for two topological relations. The doll is "in" the river when it should be, and it is at least "near" or in the proximity of the house when it should be.

At stage 2, ages four to seven, two or three reference points are used simultaneously, such as the hill and the river. Also the doll may be correctly positioned left or right or behind or in front of the house. The whole layout is still not coordinated correctly, however.

At stage 3, ages six to seven, the 180° rotation of the model causes no difficulty and the doll can be located correctly in each of the 15 positions. This 180° rotation of one model involves taking a different viewpoint or perspective; it also involves a mathematical concept of projective geometry. The two dimensions of the layout also involve a dual reference system and the coordinates of Euclidean geometry, such as to the left and above the house.

Figure 15-13. Susan, 9, is successful in locating policeman when model is rotated 180°.

This experiment is not as difficult as the idea of horizontal and vertical developed with the bottle and liquid experiment in the previous section. In this experiment only a single object, the doll, has to be located, and it is to be located in a layout already organized; that is, the river, house, and so on, are shown already positioned. Thus the six- to seven-year-old is successful as compared to the nine-year-old in the preceding section with the water-level experiment.

Construction of a Layout

In the preceding section a single object, a doll, was located in a two-dimensional layout, a village. We will now consider the ability of children to reproduce a complete layout. A number of objects have to be located in relation to each other. For younger children blocks are used to represent such objects as houses. Older children are asked to draw a reproduction of the layout as seen from above or at an angle of 45° and also in smaller size or scale. The construction of such a diagrammatic layout involves all the geometrical concepts discussed in this chapter.

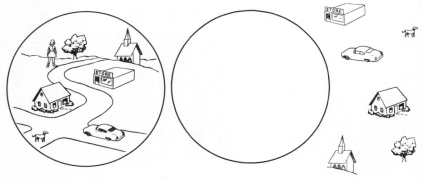

Figure 15-14

Stage 1 is characterized by inability to reproduce the layout except for a crude approach to certain proximities, such as a fence near a house. In stage 2 the child picks out pieces that correspond to those in the model and tries to locate them in similar positions, but he has no system of reference that allows him to locate the objects in correct positions. He does create small groups of objects and locates individual objects correctly as pairs, thus showing a partial coordination. However, he uses only a small part of the space corresponding to that occupied by the model.

The child may also be given a sheet of paper and asked to draw on it the objects "just as they are in the model." If the piece of paper is smaller than the model, the drawing involves a reduction in scale or ratio. It should be approximately the same size at first.

Piaget remarks that it is astonishing to observe the difficulties children have in properly utilizing the space they have at their disposal. They do not spread objects out on their copy as the objects are spaced on the model. This failure to utilize the space available is due to the fact that the child is not yet using the "surround" (edges of the model or paper) as a basis of establishing a frame of reference or coordinate axes with which he could properly locate the objects on his copy. The child is able to establish relations between one object and two or three others, but such little groups are not linked with other groups of objects. The edge of the table or model is used as a reference axis only for the objects that are near the edge of the model. At this stage of development there is no such thing as a diagrammatic layout. The child constructs a few incomplete groups, but there is no coordination between the groups in a larger context or framework.[6]

Figure 15-15. Misty, 7, has difficulty reproducing layout.

[6] Ibid., p. 435.

Figure 15–16. James, 9, very self-assured in his approach to reproducing model but has difficulty if model is rotated 180° relative to his own map.

At stage 3A, age seven to eight, the child can make a copy of the model indicating an understanding of projective and Euclidean relationships. At the first level of stage 3 the child can coordinate all positions into a simple whole, but he is unable to preserve the correct distances between objects. When one of the objects in the model is moved, he can only approximate its new position, and this he does by using only a single object as a reference point. Thus it may be incorrectly positioned with respect to other objects.

A child, asked to walk around the model containing a house stationed in the center with a pine tree in the corner, is able to draw them from four different positions. He has this understanding of projective geometry. But he is unable to describe the position of the pine tree if the interviewer could not see it.[7]

Stage 3B occurs between nine and eleven years of age. At this stage the child is able to establish correct intervals or distances between objects by measurement. This ability to use two distances or coordinates in order to correctly position objects relative to each other is not exhibited before this stage. Also, at stage 3B reduction to scale or proportion is possible.

[7] Ibid., p. 438.

Drawing to Scale (Ratio and Proportion)

The problem of drawing a map or making a model smaller than the given one involves an understanding of scale drawing or ratio and proportion. A child of ten and one-half is given a model considerably larger than the one he is asked to reproduce. Asked how he can get everything in, he replies that he can do so by making the distances less and the objects smaller. He is willing to measure but prefers to make a visual estimate. At stage 3B the child realizes that the objects on the model should be reduced in size as should the distances between the objects. A feeling for proportion emerges for simple ratios such as 1:2 or 1:4. Piaget characterizes this stage as that of mastery of distance and proportion.[8]

However, the child is still at the concrete operational level, needing physical objects such as strips of paper for a reference system in order to correctly position objects on his model.

At stage 4, age eleven to thirteen, the child is finally at the abstract or "operational" level. He no longer needs physical objects such as strips of paper to use as a reference system in order to correctly position objects. He now has in his mind abstract coordinates (one vertical and one horizontal) intersecting at the center of the model as the best means of reproducing the model. This is a transition from the concrete to the abstract or operational.

A child of twelve and one-half, asked what might help him put everything in the right place, replies that he could draw axes, which he represents by folding the paper four ways. He locates a house by comparing its position relative to one axis. Asked if that is accurate, he replies that it is not, that he must measure in two directions (from both axes) and also reduce to scale.[9]

The ability to make a map of the model using a reduced scale is also considered by Fau, a thirteen-year-old. He does not bother to draw axes or coordinates but uses them in conjunction with the edges of the paper.

> Fau. Measures everything right away and decides to make his first drawing to quarter scale. *You have to make a quarter of the house. No, that's a bit too large. No, it'll be all right.* He carries on in the same way, looking at *the corners and the edges of the paper* by way of reference. After he has made a few measurements we ask, Is it right that this distance should be less on your drawing then in the model?—*Yes, because it's a quarter of everything.*[10]

[8] Ibid., p. 442.
[9] Ibid., p. 445.
[10] Ibid.

Implications

The foregoing experiments point up the fact that the abstract operations necessary for a child to perform such tasks as map making using coordinate axes are not fully developed until age eleven to thirteen. Piaget concludes that "it is precisely the development of abstract operations [at age 11–13] which enables the child to understand maps and coordinate axes in his school work . . . a combination of individually worked out and formally learned concepts." [11]

The development of these "abstract operations" cannot be accelerated to any great extent according to Piaget. If he is correct, then serious attention needs to be given to the placement of subject matter appropriate to the child's level of development. Map making in social studies may be an example of a part of the curriculum now being taught before many youngsters have reached the necessary operational level for real understanding of the mathematical bases involved in such activities. The necessary developmental bases include an understanding of perspective, a stable reference system (horizontal and vertical), and ability to approximate distance and reduce to scale (ratio). Such developments are not fully organized until the child is ready to leave the elementary school.

The implications of these studies for the teacher are important. She may very well be proceeding to teach on the false assumption that her pupils automatically know or have at their disposal the idea of a horizontal and vertical axis frame of reference. She should carefully test the children before attempting to develop ideas that require a stable reference system in the form of vertical and horizontal axes. Various tests have been outlined for conducting such an evaluation. She cannot expect the necessary development before approximately nine years of age. It may even be two years later.

In the primary grades, an activity often used is that of making a map of where each child lives in relation to the school. This requires a stable reference system. The child cannot reproduce the map in his mind. Seeing the map on a classroom wall does him little good as a frame of reference when he leaves the classroom. He then gets turned around because he does not have at his disposal an abstract set of stable coordinates, such as vertical and horizontal with which to position key landmarks.

When the child is able to conceive of abstract coordinate axes such as vertical and horizontal as a means of coordinating the relative

[11] Ibid.

positions of objects around him, he can begin to represent space. This ability to represent or abstract can be seen by the way he draws or reproduces a map no longer visible. To do this, he will need a frame of reference. The child who can find his way home by knowing only what comes "next" does not have a coordinated system.

For the four- to ten-year-old, Piaget concludes:

> The growth of knowledge is not a matter of mere accumulation and while it is true that between the ages of four and ten children collect a good deal of information about their district they also coordinate the picture they have of it which is an infinitely more complex process of development.[12]

In the upper elementary grades the study of geography should follow and not precede the stage 3 developmental level if a true understanding of relative positions and distance between reference points such as countries or cities is desired. What meaning can geography have if space is not a coordinated whole?

Also, if map making and scale drawing are not fully understood until approximately eleven to twelve years of age, should they be taught earlier? Scale drawing involves the understanding of ratio and proportion in mathematics. This mathematical concept is being introduced at approximately the correct stage of development in some of the newer sixth-grade textbooks at eleven to twelve years of age. (For further study of proportions see Chapter 9.)

[12] Jean Piaget, Barbel Inhelder, and Alina Szeminska. *The Child's Conception of Geometry*. New York: Basic Books, Inc., 1960, p. 24.

16 Measurement in Two and Three Dimensions

Measurement in two or three dimensions brings us to the central idea of Euclidean space, namely the [ideas of vertical and horizontal] coordinates—a system founded on the horizontality or verticality of physical objects. It may seem that even a baby should grasp these concepts, for after all it can distinguish between the upright and lying-down positions. But actually the [mental] representation of vertical and horizontal lines [is not developed on the average until the age of 9]. When a child has discovered how to construct these coordinate axes by reference to natural objects, which he does at about the same time that he conceives the coordination of perspectives, he has completed his conception of how to represent space.[1]

The ability to measure in one dimension, length, was discussed in Chapter 14. As an example, if a child is shown two line segments with a point marked on one and asked to put another point in the same relative position on the other line, he can usually accomplish it by eight to eight and one-half if given appropriate tools, such as a piece of string, strip of paper, and pencil.

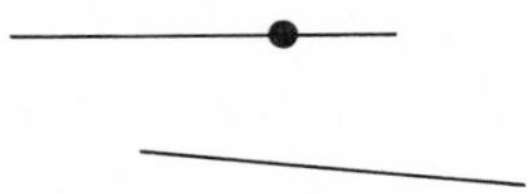

Figure 16-1

[1] Jean Piaget. "How Children Form Mathematical Concepts," *Scientific American*, Nov. 1953, p. 79. Copyright © 1953 by Scientific American, Inc. All rights reserved.

Locating a Point in Two-Dimensional Space

Two-dimensional measurement is accomplished approximately one year later. Two-dimensional space involves a **region** or area. To locate a point in two-dimensional space without an instrument to measure angles requires a coordinate reference system such as horizontal and vertical axes or rectangular **coordinates**. To locate a point, as in

Figure 16–2

requires a horizontal and vertical measure, or what are often called x and y coordinates. To locate a point such as (2, 3), one may count 2 units "right" on the x-axis and 3 units "up" on the y-axis.

Figure 16–3

Thus the rectangular x and y coordinates of the point are (2, 3).

Without this knowledge or background, how would a child attack a problem of representing on a blank piece of paper a point in the same position as a point shown on another piece of paper?

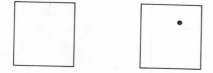

Figure 16–4

He is given as tools a ruler, stick, strips of paper, and a piece of string.

At four to five years of age the child simply guesses or makes an estimate of the position of the dot and makes no attempt to use the tools.   At stage 2 the child uses the ruler or stick and attempts to solve the problem by linear measurement—measuring the distance from the corner of the paper and guessing or estimating the appropriate angle.

At stage 3 the child discovers first by trial and error and later by logic the necessity of two measurements or operations (horizontal and vertical usually) and is able to coordinate these two measurements to locate the point.   Until stage 3 a child is not able to coordinate two measurements and so satisfies himself with one, attempting to solve the problem by linear measurement only.

A major difficulty in solving such problems is the concept of a stable horizontal and vertical, which does not develop in children until approximately nine years of age.

Area Measurement

The understanding necessary for measurement of area or volume poses a psychological or learning problem different from that of locating a point in space.   Locating a point in two-dimensional space involves two linear measures or coordinates, such as x and y.

A unit of measure that measures length or linear measure is not sufficient to measure area.   The unit of measure must be two-dimensional or have area such as 1 square inch.

How does a child try to solve a problem that necessitates a measurement of area?   The invariance or conservation concept is again a problem.

Would, for example, a cow in a pasture that contains several buildings such as barns and house have as much grass to eat regardless of the arrangement of the buildings.   This question involves the mathematical idea of Euclid's axiom: "If equals are subtracted from equals, the results are equal."

$$\text{If } A_1 = A_2$$
$$\text{and } B_1 = B_2$$
$$\text{then } A_1 - B_1 = A_2 - B_2$$

A and A_2 being area of two pastures and B being base area of buildings regardless of the positions of the buildings B_1 and B_2

To investigate these questions, Piaget used two rectangular sheets of cardboard, colored green, both the same shape and size.   After the child agrees that they are the same size, a model of a cow is placed on each and the child is told that the farmers who own the pastures have decided to put a house on them. A model of a house is put near the middle of one pasture and in the corner of the other and the child is asked whether the two cows still have the same amount of grass to eat. Houses are added in pairs, one to each pasture, but with the houses in one pasture placed together, and the question is repeated.

Figure 16-5. Child points to pasture which he thinks has more grass. Child at left is stage 3.

A child may agree that the grass areas are the same until as many as 14 houses have been added, and then suddenly he changes his mind, being overwhelmed by perception of the spread-out houses.

At five to seven years of age equality is denied as more houses are added, but on average at seven and one-half the mathematical idea of Euclid's axiom is operational; that is, the children know that if the pastures contain the same number of houses regardless of their arrangement, the pasture areas must be the same.

At the preoperational level, a six-year-old watches as two houses are placed on B_1 and B_2 as follow at the top of next page.

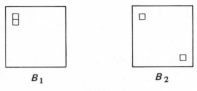

Figure 16-6

Asked if there is the same amount of grass, he says there is more on B_1. If one house is removed from both B_1 and B_2, he says they are now the same.[2]

Piaget concludes from many such experiments that children at this stage cannot maintain the invariance of the subtrahends (as when one house was removed from each field). The operation of subtraction has no meaning for them. While subtraction and addition are reversible operations (or, better, form one reversible operation), the idea of reversibility necessary for understanding conservation of area is not yet present.[3]

At stage 3 a child immediately understands, because there is an operational understanding of the addition and subtraction of areas. This allows an understanding of conservation of area as houses are added or are taken away from each field, regardless of the position of the houses on the two fields. However, measurement of areas becomes effective only when these processes are fused with the understanding that area does not necessarily change with shape. This idea is investigated in the next section.

Conservation and Measurement of Area

To investigate the concept of conservation and measurement of area, Piaget used two procedures. The first involved two identical rectangular arrangements of six blocks.

Figure 16-7

[2] Jean Piaget, Barbel Inhelder, and Alina Szeminska. *The Child's Conception of Geometry*. New York: Basic Books, Inc., 1960. p. 268.
[3] Ibid.

This arrangement was then altered for one rectangle by removing the two blocks at one end and placing them on top or below the others as follows:

Figure 16-8

The children were then asked if the rectangles were still "the same size" or had the same amount of room.

A second method, as a check on the first, involved using two congruent rectangles cut out of cardboard. One rectangle was then cut into two pieces and the pieces rearranged so as to have a different shape from the other rectangle.

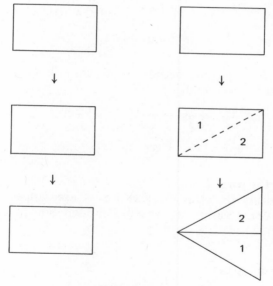

Figure 16-9

Children from five to six years of age think that the area or amount of room changes as the shape changes. They are fooled by perception on which they base their answers. One configuration is larger because it "looks" larger or because, in method two, "it has been cut."

The concept of conservation of area requires the concept of grouping of parts to form a whole and the realization that the arrangement or grouping (addition) of these parts does not affect their area (sum).

At stage 2 children begin to think in terms of subdivision of area into units that can be used to "measure," but their efforts are trial and error rather than intellectual.

At the operational or intellectual level (stage 3), with a rectangle composed of six squares transformed to a pyramid,

Figure 16-10

a seven-year-old first says there is more space in the pyramid but quickly corrects his error because there are six squares in each figure. If the pyramid is changed to

Figure 16-11

he says it is still the same because there are still six squares. If the row of squares is spaced out as

Figure 16-12

the answer is the same.[4]

It is interesting that the conservation of area appears at the same time as the conservation of length although one might think area more difficult.

Measurement of Areas

By Superposition. How would a child attempt to solve a problem of comparing two areas when the shape is not the same? Piaget used a right triangle and an irregular figure.

[4] Ibid., p. 285.

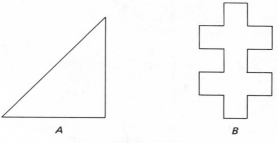

Figure 16-13

The children were given smaller figures in the form of squares that would fit on B, rectangles composed of two of these squares, and triangles formed by cutting the squares diagonally.

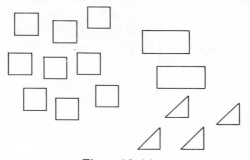

Figure 16-14

The children are asked if these smaller squares will help to find out whether the areas of the two figures A and B are the same. If this is not enough help, ask if the smaller figures will "cover" both figures. This idea generally escapes children below six years of age.

Some do not understand the basic idea that a number of smaller cutouts, taken together, can be the same area as a single larger cutout. They can only compare two areas when each is considered as a single unit.

A second and more important idea—that if the smaller cutouts do fit or cover both figures, then the two areas must be the same—is referred to mathematically as the **transitive property of the equals relation**. This idea is usually stated in the form

$$\text{If} \quad A = B$$
$$\text{and} \quad B = C$$
$$\text{then} \quad A = C$$

The smaller cutouts that fit both figures are the middle term, B. If B fits on A and it also fits on C, then the area of A must equal the area of C.

At six to seven and one-half, by trial and error, children begin to realize the transitive idea involved. From seven and one-half to eight and one-half the need of the common measure (smaller cutouts) and the transitive idea are immediately recognized.

By Unit Measurement. In the section just discussed children were given enough small cutouts to cover the two figures whose areas were being compared. The problem involved only qualitative transitivity. If, however, the child is given only one cutout smaller than the areas being compared, unit measurement (unit iteration) becomes necessary.

To investigate quantitative unit measurement, the child is given figures of several shapes and asked to compare their size or area.[5] The child is given only one small square cardboard cutout, the same size as the dashed squares. He is also given a pencil and allowed to mark on the figures, as shown.

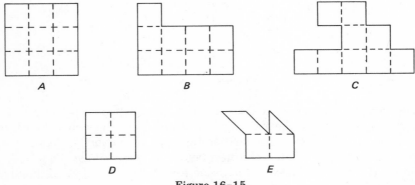

Figure 16–15

From five to six years of age children are usually unable to perform the task. Some are still unable to perform at almost seven years of age. In comparing figures A and B, they respond that "B is bigger because it has a little bit extra." If they are asked to count the squares and find nine in each figure, they will still not agree that the figures have the same area. The perceptual disparity overwhelms the number identity.

[5] Ibid., p. 296.

At the second or transitional stage, children begin to understand the idea, but it is not a general understanding. A six-year-old compares figures *A* and *B* and says there is more room in *B* because it is bigger. The interviewer then helps him by drawing two unit squares in *A* and asking in which figure one could draw more squares. The child is not sure even after filling in the unit squares. Asked if counting will help, he counts and finds nine unit squares in each figure. But asked if the squares were made of chocolate, he chooses *B*, saying that it has more chocolate.[6]

At this level, in comparing figures *D* and *E*, children do not differentiate between the areas represented by the triangles and squares, saying the figures are the same area because each has four subdivisions. They do not yet have the notion of a basic measuring unit.

At the third level children grasp the idea of a basic measuring unit. In comparing figures *D* and *E* an eight-year-old recognizes that you could cut a triangle off of *E* and fit it as follows:

Figure 16–16

Thus *E* is smaller than *D*. He also measures by using the triangle as the basic measuring unit, finding eight for figure *D* and seven for figure *E*. Thus *D* is larger.

Piaget concludes that the concept of conservation and the ability to measure occur at the same time for measuring both in one dimension (length) and in two dimensions (area). Conservation of area is the outcome of being able to compare two areas that are of different shape on the basis of counting (additive subdivision) the number of basic subdivisions in each, using a basic unit of measure such as a triangle or square.[7]

At stage 3 children can determine the area of a region by dividing or marking it off in smaller congruent regions and counting these regions. Such counting may be thought of as addition because in counting we add 1 each time.

[6] Ibid., p. 298.
[7] Ibid., p. 300.

Measurement of Area Using Linear Measures

When is the child able to develop the more sophisticated idea that multiplication or "length times width" may be used to find the area of a rectangle? Children are usually simply "told" the formula, and it has little if any meaning for them. The preceding section provides excellent readiness-type activities. Piaget classifies this ability to obtain area by multiplying length and width as stage 4, the intellectual or "operational" level for such problems. This developmental level does not generally occur until eleven or twelve years of age.

To investigate this concept, the idea of doubling an area is used. The child is shown a line segment 3 centimeters long and asked to draw one twice as long. He is given a ruler and piece of string. He is then given a square 3 by 3 centimeters and asked to draw a square twice as big, not a rectangle but another square.

At stage 2 he cannot even double lengths. The lack of the concepts of conservation of length and subdivision do not allow him to measure.

At stage 3 he can double length. Piaget remarks,

> It would seem that the child now has all he needs in order to discover the correct relationships between length and area or volume, at least for simple shapes like squares. He can find out for himself that a square with twice the sides of another has far more than double the area, and should therefore realize that area can only be a multiple of the side. In other words, he could discover that the relation between side and area is one of mathematical multiplication and not one of simple proportion. Yet he cannot do so.[8]

The problem of determining area by multiplying lengths is a much more difficult concept than the method used in the preceding section—that is, marking off a square into smaller unit squares and counting the unit squares. The difference is that one method involves simply counting a limited number of unit squares, for example, nine in the next figure:

Figure 16–17

But if only the length of the sides of the figure is considered, the problem is more difficult, because the line segment representing each

[8] Ibid., p. 348.

side represents an unlimited number of points. Its length cannot be counted.

At stage 4 a child uses a good method, although he has not learned how to extract square roots. Shown a square with sides measuring 3 centimeters he is asked to draw a square with twice the area. He finds that if he doubles the length of each side he gets a square 4 times as large. He therefore works out the area of the square: $3 \times 3 = 9$. He then doubles this, $2 \times 9 = 18$, to find the correct area of the square with twice the area. He then knows he needs the square root of 18 as the measure of each side of the new square. He has to approximate the square root of 18 as somewhat more than 4.[9]

Measurement of Volume

Conservation of Volume

The concept of conservation or invariance as applied to volume is found to develop later than as applied to such ideas as number, length, or weight.

To investigate the understanding of volume, a set of 36 building blocks is used. These are first placed on a 3- by 4-block base.

Figure 16-18

The children are asked if a house containing the "same amount" of room could be built on a smaller island shown as 3 blocks long and 2 blocks wide.

Children at stage 1 have practically no understanding. Children at stage 2 are usually unable to build a new house on the smaller base with the same amount of room. They stop their building at the same height. They do not think that the building can be made taller without increasing the volume. There is no conservation of volume with a change in shape. Toward the end of stage 2, children begin to understand.

A seven year old is able to transform a $3 \times 3 \times 4$ house and reconstruct it on a base of 2×2. He begins by making it $2 \times 2 \times 4$.

[9] Ibid., p. 352.

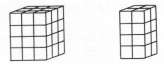

Figure 16-19

After some hesitation, he realizes he must build it higher to 2 × 2 × 7. Comparing the two houses, he then adds another story, making it 2 × 2 × 8. He then thinks it is right but is unable to explain why.

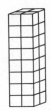

Figure 16-20

He is then asked to copy a 3 × 3 × 4 model, which he does. The experimenter then alters the model to 2 × 2 × 9. Asked if there is still the same amount of room, he says that it is because "it's the same bricks." The model is then transformed to 2 × 18 × 1:

Figure 16-21

The length at first makes him think that there is more, but then he remembers that there is the same amount of room because the same number of bricks are involved. He is again misled with a model, 1 × 36 × 1, because it's very long.

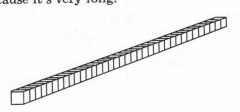

Figure 16-22

He agrees that it's the same bricks, but still thinks there is more room.[10]

Stage 3 covers a long period of time, from approximately age seven to eleven or twelve, thus encompassing most of the time that children are in the elementary school. The idea that interior volume or "room space" contained in the blocks is not changed as the exterior dimensions or length, width, and height are varied is mastered. This conservation of volume is, however, only one type of conservation. It refers only to **interior volume** of the blocks—the volume determined by the boundary surfaces of the blocks. The children's notions are still topological as well as Euclidean.

That conservation at stage 3 is only of one type, that of interior volume, is revealed by the following experiment, which involves the same type of questioning but is followed by asking what will happen if the two different shapes are immersed in water.

Salz (7;10) anticipates that the level of the water will rise when we put in a tower of 3 × 3 × 4 bricks, and this we do: *You see I was right.—*

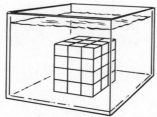

Figure 16-23

Well, now supposing we change it this way (3 × 1 × 12),

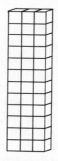

Figure 16-24

[10] Ibid., p. 367.

*will there be the same amount of room in the two houses?—Yes,
exactly the same.   You've got the same bricks.—And will they
both take up the same amount of room in the water?—No, it will
take up more room. Oh, no! That's wrong! It will take up less room
because the house is stretched out lengthways.*[11]

Thus for children like Salz the conservation of interior volume is
recognized because there is the same number of bricks, but interior
volume of the bricks is not equated with the volume of water occupied or displaced by the bricks. Attempts at true volume measurement are only begun toward the end of stage 3.

At stage 4 there are two gains in understanding. The children are
now able to measure volume by seeing its relationship between length
in three dimensions (length × width × height). Conservation of volume is also extended to include that of occupied or displaced volume.

At the beginning of stage 4 is a twelve-year-old who, although he
does not yet know how to measure volume correctly, is close to it.
Asked to build a house that is 3 × 3 × 4 on a 2 × 3 base, he says he
needs 9 × 4, or 36, bricks. Why? Because "it's 4 high and each row
is 3 and that's 4 × 3 or 12 and I multiply that by 9 because that's
the area on top."[12]   Thus his multiplying is wrong, because he
wants to multiply by 9 rather than 3, but he is close to the correct
procedure.

Finally, complete understanding by Gis, aged twelve and one-half:

Gis (12;6) with a 3 × 3 × 4 model to equal on a base of 2 × 2:
It's bound to be different in height, then (counting). *It's got to be
36 bricks in all, and that makes 9 stories.*—How did you work it out
at 36?—*It's 3 long and 3 wide which is 9, and it's 4 high: 4 ×
9 = 36.*[13]

At stage 4 children discover for the first time that "volume" is not
just the interior "contained" by some three-dimensional object such
as a brick, but that space exists in its own right whether occupied by
the brick or not occupied by the brick.

This change in concept at stage 4 is explained by Piaget as

Having understood the relation between boundary lines (or areas)
and interior volume, children inevitably deepen their sense of the
conservation of volume. *They discover for the first time that it is
not merely the interior "contained" which is invariant but the space
occupied in a wider context.* The relation between the lengths of

---

[11] Ibid., p. 375.
[12] Ibid., p. 382.
[13] Ibid., p. 383.

sides and volume remains invariant when the whole shape is transformed, and this is the essential truth which is seized upon at stage 4 and expressed in the form of mathematical multiplication: $3 \times 3 \times 4 = 2 \times 3 \times 6 = 2 \times 2 \times 9 = 36$, etc. Because interior volume can be measured and calculated from now on, its invariance now extends to the surrounding space.[14]

Construction of Equal Angles

The following construction problems require an understanding of measurement in two dimensions. Not until ages ten to eleven does the typical child develop the best technique.

How does a child (or adult for that matter) develop a solution for reproducing an angle congruent to a given angle? For example, when can he reproduce or make a copy of the following figure?

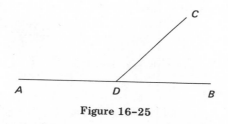

Figure 16-25

What will be his procedures?

To reproduce this figure the child is allowed to look at it as often as he wishes, but not while he is drawing. He is given a piece of paper, pencil, string, a straightedge or ruler, and a compass. He is not allowed to copy or trace the angle and he does not have a protractor to measure its interior.

Children under six years of age are unable to measure a line segment, so that a problem involving measurement of two line segments and an angle is too difficult for them. Even beyond six years of age they may make a very rudimentary approach to the problem. Children of six to seven make little if any use of the tools provided. Their method is a trial-and-error one based on visual estimation only, finding their angle too big or too small or being satisfied with a rough approximation.

At the second stage children can measure the length of line segments and thus locate point D correctly on line segment AB; but to

[14] Ibid., p. 385.

draw *DC*, they estimate the angle, not knowing what else to do. They make no attempt to use the tools provided.

At the beginning of the third stage, children try to slide the ruler from a position on *CD* to their own drawing without changing the "angle," thus attempting to use the idea of parallel. They are able to solve problems of linear measurement but are still unable to solve the problem of angular measurement. It is a trial-and-error method. During the latter part of this stage children begin to see the figure as a system of angles and make the necessary measurements of *AC* and *BC*. Measuring *AC* on the model with a compass, he draws an arc the length of *AC* on his figure from point *A*. He then measures *CB* on the model and draws an arc the length of *CB* from *B* on his figure. Where the arcs intersect is point *C*. He can then draw *DC* at the correct angle.

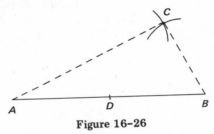

Figure 16-26

At stage 3,

> Ren (9;8): *To do that drawing I need that line (AC).—Why?— Because I know where that line (DC) begins but I don't know where it ends (C).—Can't you measure it?—No, because measuring it will only tell me how long it is, but I have to know how much it slopes as well.* He measures *AC* and *DC* to find point *C*[15] [as in the drawing above].

At stage 4, the operational level, the method of attack is no longer trial and error but intellectual. The problem is solved by measuring on the given drawing the shortest distance from *C* to line *AB* (the perpendicular),

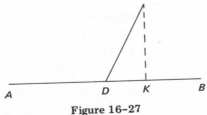

Figure 16-27

[15] Ibid., p. 181.

thus finding K. He can then locate K on his own drawing by measuring DK on the model. Using the measure CK on the model, he draws it on his own figure from K perpendicular to AB. He then has point C, so that he can draw DC at the correct angle.[16]

An eleven-year-old measures AB and AD and then plots a provisional point at C. He then draws a line segment from point C perpendicular to AB. He measures this line segment to find where the vertical distance CK coincides with DC. Asked why he did it that way, he responds that he did not know where to draw the line segment DC, but by finding the length of the perpendicular CK and the length of DC he could then find C.[17]

Piaget concludes that the introduction of a perpendicular measurement is highly significant, and that as a procedure it does not predominate until stage 4. It demands a higher degree of imaginative construction than that of measuring arcs AC and BC to find point C.[18]

In recognizing that the measure of angle CDK is based on the relationship of the lengths of line segments CK, DK, and DC, children are on the verge of the mathematics of trigonometry.

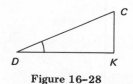

Figure 16–28

While Piaget characterizes stage 4 or the operational level as occurring at ten to eleven years of age for copying an angle, we found that in testing 90 ten to eleven-year-olds (all in the fifth grade), fewer than half of them could make this construction correctly.

The children were given worksheets as shown and asked to reproduce the angle on the left using the line on the right. Only a pencil, straightedge, and compass were allowed as tools.

This problem is somewhat less difficult than the one described in the preceding section, since showing point B directly below C suggests its use in reproducing the figure. Even so, fewer than half of the ten- to eleven-year-olds were successful.

[16] Piaget does not describe how the child is able to construct a perpendicular or whether he is able to. Apparently the interest is not in whether the perpendicular is drawn correctly, but whether the child can use the idea of perpendicular to solve the problem.
[17] Piaget, Inhelder, Szeminska, op. cit., p. 183.
[18] Ibid., p. 184.

NAME LINDA   Age 10 YRS. 10 Mos. 8

Geometry Experiment (Constructing an angle
                          from a given angle.)

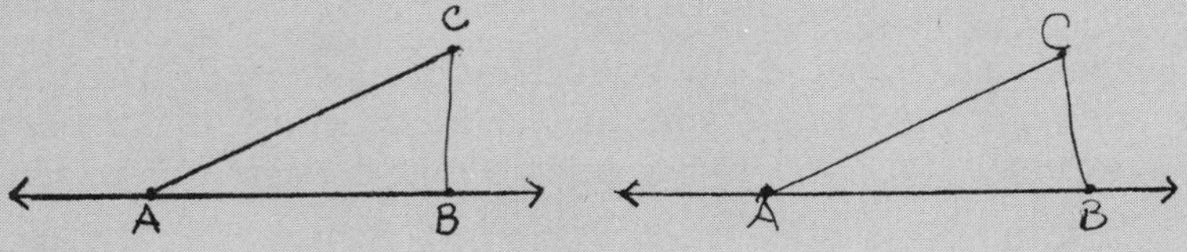

Directions:

Using a compass, ruler or protractor, copy
the angle BAC on the line next to it.
Tell how you did this by writing down
each step, below.

1- First I measured everthing.
2- Then I drew a line from A to C.
3- Then I measured from C to B
4- Then I drew a line from C to B
5- Then I measured both of them.
6- Then I thought about it.

Figure 16-29

NAME Susie   Age 10   YRS. 10   MOS. 3

Geometry Experiment (Constructing an angle from a given angle.)

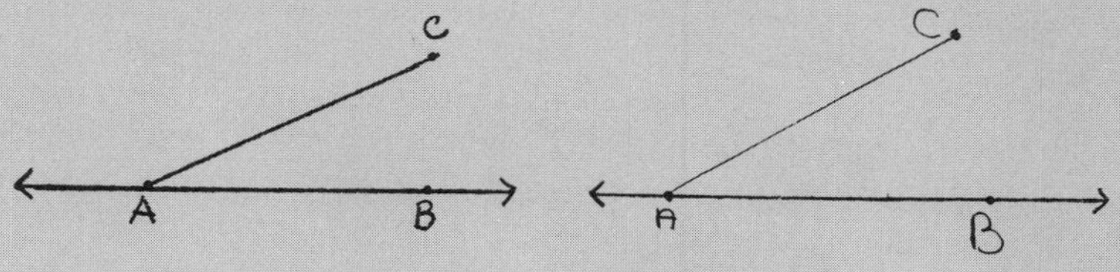

Directions:

Using a compass, ruler or protractor, copy the angle BAC on the line next to it. Tell how you did this by writing down each step, below.

Well first I look at the picture above.

1- Then I got only ruler and measured the picture.

2- So I put the ruler and put the right measurement

3- And then I took my pencil and put the dots on.

4- Then I put a — b — and c.

5- But the verry first thang I did

6. was look and read the Directions

Figure 16–30

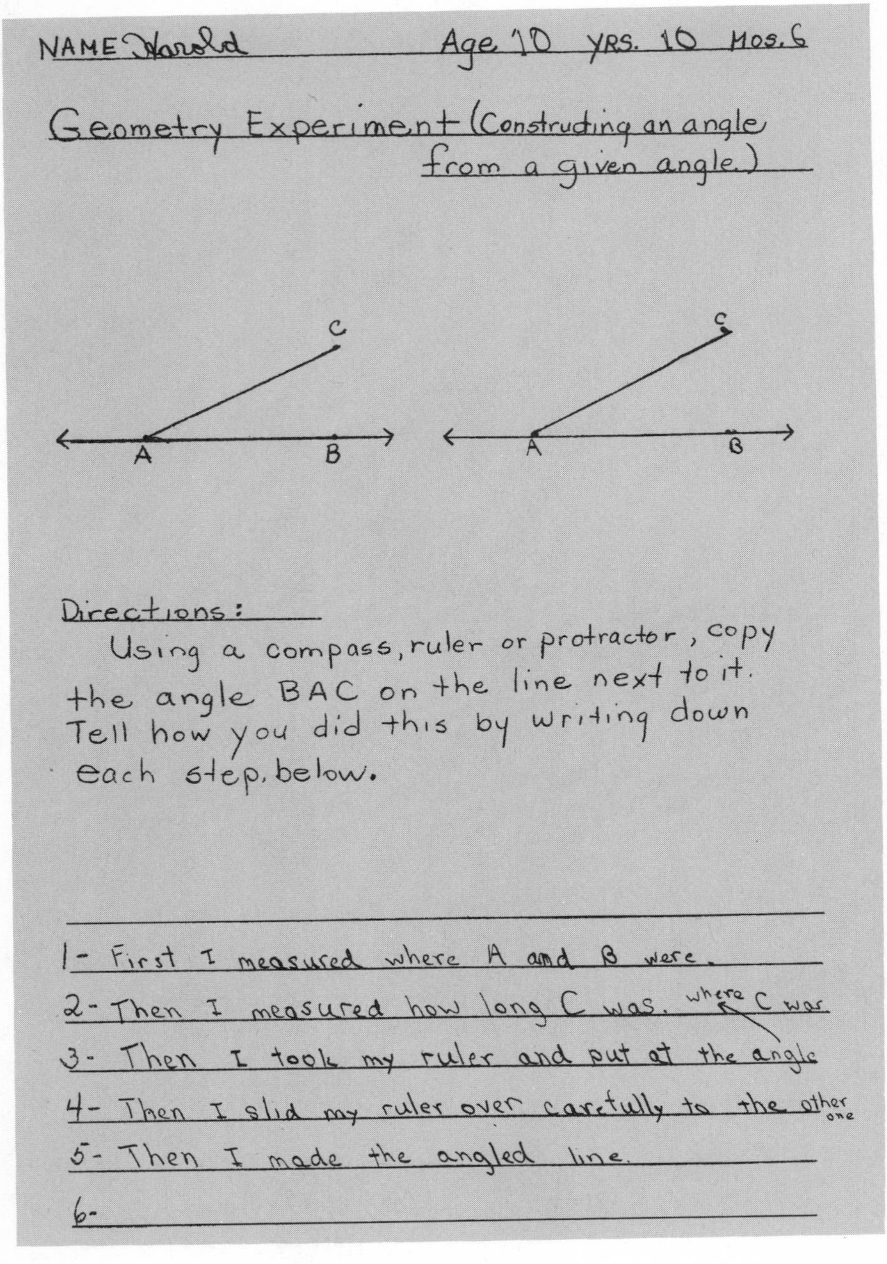

NAME Harold   Age 10 YRS. 10 MOS. 6

Geometry Experiment (Constructing an angle
                         from a given angle.)

Directions:
    Using a compass, ruler or protractor, copy
the angle BAC on the line next to it.
Tell how you did this by writing down
each step, below.

1- First I measured where A and B were.

2- Then I measured how long C was. where C was

3- Then I took my ruler and put at the angle

4- Then I slid my ruler over carefully to the other one

5- Then I made the angled line.

6-

Figure 16-31. Stage 3.

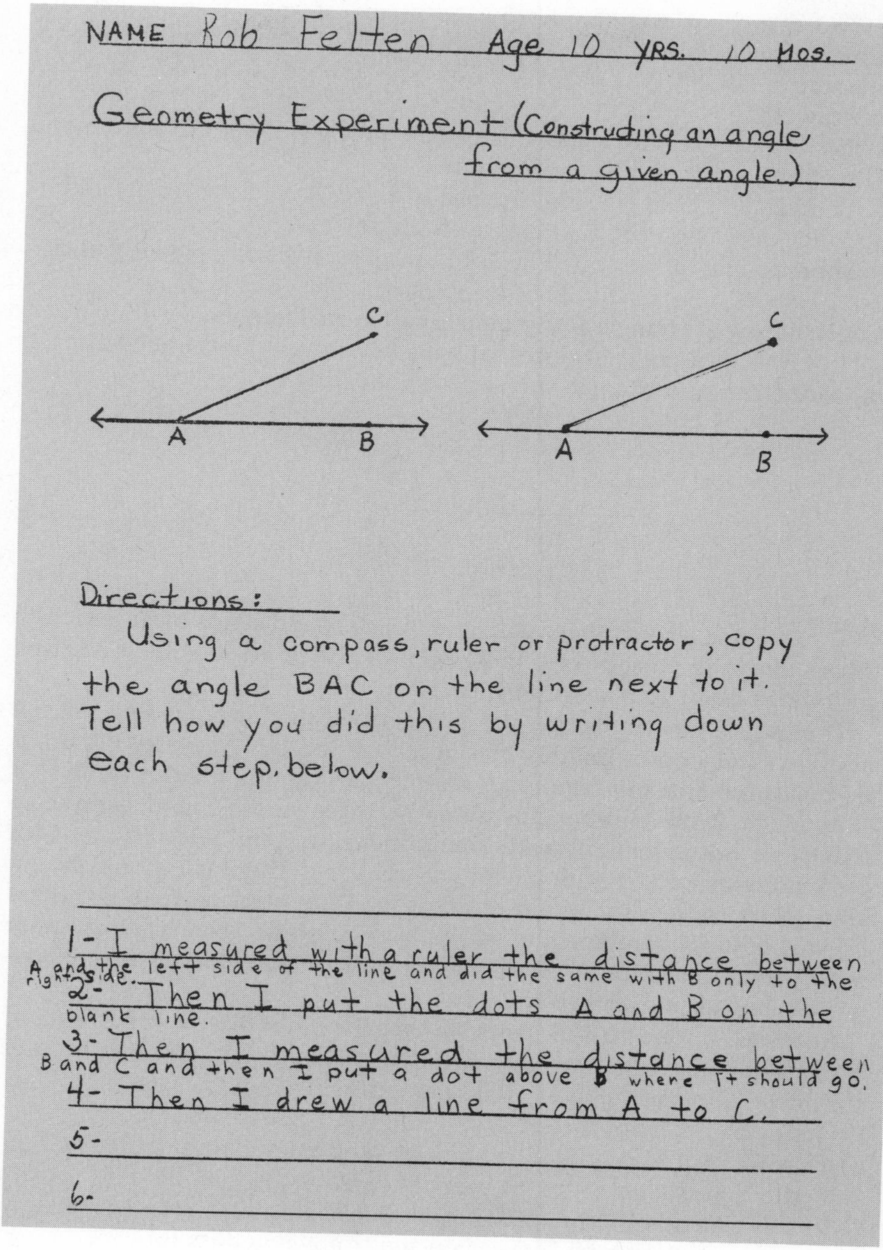

NAME Rob Felten Age 10 YRS. 10 Mos.

Geometry Experiment (Constructing an angle from a given angle.)

Directions:

Using a compass, ruler or protractor, copy the angle BAC on the line next to it. Tell how you did this by writing down each step, below.

1- I measured with a ruler the distance between A and the left side of the line and did the same with B only to the right side.
2- Then I put the dots A and B on the blank line.
3- Then I measured the distance between B and C and then I put a dot above B where it should go.
4- Then I drew a line from A to C.
5-
6-

Figure 16-32. At or approaching stage 4.

Two responses were humorous in terms of their last statements. Linda measures and then "thinks about it." She draws *AC* before measuring *CB*, so it is not clear how she chooses the angle at which to draw *AC*.

The impact of the teacher is evidenced by Susie's last statement, "But first I must read the directions."

At stage 3 Harold is using the idea of parallel to draw *AC* by sliding his ruler over from the first figure to the second.

Approaching or at stage 4 is Rob, using the idea of perpendicular.

Constructing a Triangle Congruent to a Given Triangle

How would a child attempt to solve a problem that called for the reproduction of a triangle such as the following?

Figure 16-33

The child is given a sheet of paper, a ruler, and strips of paper. The figure above is placed on a table behind the child, but he is allowed to look at it as often as he wishes.

The stages are similar to those described in the preceding section and occur at approximately the same age levels. At stage 1 there is no measurement, but simply an attempt at copying the figure.

At stage 2 the children measure the three sides, one at a time, so that their measurement is still one dimensional and not sufficient for a two-dimensional figure such as a triangle. They are therefore unable to reproduce the angles correctly. They assume that the three sides should fit together if each side is measured. They are not aware of the fact that the angle of inclination of one side to another requires another measurement.

At stage 3, nine to ten years of age, the child discovers the idea of a perpendicular as a way to solve the problem. Apparently he uses the idea of perpendicular, but, not knowing how to construct one, he estimates it, from *B* to *AC*.

At stage 4 a child often prefers to construct a perpendicular outside the triangle in order to reproduce an angle such as *BAC* (from *C* to *AB* extended). In so doing he demonstrates a greater freedom from perception, which focuses on the triangle and its interior.

To do this, first *AB* is extended on the model; then the shortest distance from *C* to the extension of *AB* is measured (the perpendicular *CK*). The figure can now be copied by measuring line segments *ABK* and *CK* on the model. After *ABK* is measured and drawn, *CK* is measured and drawn perpendicular from line segment *AK*. Line segment *AC* can then be drawn at the correct angle from *AB*. Filling in with line segment *BC* completes the triangle as a copy.

Implications for Teaching

Area

The implications for teaching measurement in one dimension (length) are discussed in Chapter 14. The experiments in this chapter reveal that conservation of area develops in the child at approximately the same time as conservation of length. Conservation is a necessary prerequisite for an understanding of measurement in either one or two dimensions.

Often measurement in one dimension is taught before the child is at the operational or readiness level to understand it, and yet two-dimensional or area measurement is deferred several years past the age at which children can understand it. Children at age nine in general are ready for measurement in two dimensions using the method of superposition of a unit square

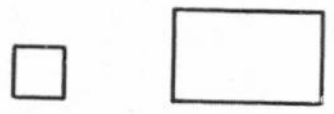

Figure 16-34

For example, given a unit square such as that shown at the left, the nine-year-old is able to superimpose it on the figure at the right, dividing it into subunit squares, thus finding the area to be six unit squares.

Children in the age range seven to nine should be tested first for an understanding of conservation of area using experiments such as those described. When they are at the conservation or operational level, they are ready to begin measurement using a unit square and counting the number of times it is contained in the figure being measured.

The method of determining area by using linear measures of length and width and multiplying should not be expected to develop until eleven to twelve years of age. This means deferring a consideration of this method until fifth, sixth, or seventh grade, depending on the operational readiness of the children involved.

Volume

The experiment with blocks to see if a house can be built with a smaller base to contain the "same amount" of room is an interesting experiment to explore the child's understanding of conservation of volume.

Children around the age of eight begin to conserve interior volume (volume inside the house); that is, they begin to realize that the outside shape (length, width, height) of the building may be changed without changing the volume inside the building since the same number of bricks are involved. But it is not until eleven to twelve years of age that children reach stage 4 and can understand the idea of conservation of occupied or displaced volume, as revealed by immersing the building in water. At this stage they also begin to see volume in terms of changes in linear measures of length, width, and height, which allows for the development of the formula for determining volume: $v = l \times w \times h$.

Stage 4 thus occurs at about the time the child completes the elementary school. Since measurement of volume is not usually taught until the junior high school level, children should be ready for this concept at that time. At whatever age volume measurement is taught, it would be most worthwhile that there be readiness experiences of the sort described in this section so that the child has a chance to develop the necessary concepts in a meaningful context, rather than being "told" a formula that has little meaning for him. It would be very worthwhile in grades 5 and 6 to begin exploring the idea of volume, using blocks, to see how well the children can solve such problems. In any case, the formula for volume measurement should not be taught until the children have had experience with three-dimensional objects and are beginning to understand the necessary concepts for the formula

$$v = l \times w \times h$$

Constructions

In the middle and upper elementary grades construction activities with a compass and straightedge provide a medium for exploration of space and for creative activity. Children should be encouraged to develop many types of patterns. Beginning with a circle, they can explore ways of inscribing polygons such as a square by drawing a diameter for the circle and then another diameter perpendicular to the first and then connecting the end points of the diameters.[19]

As far as more formal construction problems are concerned, Piaget finds ten- and eleven-year-olds at stage 4 able to use the idea of perpendicular to reproduce angles or triangles that are congruent. However, we find many college students and adults not at stage 4 in this type of construction. Apparently, some children are ready for construction problems in upper elementary school (grades 4–6), and many schools are beginning to provide more geometry experiences of this sort. In the past, this type of geometry was not taught until the tenth or eleventh grade.

[19] As a review for the necessary construction procedures, such as drawing one line as a perpendicular bisector for another, see Richard W. Copeland, *Mathematics and the Elementary Teacher*, Philadelphia: W. B. Saunders Company, 1972, pp. 208–213.

17 Projective Geometry

Drawing or imagining a straight line presupposes a projective or Euclidean space . . . notion [that is] far from elementary whatever may be the opinions expressed in textbooks of geometry.[1] . . . perspective appears at a relatively late stage in the child's psychological development.[2]

The mathematics of topology involves a study of relations within the figure itself. For example, in the line segment

Figure 17-1

the order relation of the points from left to right is A, B, C, D. The relation between the points is a topological idea. The idea of proximity, that B is next to A, C next to B, and so on, is a topological relation between the points. The relation of enclosure or between is also a topological relation. B is between A and C, and C is between B and D.

In **Euclidean geometry** the relations between different rigid figures are studied. For example, in considering two line segments, are they the same length, or, in considering two triangles, are they congruent or similar? Locating objects correctly in **relation** to each other in space, such as by distance, angle, or direction, also may be thought

[1] Jean Piaget and Barbel Inhelder. *The Child's Conception of Space.* New York: Humanities Press, Inc., 1963, p. 155.
[2] Ibid., p. 209.

of as Euclidean geometry. If the ideas discussed involve only two dimensions, as on a flat surface or plane, the mathematics is plane geometry.

In **projective geometry**, an object or idea such as a straight line is not considered by itself or in isolation, but in relation to how it looks from a particular **point of view**. This may involve three dimensions or solid geometry. Consider, for example, a pencil.

Figure 17-2

How it "looks" here is quite different from an end view. These points of view or relations of the observer to the object represent a **perspective** relationship. Perspective is a part of projective geometry.

Also involving a point of view in projective geometry is how one object would "look" if projected on another. This idea can be studied with children in terms of predicting what the shadow of an object such as a pencil would look like if projected on a screen.

Linear Perspective (Straightness)

Although the study of linear perspective seems to be a very limited study, it is found that there is a great difference in children's ability to **perceive** or recognize something that is straight and their ability to **reconstruct** something that is straight. It is this difference in perceived space and representational space in which we are interested.

As an experiment, a set of match sticks in plasticine is used. Two match sticks are placed at the same distance from the straight edge of a table.

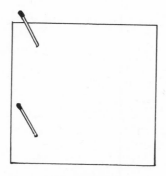

Figure 17-3

The children are asked to think of the match sticks as being telephone poles and to fill in the space between the two telephone poles with others so that the row of poles will be straight. Modifications of this experiment involve building straight rows of poles not parallel to the edge of the table to determine if the child can solve the problem without the edge of the table as a frame of reference.

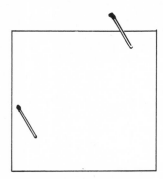

Figure 17-4

The concept of "straightness" is studied through observing at what point the act of "taking aim" or sighting is used by the child to determine straightness. Such an act involves perspective or the viewpoint of the observer as well as the object being studied. The match sticks can be aligned or placed in a row by "projecting" one on the other if an end view is used.

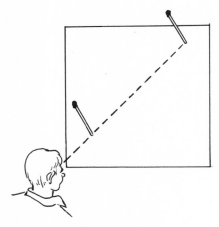

Figure 17-5

Not until approximately seven years of age does a youngster generalize to "sighting" or perspective in order to determine straightness.

Our concern is with the youngster's ability to preserve straightness
as the match sticks are moved about. This is a projective or Euclidean
concept rather than a topological one, since preserving shape (straightness) is not a factor in topology.

If the length of the set of match sticks is varied, the Euclidean idea
of length or distance changes, but the topological relations of order
and proximity between the match sticks do not.

The perspective or projective geometry involved in sighting or taking aim at the set of match sticks depends on the position of the
observer and changes as the position of the observer changes. The
straightness of the line is the sole aspect of shape which remains
unaffected by perspective changes.

Stages of Development

At stage 1 children can recognize a straight line and distinguish it
from a curve, but they cannot reproduce a line even parallel to a
straight edge, such as the edge of the table. Their line of match
sticks or fence posts will be a wavy or crooked one. They can form
a line only by having it touching another straight edge. Thus they
may line up match sticks in a straight row only by placing them
against a straight edge of some sort, such as a wall.

Their approach is topological. Without a straight edge as a guide or
model, the line of poles is wavy or crooked, but at least the proximity relation of A to B, B to C, and so on, is correct. Also the order
of B following A and C following B is preserved.

At stage 2 the child can form a straight line only when it is placed
near a model of a line, such as a table edge.

A child of four and one-half is asked to put the dolls in a straight
line on the floor. If he attempts to space the dolls farther apart, his
line becomes crooked. Using match sticks in clay on a table, he can
construct a straight line parallel with the edge of the table, but only
when the posts are brought close together.

When he tries to form a line diagonal to a corner of the table, he
uses as a reference the two sides of the table that intersect at the
corner, making first a right angle (A) with the match sticks and then
an arc (B).

Asked to indicate with his fingers how the line should "look," he
is successful, but trying with the match sticks again he makes the
same error.[3]

[3] Ibid., pp. 160–161.

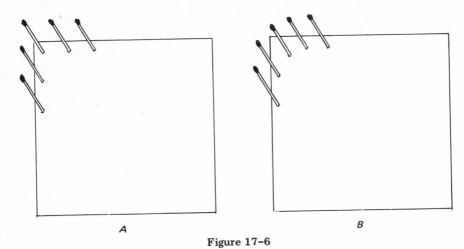

Figure 17-6

Lil, a five-year-old, is unable to represent a straight line on a round surface. He thinks he should stand near the middle of the line rather than at the end to determine straightness.

> He is shown an absolutely straight line cutting a corner of the table: Is it quite straight?—*Yes*—Where is the best place to stand to find out whether it's straight, here or there (in line or in the middle)?—*There* (the middle)—Now let's move to this table (a round one). I want you to make a straight line between these two posts (A and E, 30 cm apart)—(Lil fits in B, C and D, but following the round outline of the table)—Is it straight or round?—*It's round*—But you're supposed to make a straight line—(Lil begins again) *It's the same thing! I can't do it. It ought to be put there* (on a diameter of the table).[4]

By stage 3 the child has discovered the operation of "sighting" or "taking aim" as the best method of constructing a straight line. Thus the concept of a representational straight line has developed in place of the perceptual straight line of stage 2, which required a model such as a table edge. The child is no longer tied to such perceptual notions. He can now build a line of fence posts without an external reference system such as a table edge. He has grasped the idea that the projective relationship depends on the position of the observer or point of view.

In analyzing the psychological reasons that the child, before approximately seven years of age, is unable to develop an "aiming" or

---

[4] Ibid., p. 162.

"sighting" procedure as a means of determining straightness, Piaget concludes that the idea of even having a particular viewpoint is not realized by the child. The discovery by the child that he does occupy a particular viewpoint is much more difficult than the adult might think. Also, the operation of sighting involves discriminating between all the points of view and choosing the correct one. It is not a simple action but involves the coordination of all points of view.[5]

Piaget also points out that there is nothing in the design of the experiment to encourage the child to use a projective method such as sighting, as contrasted to the Euclidean methods of keeping to the shortest route between the two end points of the line segment or once starting out in a particular direction to continue in that direction. He found that both the projective method and Euclidean method developed at the same time, psychologically.[6]

Objects Seen in Perspective

To investigate children's understanding of perspective or apparent shape, Piaget also used a doll seated at right angles to a child. The child is asked to draw how an object such as a stick looks to him and how it looks to the doll. Thus a stick in the following drawing is seen lengthwise by the child and as an end view by the doll.

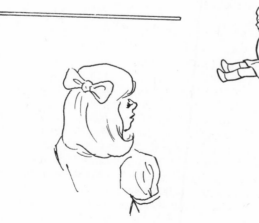

Figure 17-7

[5] Ibid., p. 165.
[6] Ibid., p. 166.

Three stages were observed. Children below four years of age showed no understanding. Children from four to seven years of age showed total or partial failure to distinguish between different points of view. At the lower level of this stage (four to five and one-half), children draw the object independent of perspective, not as it appears from a particular point of view. At the upper level of this stage (five and one-half to six) children begin to distinguish between different points of view. In the third stage there is a clear distinction between different points of view. At the lower level of this stage (seven to seven and one-half) only general shape changes are noted. At the upper level (eight and one-half to nine) detailed changes are noted and the child can portray the quantitative changes that take place.

In stage 2, Zum (aged 5; 2) is correct in some answers but wrong in others. He is able to draw the stick vertical when it is vertical for the doll and horizontal when it is horizontal for the doll. But he is unable to draw the end view when the stick is pointing toward the doll, drawing it first horizontal and then, asked if he is sure, drawing it vertical.[7]

Similarly, for a circular metal disk such as a coin, Zum can draw or represent it correctly as a circle, but for a side view he also draws a full circle.

> Do you see the same thing this way (full view) and that way (edge)?—*No*—Why not?—*I don't know*—Try to draw it—(Another circle)—Look at these drawings and try to find the circle you see like this (full view)—(He selects the full circle)—And like this (edge)? (He chooses a half-circle picture.)[8]

Thus a circle is a circle regardless of the position of the observer. Another child, a six-year-old, is shown a picture of railroad tracks that converge in the distance and asked to reproduce the picture.

> Mer (6; 0) draws the rails as parallel: Are they as big over there as they are here, when you see them a long way away?—*They're both the same*—And a fence like this (the beginning is drawn for him), continue it to the end of this long road—(He carries it on at the same height all the way)—And at the end of the road, do you see it the same height or shorter?—*The same*—Carry it on further still—(He does so but makes it slightly shorter, a difference he promptly corrects to make it the same height again) *I drew it smaller*—But if you look at something a long way away, does it seem bigger or smaller?—

[7] Ibid., p. 176.
[8] Ibid.

Smaller—Well then, draw this fence the way it looks when it's a very long way away—(He still makes it a constant height)—At the end, over there, does it seem smaller or not?—*It's no smaller.* [9]

At stage 3 the child is thinking at the operational, intellectual, or abstract level in contrast to previous levels in which his thoughts were based on perception or perceptual images. He generalizes the idea that as an object is tilted away from the observer it appears to become smaller. An eight-year-old (Han, stage 3) correctly draws or represents a vertical stick. "And if its tilted back a little? "You must make it smaller." And if I tilt it back farther still? "You must draw it smaller still." And laid down flat? "You'll see nothing but a little round bit." [10]

Han is also shown a metal disk, full face view. He draws it as a circle. What if it is tilted back a little? Han draws an ellipse. And a little farther? A flatter ellipse is drawn. And finally? A line.[11]

Not until age eight or nine then does a child draw things correctly from different points of view or perspectives. Perspective appears at a relatively late stage in the psychological development of children.

Projection of Shadows

These studies in perspective were extended by Piaget to include a study of shadows cast by various objects, such as a coin, pencil, and rectangular cutout, inclined at various angles and rotated to various positions such as side and end view with the child attempting to predict by a drawing how the shadow will appear. This activity provides additional experiences in perspective or point of view and helps challenge children to think of points of view other than their own. Such activities will find children at various stages of development similar to those described in the preceding section.

Using a light source that can be turned on or off as a point of view and placing an object on a thin mount between the light and a vertical screen, children can be asked to predict by drawing, or to select from a collection of sample drawings, what the shadow of the object will look like.

[9] Ibid., p. 177.
[10] Ibid., p. 189.
[11] Ibid.

Using a pencil as an object, shown first vertical, then tilted toward the screen, then horizontal or end view, the same stages of development can be observed.

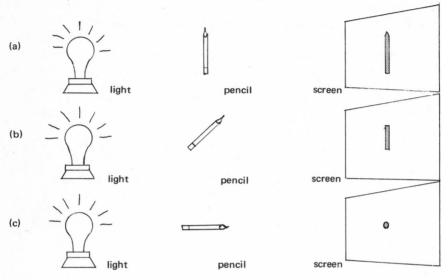

Figure 17-8

Preoperational children, below the age of seven or eight, can think only from the point of view of the object itself, a topological concept. They place themselves at the object point of view. Their perception is dominated by egocentrism (one point of view)—that of the object. They cannot think of it from different viewpoints. The object is always drawn the same way, regardless of how it is positioned relative to the light source.

At stage 2 children represent the object as seen from their position rather than the light source. If the pencil is pointed toward the screen (from the light source), the child draws it as a horizontal line rather than a circle. When the light is turned on, he is surprised to see the shadow is a circle. Similarly, when the pencil is slanted toward the screen from the light, instead of drawing it as a shorter line, he draws it as a tilted line the same length as when the pencil was vertical. He is surprised to see that the shadow is shorter than the pencil.

At the operational level the child can think from different points of view and correctly predict the shadow of the pencil in different positions.

The same stages are observed using a circular disk as an object—predicted as round, regardless of position relative to light source, by the five- or six-year-old.

At stage 2 the child may describe the tilted circle as being tilted, but he either draws it as a circle or alters it incorrectly. At stage 3 the shadow can be described correctly as a circle when the disk is vertical, as oval or an ellipse when tilted toward the screen, and as a line when flat.

Using a rectangular cutout produces similar results. The shadow is always the same rectangle regardless of its position relative to the light source for the five- to six-year-old. At stage 2, for a rectangle tilted toward the screen, children predict a different incorrect shape, such as a square. At stage 3 the rectangle is described correctly as "thinner" when tilted, until when it is flat, "a line" is produced as a shadow.

Using a three-dimensional object (such as a cone) makes prediction considerably more difficult than for the simpler two-dimensional shapes (circle or rectangle). Piaget reports a distinct time lag in ability to conceptualize shadows of such objects. This he characterizes as stage 4, which does not occur until eleven or twelve years of age.

A seven-year-old, at stage 2, is shown a vertical cone. He is able to predict correctly the shadow, drawing it as a triangle.

  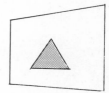

Figure 17-9

With the base of the cone toward the light, he draws it as a circle with a point placed above the circle. With the light turned on, he sees that the shadow is a circle but cannot explain why.[12]

Such children cannot conceptualize how the object will project on the screen.

During stage 3, which occurs over a relatively wide age range (from seven to eleven), children begin to obtain correct answers based on trial-and-error experiment.

[12] Ibid., p. 204.

At stage 4 children immediately conceptualize correct answers without having to resort to experimenting with the light and object.

Mon (12; 0). Single cone, horizontal:

Figure 17–10

It's a circle because it gets bigger and bigger, and the point is hidden by the big circle (i.e., enclosure by increasing cross sections)—And this (cones, base to base, horizontal)?—

Figure 17–11

A circle, because the points are hidden—And this (double cones point to point)?—

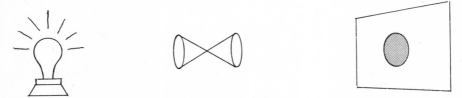

Figure 17–12

It's a circle as well, because the two circles are alike and the one in front hides the one behind.[13]

---

[13] Ibid., p. 207.

18 The Mathematics Laboratory— An Individualized Approach to Learning

> Without interchange of thought and cooperation with others the individual would never come to group his operations into a coherent whole. . . .[1]

Children are very much a part of the physical world. They like to explore the many objects they see, sometimes to the dismay of parents. Physical objects such as plants, rocks, a bird's eggs, and cows are all subjects worthy of attention. Boys much prefer wading through a puddle of water to walking around it. First-hand experience with objects is very necessary for learning. It is a basis for Piaget's concrete operational level of thought.

Children should be encouraged to compare objects—to determine the **relations** that exist between their characteristics or properties and the properties of other objects. Mathematics is a study of relationships. Is one object heavier, lighter, darker, smoother, rougher, bigger, smaller, taller, shorter, thicker, thinner than another? The same shape? Younger children will study such relations; later they will measure to make more precise determinations. It is necessary that the children themselves make these determinations, as in a laboratory setting, for a real idea of number and geometry to develop.

The mathematics laboratory approach is a recognition of this need for first-hand experience by each child with objects in his physical world. If real learning is to take place, mathematical ideas should be

---

[1] Jean Piaget. *The Origins of Intelligence in Children.* New York: W. W. Norton & Company, Inc., 1963, p. 193.

abstracted from the physical world. The relation of geometry to the physical world is often less difficult to see than that of number. The child cannot pick up and handle a number.

Number is an idea or abstraction and not an object in the physical world, but it does need a physical framework in which to develop for children. Dogs, cars, and houses are objects in our physical world, but a "two" is not. The world of number is completely separate from the physical world. And yet, we can use ideas from the world of number to describe **relationships** between objects in our physical world. For example, which is heavier, longer, wider, or taller and by how much? Measurement is an important activity in the mathematics laboratory. It is also important to find ways to record or express these relationships to systematize our work and for others to see or use. Charts and graphs will be useful.

Number, in its cardinal sense, may be thought of as a **property** of a set. For example, in considering the following three sets,

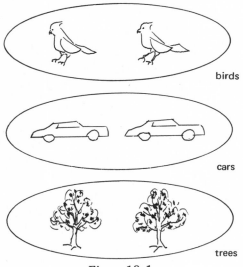

birds

cars

trees

Figure 18-1

one finds that each has the same number property, which we call "two." Each set contains two objects, although we see no "two" in the picture. The number two is a property of each set. We find that there are two by matching the objects in each set with the corresponding set of counting numbers.

Matching of objects in one set with objects in another set is a prelude to counting. In comparing two sets, are they the same (in number) or is one larger? Which one? How much larger?

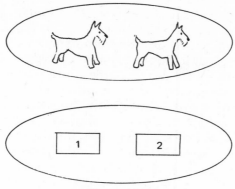

Figure 18-2

This is in sharp contrast to the way children have often learned to count by simply memorizing a sequence of sounds "one, two, three, ..." The futility of such a process is seen by asking such a child to tell you how many objects you hold in your hand. If he has just learned to memorize a sequence of sounds, he is unable to match the number names with objects in your hand. He has not established the idea of one-to-one correspondence that is basic to counting.

Similarly, the child may learn the addition facts by memorizing sums from a table with no real understanding. He may memorize 3 + 4 = 7 and still tell you there are more coins in the box on the right than on the left.

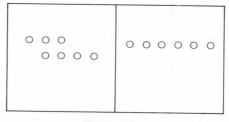

Figure 18-3

Children must develop mathematical concepts from operations they perform on physical objects. The many experiments described have shown that this involves an individual developmental process. Each child has his own span of development of necessary concepts.

To help meet such needs, schools may include classrooms designed as mathematics laboratories, a classroom designed to allow children to individually perform the necessary physical manipulations or concrete operations that are necessary for real learning of mathematical concepts.

Such real learning, based on first-hand experiences in the physical world, places mathematics in the realm of something that is fun, that can be enjoyed, and that can be understood. The child sees some purpose in what he is doing; number is not just tables and sums to be memorized. From a psychological standpoint, this consciousness of purpose is most important. The method of inquiry is an experimental one—can you find out? Did you discover anything? Important from a psychological standpoint is the inductive or discovery approach to learning. The child is provided a situation from which he should discover for himself or "disengage" the mathematical structure involved.

For example, does each of the two sets shown below contain the same number of objects?

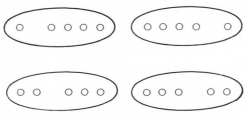

Figure 18–4

How about these two sets?

Would the number always be the same when the order of the subsets is reversed? Could you give us a general rule? (The commutative property.)

How to Begin
a Mathematics Laboratory

Many teachers have used a laboratory situation for part of their mathematics program, such as in playing store. Children are allowed to go to the store and buy something and then asked to make the proper exchange in terms of money for goods purchased. Children may also take a train trip or figure the cost of their morning milk. Such practical activities give some meaning to the mathematics learned.

Such procedures are, however, still not a laboratory learning situation in terms of an individualized approach to learning; they are usually a total class endeavor with the whole class doing or attempting to do the same problems at the same time. For some, it has meaning; for others, it does not.

A laboratory situation should allow for individual work as a basis for learning. It may, however, be advantageous in many situations for children to work in pairs or even in small groups. This will allow each child a measure of freedom to develop concepts on his own. Working in pairs or small groups may contribute to social needs and build vocabulary development. Vocabulary development is important in mathematics as elsewhere.

In starting a mathematics laboratory a teacher often begins in a small way, such as with an arithmetic corner in the classroom containing such useful apparatus as counting frames, abaci, blocks, measuring tools (see illustration next page).

A spare room, if one is available, may be used to which children may go when they want to work with the available materials when they have finished their regular lessons. There are enough interesting things, such as mathematical games, in the laboratory to draw children to it.

Class Organization

In a conventional classroom situation, children may be working problems in a textbook. If grouped for instruction, they may be working in different books. The emphasis may be an individualized one, but it is still a vicarious type of experience with possibly little meaning.

In a laboratory situation, children may be given "assignment" cards that are usually problems that require using some of the materials in the mathematics laboratory. There is much measuring, comparing, sorting, and questioning.

Assignments may be on an individual basis or in the form of some type of grouping. Allowing children to work in pairs provides for much first-hand experience and also allows opportunity for discussion of the problem. In experiments, one child may perform and the other record. After evaluating their findings, they decide on the best way of making a record of their findings, for example, a graph, model, or table. While pairing or grouping is important for vocabulary development and sharing ideas, it may mean that only one person is learning and the other simply following. The teacher can observe easily enough and make grouping changes as necessary. It may be advisable to make grouping changes as new assignments are undertaken.

Figure 18-5. Children in Hazelmere Infants' School, Colchester, Essex, England performing experiments of weight relations. Note other weighing scales in background. (Courtesy: Miss Lena Davidson, Head of School)

Children may be grouped by friendship, mixed ability, or common ability. Each has its advantages and disadvantages. The Piaget experiments can serve as a basis for determining common ability groups.

(See Copeland, *Diagnostic and Learning Activities in Mathematics for Children.* New York: Macmillan Publishing Co., 1974.)

A beginning teacher may allow only one group a day to do the practical "discovery" work while the others continue their regular routine. This will allow a pilot approach to the new procedure to see how it works, and later the program can be broadened as the teacher feels more secure with it. This will also allow time for obtaining additional materials. Friday afternoon, as an informal time, may serve as a basis for beginning a laboratory program.

Children who have been in a formal classroom atmosphere will need some time to develop self-sufficiency and confidence. Some have not been allowed to pick up a pencil until told to do so. They have become used to doing only what they were told. There will be some noise and confusion in the changeover and the teacher will have many questions to answer, but gradually the children will proceed more and more on their own. This will finally allow the teacher to perform her true role of advisor and questioner as she moves from group to group.

Figure 18-6. Mathematics Laboratory—Hazelmere Infants' School, Colchester, Essex, England. (Courtesy: Miss Lena Davidson, Head of School.)

Figure 18-7

Classroom Arrangement

In the traditional school, desks are placed in rows so that all children face the blackboard and the teacher. For a teacher-centered learning situation, this is a logical arrangement. Class discussion is largely recitation. The entire class considers the same question and reads the same page at the same time. Pupils do not leave their desk without permission.

If learning is to be on an individual basis with actual rather than vicarious experience, a different physical arrangement of the classroom is necessary. Also a more permissive classroom atmosphere must exist. Children should be allowed to move about as they seek answers to questions.

In many elementary classrooms there are now tables and chairs in place of desks. The chairs and tables may be moved about as necessary for various work and grouping. Since children will be working as individuals or in small groups, and often in different activities, cupboards and partitions should be placed at right angles to the wall to allow for some separation of the learning groups. The back of the cupboards and the partitions can serve as display areas for the results of the group work. Children often prefer to work at the tables in a standing position, in which case chairs should be stacked, as shown in the following illustration.

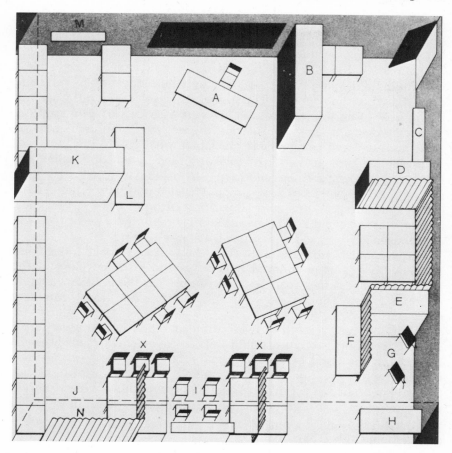

Figure 18-8. A classroom designed for active learning. From: *I Do and I Understand*, Nuffield Junior Mathematics Project. (Courtesy: John Wiley and Sons, New York, N.Y.)

In some experimental "open" schools, children are not grouped by grade or age. Instead there may be 90 to 120 children in a large room with several teachers. The children move from one activity to another as they are able. The range of activities will be greater than in the conventional classroom as will the variety of learning materials.

Moral Behavior

Discipline and Justice

The conservation of moral values depends upon the ability to think logically, just as does the conservation of such mathematical concepts as numbers. Children's thoughts on such moral questions as cheating, lying, or tattling are, of course, extremely important in their developing into wholesome adults.

As Brearley and Hitchfield[2] point out, a study of children's ideas on punishment leads one to rethink the whole question of rules and regulations in the school.   The ability to resolve a conflict by not giving way to an immediate urge involves a process of **decentration**. This includes not only considering the act itself but remembering what preceded and being able to anticipate what will follow.

Justice does not grow out of rules imposed by an adult, which are often not understood by children.   In asking children why they should not "copy" from a neighbor, Piaget found only 5 per cent of eight- and nine-year-olds, and 10 per cent of ten- to twelve-year-olds, define it as deceitful.[3]   The great majority reply in terms of "we will get punished," or in today's vernacular, "it is a no-no."

Justice requires nothing more than the mutual respect and solidarity that holds among children themselves and often develops at the adult's expense rather than because of him. As the solidarity among children grows, the notion of justice emerges in almost complete autonomy.

Children come to see that retribution or the infliction of suffering to right a wrong is only justified to make the offender realize that he has broken the bond of solidarity and is largely ineffective. The law of reciprocity, the ability to put oneself in another's place, tends toward a morality of forgiveness and understanding. Young children, of course, are only groping toward reciprocity and have many regressions.

Piaget concludes that

> Equalitarianism would therefore seem to come from the habits of reciprocity peculiar to mutual respect rather than from the mechanism of duties that is founded upon unilateral respect.[4]

In a laboratory where children are pursuing their work at their own rate and level with purposes that they have made their own, cheating does not appear. It would be pointless. It is the externally imposed standard exercise and correctness that encourages cheating to avoid humiliation.[5]

---

[2] Molly Brearley and Elizabeth Hitchfield. *A Guide to Reading Piaget.* New York: Schocken Books, Inc., 1966, p. 130.

[3] Jean Piaget. *Moral Judgment of the Child.* New York: The Free Press, 1932, p. 285.

[4] Ibid.

[5] Brearley and Hitchfield, op. cit., p. 138.

Materials and Their Use

We have emphasized the use of various concrete materials that children can see, handle, measure, and so on, to develop mathematical ideas. Such materials should include objects of an appropriate size for children to handle and that do not roll easily and are harmless. Ease of storing when not in use is also a factor.

For the lower grades, such materials might include wooden blocks, dried peas or beans, match boxes, plasticene, bricks, milk straws, sand, pipe cleaners, tongue-depressor sticks, counting frames, such as a coat hanger with wooden beads on it, and for place-value concepts an abacus and pocket chart. Containers are needed for most of these materials. Large sheets of polyethylene are needed as a floor or table cover when working with sand as are tools for transferring sand. Containers should be provided that hold the same amount but are different in shape to determine whether the children have reached the stage of conservation or invariance of quantity.

Vocabulary development is a valuable part of such activities. The containers may be described as wide, narrow, tall, thin. The mathematical relations of the same as, more than, and less than can be studied.

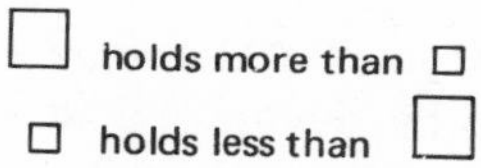

holds more than ☐

☐ holds less than

Figure 18-9

In studying length children may compare ribbons of different colors and lengths. They may be first asked: Which is longer, the red or the black? "Which is shorter?" Finally, they may be asked to "order" the ribbons by finding the shortest, the next longer, and so on. They should order from shortest to longest and also longest to shortest.

Children can compare the many lengths around them, such as pencils and table edges. They will also need to be tested on conservation of length. Children should not begin a systematic study of linear measurement until they are able to understand the conservation-of-length concept.

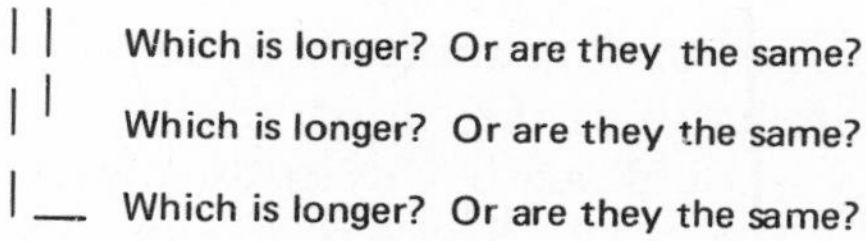

| | Which is longer? Or are they the same?

| | Which is longer? Or are they the same?

| __ Which is longer? Or are they the same?

Figure 18-10

Measurement is an important part of science and mathematics when the youngster is ready for it (nine to ten years of age). There are many materials needed for experiences in measurement. These include balance scales, weights, rulers, yardsticks, tape measures, micrometers, protractors, compasses, stopwatches, clocks, thermometers, trundle wheels, and plastic containers of various sizes.

Younger children may use balances of the following type:

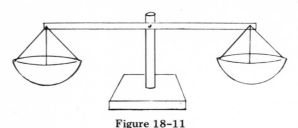

Figure 18-11

Older children will use the measuring instruments that are more precise after the conservation concept has been mastered.

Learning the Basic Addition and Multiplication Facts

The basic addition and multiplication "facts" involving the single-digit numbers (from 0 + 0 to 9 + 9 for addition and 0 × 0 to 9 × 9 for multiplication) should be developed **by each child** using concrete materials. An addition family such as twelve (6 + 6, 5 + 7, 8 + 4, 9 + 3, 7 + 5, 4 + 8, 3 + 9) should be developed by asking the child to count out 12 objects and see how many ways this set can be grouped as a pair of sets or into two sets. The restriction to two sets is important, since addition is a binary operation that involves two elements at a time.

To develop the multiplication facts for 12, the children are allowed to use as many sets as they wish, but each set must contain the same number of objects. Hence 12 = 2 × 6 or 2 sets of 6, 6 × 2 or 6 sets of 2, 3 × 4 or 3 sets of 4, and 4 × 3 or 4 sets of 3.

For learning the multiplication facts in table form, such as the fourth table, the child should use sets each containing four objects and should find the products for 1 × 4, 2 × 4, 3 × 4, 4 × 4, 5 × 4, 6 × 4, 7 × 4, 8 × 4, and 9 × 4.

As children learn the basic addition facts, such as 3 + 2 = □, they should learn the corresponding subtraction facts, such as 3 + □ = 5 and □ + 2 = 5. Similarly, as they learn multiplication facts such as 3 × 4 = □, they should learn the corresponding division facts, 3 × □ = 12 and □ × 4 = 12. These problems can be worked out as necessary with concrete objects such as popsicle sticks.

Use of Commercial Materials

More expensive but also useful are various commercially prepared materials, such as logic blocks, trundle wheels, stopwatches, mathematical balances, Cuisenaire rods,[6] Multibase Arithmetic Blocks,[7] Multimat,[8] Number Blox,[9] and, for diagnostic work, *Diagnostic and Learning Activities in Mathematics for Children.*[10] Catalogs describing these and other materials can be obtained at no cost from sources listed at the bottom of the page.

The Multibase Arithmetic Blocks, Multimat, and Number Blox all serve the purpose of rationalizing the operations of addition, subtraction, multiplication, and division with concrete materials. They are similar to the illustration on page 340.

These or similar homemade materials provide a much firmer basis for understanding the basic operations. For the necessary practice or reinforcement activities these commercial sources also have a number of games that can be fun and yet provide much of the necessary drill, such as learning the basic multiplication facts.

The Cuisenaire rods are wooden rods of different lengths. They allow children to explore number relationships by fitting the rods together. They serve as a concrete number line. For example, a rod 3 units long and another rod 3 units long is the same length as a rod 6 units long.

The mathematical balance is also useful in developing the basic addition, subtraction, multiplication, and division facts.

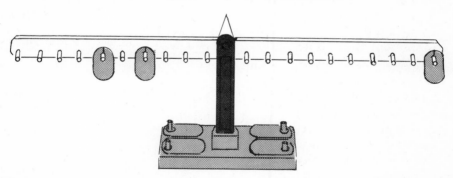

Figure 18–12. Invicta Mathematical Balance. (Distributed in the U.S. by Selective Educational Equipment, Inc., Newton, Mass.)

[6] Cuisenaire Co. of America, Mt. Vernon, N.Y. 10550.
[7],[8] Selective Educational Equipment, 3 Bridge St., Newton, Mass. 02158; in England by Tiger Toys Ltd.
[9] Creative Publications, P.O. Box 328, Palo Alto, Calif., 94302.
[10] Macmillan Publishing Co., Inc., 866 Third Ave., N.Y., N.Y. 10022.

To solve 2 + 3 = □, represent 2 + 3 as one weight on the 2 hook and one weight on the 3 hook. To balance, one weight must be placed on the 5 hook on the opposite side of the balance.

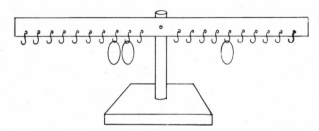

Figure 18-13. Homemade balance.

For a problem in subtraction (the inverse of addition), 2 + □ = 5? If a weight is placed on 2 on one side of the balance and on 5 on the other side of the balance, then where must a weight be placed to balance?

For a multiplication such as 3 × 2 = □, 3 weights are placed on the 2 hook. To balance, one weight must be placed on the 6 hook on the opposite side. For the problem, 4 × 3 or 4 weights on the 3 hook, a balance can be made by weights on the 10 hook and the 2 hook on the opposite side. For division, 3 × □ = 6, a weight is placed on 6, and 3 weights must be placed where on the opposite side to balance?

To explore geometric or spatial relationships, the geoboard is a very useful device. Rubber bands can be fitted on the pegs or nails to represent the various basic shapes and such ideas as perimeter and area relations explored.

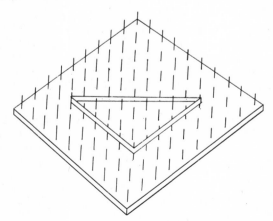

Figure 18-14

A trundle wheel is useful for measuring long distances. It has a counter to determine number of rotations (see illustration).

Figure 18-15

Learning Procedures or Algorisms for the Basic Operations— Addition, Subtraction, Multiplication, and Division

After children have learned the basic addition facts to 9 + 9 and the multiplication facts to 9 × 9 with appropriate concrete materials, they need to develop procedures for solving problems with larger numbers. Again, the beginning should be with concrete materials since to begin at the abstract level is not conducive to understanding.

Our algorisms for addition, subtraction, multiplication, and division are based on the principle of place value. Each **number** has a place value. Not having such a system of numeration, older cultures used an abacus to help with place value. An abacus is useful for children, but it has limitations as far as learning our procedures for addition and multiplication.

The problem is to find appropriate concrete materials to represent our base-ten system of numeration. Simulated money with paper or cardboard cutouts to represent pennies, dimes, and dollars may be very useful. Children seem to understand problems with money more readily. It is a necessary commodity in their lives. The pocket chart is also a useful device for exploring basic operations with concrete materials.

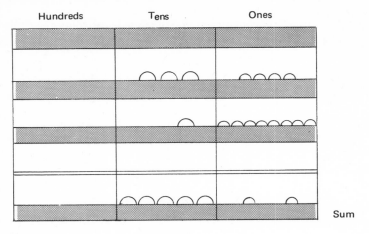

Pocket chart

Figure 18-16

Several commercial sources provide wooden blocks cut out to represent both base-ten and other base systems. The Multibase Arithmetic Blocks and Multimat, for example, use wood shapes in the form of units, longs, flats, and blocks. The terminology of "longs," "flats," "blocks," and "long blocks" is that of Dienes. The number 1245_{ten} represented with blocks would be

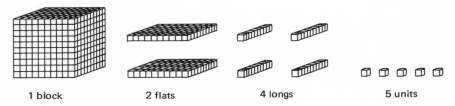

| 1 block | 2 flats | 4 longs | 5 units |

Figure 18-17

To consider the concept of division as we perform it, the child may be asked to divide the blocks equally among three children. To do this, the large block (1000 units) has to be renamed as 10 flats and placed with the 2 flats (each 100), thus producing 12 flats. The 12 flats divided into 3 sets produces *4 flats* in each set. The next step is to divide the 4 longs (each ten) into 3 sets. Thus *1 long* goes into each set with 1 long left over. The undivided long is renamed as 10 units and placed with the 5 units producing 15 units. Dividing the 15 units into 3 equal sets produces *5 units* in each set. Hence

$$1245 \div 3 = 4 \text{ flats } (100) + 1 \text{ long } (10) + 5 \text{ units } (1) \quad \text{or} \quad 415$$

The same procedure can be explored with the more conventional pocket chart. The column headings may be tens and ones or dimes and pennies, and paper or cardboard cutouts may be used to represent the numbers being studied. For example, in an addition problem such as

$$34$$
$$+18$$

the 4 ones and 8 ones are joined making 12 ones, which are renamed as 1 ten and 2 ones. The 1 ten is placed in the tens column.

Nondecimal Bases

Nondecimal bases such as base five will have more meaning for the teacher and student if first explored with concrete materials such as the blocks just described. The exploration helps the teacher as a learner to see how the use of concrete materials aid with a new concept. The undergraduate student planning to teach and who already understands base ten often wonders if concrete materials are necessary for children or whether it is just wasted time. Since her own understanding of base five may be somewhat limited, she may see the importance of concrete material in solving a problem such as $1133_{five} \div 3$.

Representing 1133 with blocks in base five,

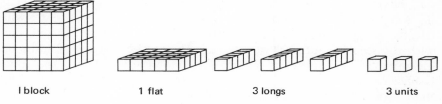

I block   1 flat   3 longs   3 units

Figure 18–18

To solve the problem of dividing this set of objects into 3 equal sets, the single block (125 units) is renamed as 5 flats (each 25 units). There are then 5 + 1, or 6, flats. Dividing these into 3 equal sets produces *2* **flats** in each set.

The 3 longs are then divided into 3 sets, producing *1* **long** in each set. Similarly, the 3 units divided into 3 sets produce *1* **unit** in each set. Thus

$$1133_{five} \div 3 = 211_{five}$$

The result, using blocks, would be three sets each containing

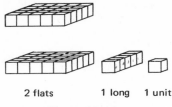

2 flats   1 long   1 unit

Figure 18–19

Division problems such as 1133 ÷ 3 should not be verbalized as "divided by 3" since this has no meaning at the concrete level. Instead it is a set of 1133 "divided into 3 sets."

These wooden blocks are also useful in developing the basic addition and multiplication tables. In base ten, 2 × 6 = □ and 6 + 6 = □? Using the units, 2 sets of 6 units is 12 units, which, represented with the smallest number of objects, is renamed as 1 long and 2 units.

The Algorism for Multiplication, Base Ten

To introduce the conventional algorism for multiplication in base ten, how would the problem 2 × 36 be solved? Using the blocks, 36 is represented as 3 longs and 6 units. Two sets of this many will be how many in all? The rule of the game is to represent the answer with the smallest number of objects. Hence the 2 sets of 6 units or 12 units are exchanged or renamed as 1 long and 2 units. This long is placed with the 2 sets of 3 longs, making 7 longs. The answer is then 7 longs and 2 units or 72.

A problem involving two-digit factors such as 12 × 34 or

$$\begin{array}{r} 34 \\ \underline{\times 12} \end{array}$$

using concrete materials such as the blocks would involve 12 sets of 3 longs and 4 units. If the 12 sets are grouped as 10 sets of 3 longs and 4 units and 2 sets of 3 longs and 4 units (the distributive property of multiplication with respect to addition), the problem is simplified and solved in a manner similar to our conventional algorism.

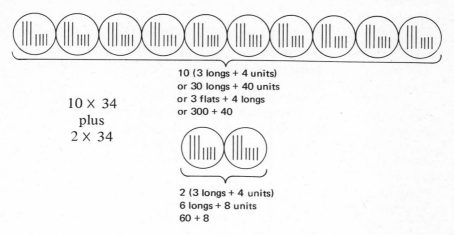

10 × 34
plus
2 × 34

10 (3 longs + 4 units)
or 30 longs + 40 units
or 3 flats + 4 longs
or 300 + 40

2 (3 longs + 4 units)
6 longs + 8 units
60 + 8

Figure 18-20

The procedure children use in solving mathematical problems with concrete materials can be set up in the form of "assignment" cards. This type of programmed learning material is described in sample lessons later in the chapter. Such material may make learning more meaningful for the pupil and free the teacher to serve as a resource person.

Care of Materials

The responsibility for the use of learning materials should be clearly defined.

Responsibilities of Teacher

1. Obtain and assemble the necessary materials.
2. Organize and label storage areas and containers.
3. When certain procedures are necessary, as in the use of delicate tools, to introduce their use with great care.
4. Trust pupils to use materials. The teacher should not spend her time checking materials in and out.

Responsibilities of Pupils

1. To select appropriate material.
2. Use the material with care.
3. Return material to its proper storage space (chairman of group responsible).
4. Clean up working area.

Books

Textbooks are now much better than they used to be. The mathematical content is better. Also they are better organized, more attractively illustrated, and often related to the needs of the learner in terms of practical usage.

In the conventional classroom there may be one graded textbook series through which the children proceed, page by page, lesson by lesson, with problem exercises for reinforcement. The teacher presents the idea, does some sample problems, and the children then do other similar problems. Only one book may be used but each child has a copy.

Many teachers, however, recognize the wide range in ability and achievement that they have in any group of the same chronological age. To remedy the problem, they may group children for instruction and use books written for different levels of achievement and ability. The trend toward the nongraded school is another way of attacking the problem. Such a procedure calls for a variety of books.

In the experience-centered, mathematics laboratory approach to learning, books are also necessary. Their use, however, is as a resource material, just as are the other materials in the mathematics laboratory. They are not the only basis for learning mathematics as is the case in many classrooms.

Practice in computation is necessary, but it should not be the whole mathematics program as it is in many schools. As the children attempt to solve such a problem as how many posts 4 feet apart will be needed to fence the playground, they will need to find the perimeter of the playground and know that the necessary operation is division. They will also need to know the necessary multiplication facts. They will need practice in order to remember the basic multiplication facts and also to remember the division algorism.

It is more meaningful if such computational practice grows out of a need to solve a problem. If the children do not know the multiplication facts, they see quickly enough that the division problem becomes very laborious.

Practice with the multiplication and division operations, however, should come **after** experience with concrete materials. Otherwise, it may have little meaning. The adult reading this book probably learned multiplication facts from a "table" rather than developing them for himself using such materials as beans or blocks. Fraction problems are not understood by many adults because fractions were "taught" at the abstract level. For example, what problems in the physical world would be solved by the notations $3 \div \frac{1}{2}$ or $\frac{1}{2} \div 3$ or $\frac{1}{2} \div \frac{1}{3}$? Can you represent these notations with concrete materials?[11]

Books or worksheets of duplicated problems can serve as reinforcement or practice material once the ideas have been abstracted from objects by children at the concrete operational level. Books are also an important source for problems to be used as reinforcement. Problems in a mathematics laboratory learning situation are more often in the form of assignment cards.

Assignment Cards

In using a book as *the* learning material, assignments are in terms of pages or problems. In a laboratory situation, the material to be learned in a given concept area may be divided into "units." The units are in the form of "assignments," "jobs," or "work" cards. The assignments or lessons are placed on individual cards or sheets of paper and kept in a pocket or card file. This allows for modifications, additions, or deletions from the file as the assignments are improved.

Examples of Assignment Cards

I

1. Put out two piles of money using both dimes and pennies in each pile (or use paper cutouts of money).
2. Make a column on your paper for dimes and one for pennies.

Dimes   Pennies

3. Write down the amount in each pile in the appropriate column.
4. Write down how much there is in all. Can you represent this number with fewer coins? If so, how should it be written?
5. What is the best way of doing this kind of problem? What you have just done is called **addition**.

II

1. Using dimes and pennies, show 26.
2. Double this number, first estimating what your answer will be.
3. Can you use fewer coins to represent your answer?
4. Write down what you did in solving the problem.

26
X 2

[11] See Richard W. Copeland, *Mathematics and the Elementary Teacher*, pp. 279–281. Philadelphia: W. B. Saunders Company, 1972.

5. Solve the following, first by using coins and then by writing the problem with numerals.

$$\begin{array}{ccc} 13 & 12 & 14 \\ \times\ 4 & \times\ 5 & \times\ 3 \end{array}$$

III

1. Using dimes and pennies, show 32.
2. Divide this amount equally between yourself and a friend.
3. How much will each have?
4. What you did can be expressed as

$$2\ \overline{\smash{)}32}$$

Write the answer above the line putting the number of dimes for each person over the number of dimes that there were altogether.
5. Now try some more division problems like this, beginning with a different amount of money.

IV

1. Get the bag of logic blocks and empty them in the place where you work.
2. Put them in sets so they are alike in some way. Write down how each set is alike.
3. Can you group them so they are alike in another way? Write how they are alike now.
4. Are there still other ways that they can be grouped so that they are alike? If so, write the other ways they are alike.

The teacher should be available for discussion as the child records what he has done and to see if he has discovered the important patterns involved. When first using assignment cards, children may work through the assignment and miss the important ideas, feeling the game is to finish the assignments. If the child has not discovered the idea sought, the teacher should ask additional apporpriate questions. After the child completes an assignment and records his result and conclusion, he moves on to the next assignment. It is a "doing"-type activity or assignment. The youngster solves problems for himself as a basis for learning, rather than having ideas "explained."

Records
Records kept by children can be an important part of a learning experience, but it can also be a deadening one. Some experiences involve recording, others do not. The criteria should be whether recording enhances or detracts from the experience, as will be easy

to observe in the behavior of the children as they make their records. Making records can be an enjoyable experience in the form of displays for other members of the class to see.

The first kind of recording by children is of a personal matter in the form of words in their individual diaries or workbooks. As their skill in writing develops, they love to write long rambling stories. If they have experiences of a mathematical sort, these will be included in their diaries.

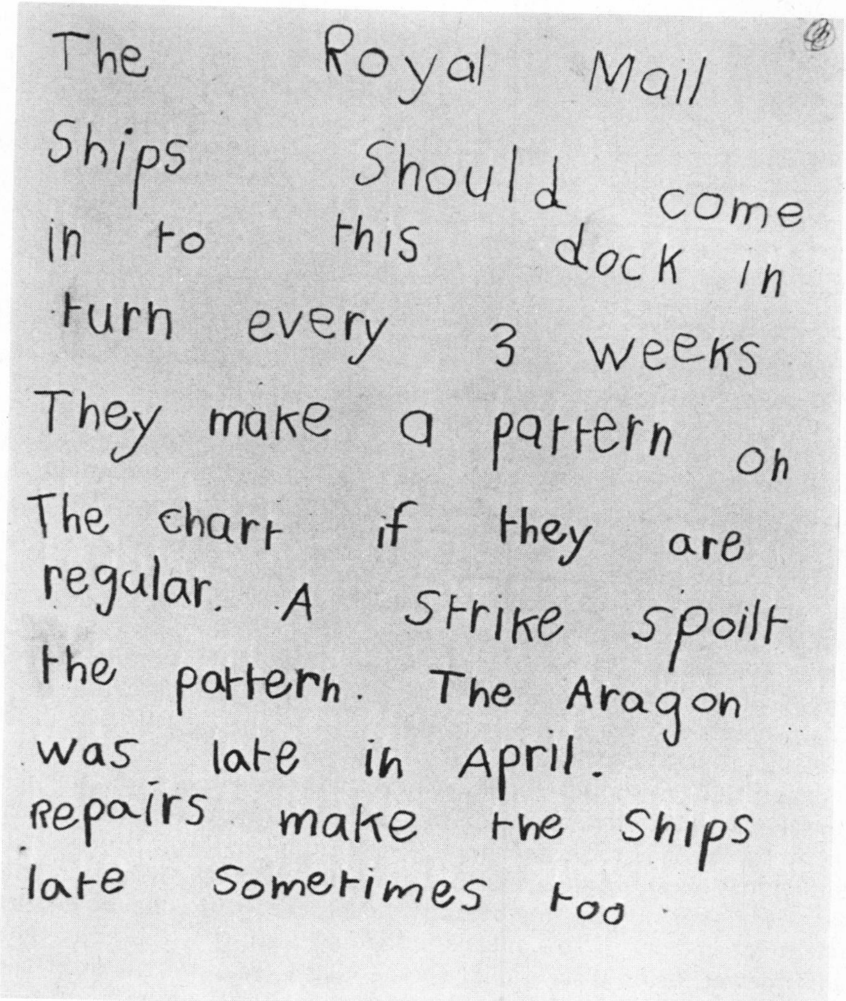

The Royal Mail Ships Should come in to this dock in turn every 3 weeks They make a pattern on The chart if they are regular. A strike spoilt the pattern. The Aragon was late in April. Repairs make the ships late Sometimes too

Figure 18-21. From: *Beginnings*, Nuffield Junior Mathematics Project (Courtesy: John Wiley & Sons, New York, N.Y.)

The second type of recording will be in the form of displays—charts, graphs—for other members of the class to see (see illustrations on this and following pages).

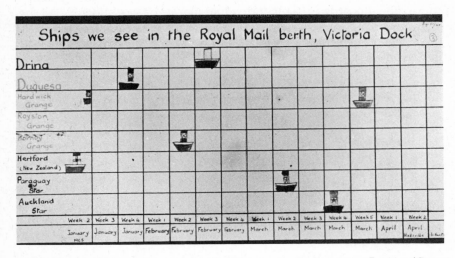

Figure 18-22. From: *Beginnings*, Nuffield Junior Mathematics Project (Courtesy: John Wiley & Sons, New York, N.Y.)

If assignment cards are used, a progress chart can be kept on the wall or in an ordinary exercise book. As a child completes an assignment, the date is recorded on the chart by his name in the proper assignment column.

The Nuffield Project material recommends that the teachers also keep a diary of the activities developed during the week—which succeeded and which did not and why; which children excelled or failed and why. Also individual cards or a notebook should be kept on each pupil. These individual records should include the dates assignments are completed, achievements, and difficulties, including attitude toward mathematics.

The principal should keep a record of the general development of mathematics in the school. This can be a summary of the diaries kept by the classroom teachers. The second important record is of individual pupil progress, assessed at regular intervals (i.e., six months or every year). Measures of individual progress in **concept development** are needed. This means individual testing of the child by an interviewer, using tests similar to the Piaget tests described throughout this book. A standardized achievement test in number manipulation is a mechanical process for the child and does not usually measure concept development.

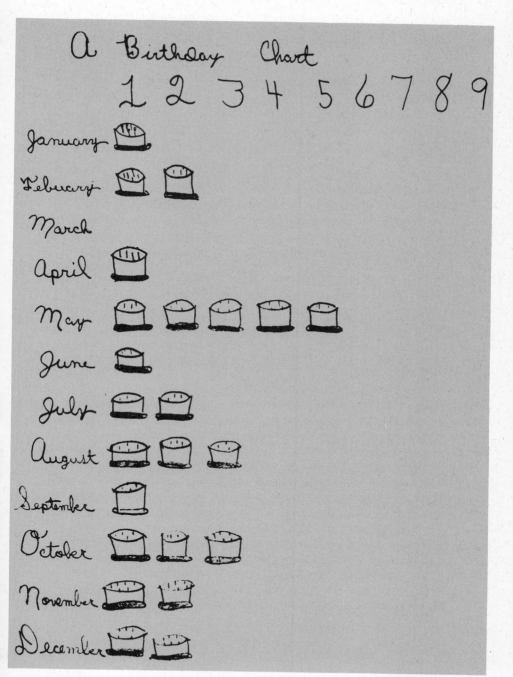

Figure 18-23. Birthday Graph of Class by 9 year old. (Courtesy: Miss Barbara Bittner, Henderson Laboratory School, Florida Atlantic University, Boca Raton, Florida.)

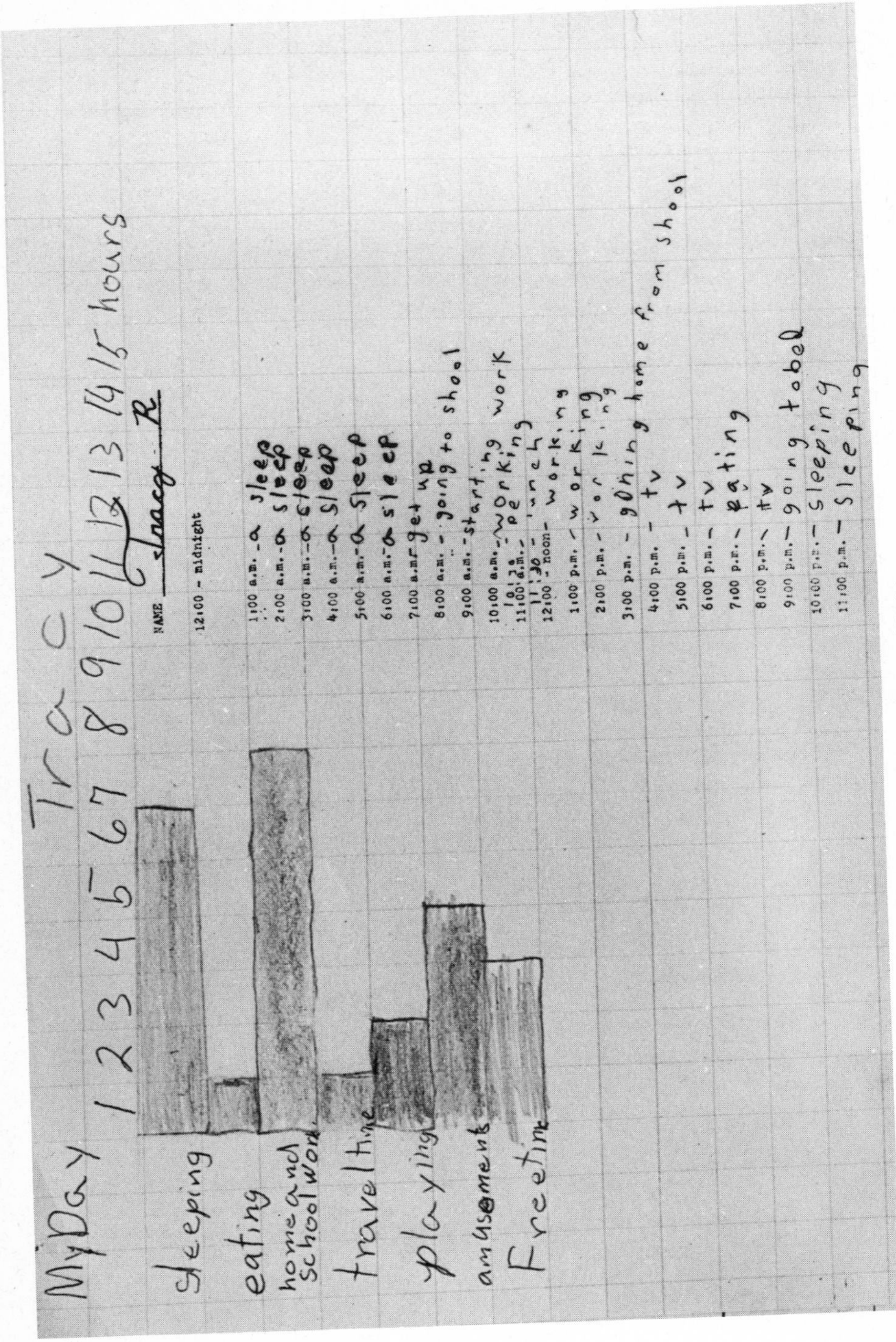

Tracy

My Day   1 2 3 4 5 6 7 8 9 10 11 12 13 14 15 hours

NAME   Tracy R.

sleeping

eating
home and
school work

travel time

playing

amusement

Free time

12:00 – midnight

1:00 a.m. – a sleep
2:00 a.m. – a sleep
3:00 a.m. – a sleep
4:00 a.m. – a sleep
5:00 a.m. – a sleep
6:00 a.m. – a sleep
7:00 a.m. get up
8:00 a.m. – going to shool
9:00 a.m. – starting work
10:00 a.m. – working work
11:00 a.m. – peing work
11:30 – lunch
12:00 – noon – working
1:00 p.m. – working
2:00 p.m. – working
3:00 p.m. – going home from shool
4:00 p.m. – tv
5:00 p.m. – tv
6:00 p.m. – tv
7:00 p.m. – eating
8:00 p.m. – tv
9:00 p.m. – going to bed
10:00 p.m. – sleeping
11:00 p.m. – sleeping

Figure 18-24

Assignments Completed

	1	2	3	4	5	6	7	8	9	10
Sue Jones	3/18	3/24								
Bill Smith	3/18	3/21	3/25							

Figure 18–25

Sample Assignments for Children

Each assignment should involve:
1. Performing the experiment.
2. Expressing the results pictorially, if possible, such as with a graph or chart.
3. Writing down findings or conclusions.

Weight Relations

1. Using a pan balance, put a larger number of objects (shells, buttons, sand, etc.) on one pan than the other. Estimate the weight relation and describe different ways of determining this relation.
2. Estimate the weight relations between the following pairs of objects (check estimates with a balance scale):
   a. A toy car and a pencil.
   b. A 2-inch and a 4-inch nail.
   c. A large and a small object.
3. If two bags are the same size, which is heavier?
   a. A bag of beans or a bag of marbles?
   b. A bag of shells or a bag of sand?
   Determine the weight relation using a balance.
4. What are the weight relations among a penny, nickel, dime, and quarter? Make a graph to show these relations. Write down your findings or conclusions.

Volume Relations

1. Using different shapes and sizes of containers, which holds more?
2. Using a set of plastic containers of different sizes, find the volume relation between them. Make a chart or graph of your findings.
3. Using three drinking glasses of the same type and size, put different amounts of water in each until you get a musical scale. Test by striking glasses with a stick. Measure the volume of water in each glass. What is the mathematical relationship? Show with chart or graph.

Time Relations

1. Make a birthday graph for children in your room. Show number of children born each month. What are your conclusions?
2. Using a piece of string and a weight on one end as a pendulum, make a timing device. Experiment by shortening or lengthening the string. Can you graph your results? Write down your conclusions.
3. Make a graph of how you spend your time during a 24-hour day.

Size Relations

1. Draw an animal that looks large to a dog and also one that would look small. Express the size relationship between the objects. Can you graph this relationship? Write down your conclusions.
2. Using a piece of string, measure around your head, neck, waist, and knee. Can you make a graph showing the relationships? Compare these relations with those of a partner.
3. Measure with a piece of string the arm length or foot length of five children in your class and make a graph or chart to show the relationships.
4. Classify the children in class by height using 2-inch intervals. How many are there in each interval. Can you show this relation with a bar graph? Conclusions?
5. Classify a set of buttons, or dolls, by size, and draw a graph of these relations.

Shape Relations

1. Find how many models of triangles, squares, rectangles, and circles there are in your room (such as the blackboard as a rectangle). Make a graph showing the number relation among these shapes.
2. Draw a tent and describe the shapes you use. Write the relation of height to width. Of width at the top to width at the bottom.
3. Look at a picture of, or draw, a boat or ship. What shapes are used to make a boat or ship? What is number relationship between the different shapes used? Can you make a graph of these relations? Write your conclusions.

Exercise for Teachers

Select and develop a set of concrete materials designed to teach a mathematical concept and prepare an assignment card or cards for the pupil to use in learning the concept.

19 Conclusions

The implications of Piaget's theories for mathematics education have not yet been realized. Studies by competent researchers involving American children are badly needed. New curricular materials, based on sound psychological evidence should be written. And, in teacher education, more work involving Piaget's theories and their implications would serve as landmarks in improving instruction in the elementary school.[1]

Mathematics educators are beginning to think of the implications of Piaget's research for teaching children mathematics, but implementation still seems to be a long way off. One reason is the demand for more supporting research. Another is the unwillingness to consider the psychology of the learning process, preferring to treat mathematics as a logical process. A third reason is an unwillingness to explore the voluminous work of Piaget. And still a fourth is opposing points of view, such as that of Skinner. Piaget's evaluation of the Skinner position is described on pages 9 and 22.

Piaget's own rather negative conclusions on education today were described in Chapter 3. They should probably be read again as part of the conclusions for this book.

---

[1] Paul Rosenbloom. "Implications of Piaget for Mathematics Curriculum," *Improving Mathematics Education for Elementary School Teachers—A Conference Report*, edited by W. Robert Houston. East Lansing, Mich.: Michigan State University, 1967. Sponsored by the Science and Mathematics Teaching Center and The National Science Foundation, p. 49.

The Importance of Developmental Stages

We have explored in detail the difficulties children have with mathematical concepts. We have demonstrated the necessity of readiness for learning mathematics with many experiments. Yet many teachers have difficulty adjusting to the idea of developmental stages as a basis for planning their instructional programs.

Until children reach the concrete operational stage (stage 3), such as in the conservation of number, they are unable to understand such ideas as more or less than or addition and subtraction. Unfortunately, many teachers think they can teach number to the average child of six, or measurement to the child of seven, or logic to the child of eight.

But this does not mean that the teacher has nothing to do. She should provide many experiences with manipulative materials so that when the child is able, he is provided with the necessary environment or learning situation that will provoke the desired logical process necessary for such a concept as conservation or invariance. This means testing and retesting in an interview situation until the child is ready for the concepts. If the child is not provided the proper learning situation, as is the case for many disadvantaged youngsters, he may still be at the nonconservation stage for number when he is in third or fourth grade (ten or eleven years old).

Isaacs describes how foreign number concepts are if taught too early:

> Average children of 4–5 years may be able to count readily up to perhaps eight or ten, not only in words, but in terms of real objects, and a little later they may be able to produce the right answers to simple questions in addition or even in the beginnings of the multiplication table. . . . But the illuminating sequence of experiments of Piaget and his collaborators show that behind this verbal facade these self same children have in reality not a glimmering of the idea of number. It is all mixed up with size and shape and arrangement and they cannot apply the (number) concept to the most obvious situations. . . . Average children of 5–7 have meanwhile made some progress in their ability to count and to "perform," in appearance, simple numerical operations, but this is all still mere surface semblance, practically meaningless and valueless, *for the foundation is not yet there.* We can actually watch them, through this stage, advance slowly [groping for each aspect of conservation as shape and arrangement are changed]. And so, as we might suspect when Piaget's experiments are applied to children another year or two older, we find ourselves back in our familiar world, almost indeed as

though the earlier ones had not existed. The right answers are now
given without hesitation as a matter of course [pp. 24-25].[2]

The pervading importance of the conservation or invariance concept
according to Inhelder[3] is that the most elementary forms of reasoning—logical, arithmetical, geometrical and physical—all rest on the
principle of invariance of quantity.   The concept of invariance involves many difficulties for the child unsuspected by the teacher.

Basic to the concept of conservation or invariance is that of
reversibility.   The preoperational child cannot reverse his thought
process. When the shape of an object is changed, such as water being
poured into a different-shaped container, the preoperational child
thinks there is more or less based on the appearance of the new shape.
He is unable to grasp the idea that the process can be reversed and
the water poured back to its original shape. Hence the amount has
not changed. Similarly, he may be able to solve $3 + 2 = \square$ but cannot
solve $3 + \square = 5$. Bruner[4] points out that teachers are severely limited
in transmitting concepts to a child at this stage, even in a highly
intuitive manner.

When, then, does the child reach the operational thought level?
Complete logical thought structures are not fully developed until
twelve or thirteen years of age, but many concepts can be mastered
in the preceding stage, the concrete operational level. One of these
is the inclusion relation, which develops in the average child at seven
to eight years of age. When the child understands this concept, the
teacher can begin to teach addition in an effective fashion. Such
teaching should, of course, not be the conventional telling, rather provide a situation in which the youngster can learn for himself. This
will involve many activities with concrete or manipulative materials.

The intent of each chapter is to include ideas useful to the teacher
in deciding when to begin instruction in each of the basic mathematical ideas. The results of the Piaget studies have been confirmed
by other studies.   Elkind,[5] for example, reports confirmation

---

[2] With acknowledgment to the late Nathan Isaacs, from whose pamphlet *Some Aspects of Piaget's Work* (published by the National Froebel Foundation, London, 1965) we have permission to quote.

[3] Barbel Inhelder. Memorandum for Woods Hole Conference. Reported by Jerome Bruner in *The Process of Education*. Cambridge, Mass.: Harvard University Press, 1963, p. 41.

[4] Jerome Bruner. *The Process of Education*. Cambridge, Mass.: Harvard University Press, 1963, p. 35.

[5] David Elkind. "Children's Discovery of Mass, Weight and Volume" *Logical Thinking in Children*, edited by I. E. Sigel and F. H. Hooper. New York: Holt, Rinehart and Winston, Inc., 1968, p. 17.

concerning the average age at which children can grasp number conservation concepts. He reports the conservation of quantity (which is necessary to study number) as occurring from seven to seven and one-half, a full year later than number is being "taught" in most schools. Almy[6] found conservation occurring at approximately seven years of age in three basic experiments. Other studies found that conservation of number occurs somewhat earlier than seven years of age. There is a variance in the child's development, and the only way a teacher can know about her own pupils is to test them herself as a basis for planning her program of instruction.

Since around seven years of age is a critical development time, one might be justified in concluding that the six- to seven-year-old is in reality a preschooler as far as systematized instruction in mathematics is concerned. The six-year-old is more like the five- than the seven-year-old. The first grade as well as the kindergarten should probably be devoted to readiness activities as far as mathematics is concerned. This means a drastic change in many of the current first-grade mathematics curricula. There should be more work with concrete material and less work with mathematical symbols, such as $+$, $-$, and $\div$.

While six and one-half to seven and one-half is an important readiness stage in learning many number concepts, other number concepts such as proportions and time are not developed until considerably later.

In the chapters on geometry and measurement (Chapters 12–17) we found that critical developmental changes occur between nine and eleven years of age. Thus it is not only the primary-grade teachers who are concerned with readiness in learning mathematics. A child's concepts of mathematics and logic continue to change and develop until he is approximately twelve years of age or at the point of leaving the elementary school. Also, in speaking of seven as the average age at which certain concepts develop, it should be remembered that such concepts will be present in some five-year-olds and not present in some nine-year-olds.

The study of the child's understanding of space is most illuminating. It is not something that is "given" or automatic but develops over a long period of time. This understanding is constructed in the mind of the child at a certain stage of development after many experiences with the physical world. To locate himself and other ob-

---

[6] Mildred Almy. *Young Children's Thinking.* New York: Columbia University Teachers College Press, 1967, p. 90.

jects correctly requires an abstract reference system such as vertical and horizontal coordinates.   This he is unable to do until approximately nine years of age.   Yet little attention has been paid to this inability.   For example, in primary grades children are asked to perform such activities as making maps of their neighborhood; such activity can have little if any meaning at this stage of development.

A study of the child's understanding of measurement is also most illuminating.   Again concepts must develop before teaching measurement can be meaningful.   Unfortunately, many teachers still skip geometry, feeling that computation with numbers is all that is necessary.   Geometry can give meaning to work with numbers.

Piaget has done an exhaustive study of children's concepts of time (Chapter 10), and yet the results of this research were not available in English until 1969.

Testing

Concerning the importance of the concept of conservation or invariance, Almy found that both the Pinter and the Reading Readiness tests show considerable relationship to progress in conservation, and she suggests an underlying common factor that teachers call "mental maturity."[7]   She concludes that the success of the various "new" programs in mathematics is largely dependent on the conceptual abilities of the children involved.[8]   The structuring of a mathematics program based on these conceptual abilities has been the main concern of this book.

Concerning diagnostic tests, Almy also maintains that the Piaget studies and method have important implications for appraising the progress of children, that his interview procedures provide information that standardized tests do not.   In the interview procedure the ways a child organizes or fails to organize information are revealed as they occur.[9]   (For a battery of 32 diagnostic tests see Copeland, *Diagnostic and Learning Activities in Mathematics for Children*.   New York: Macmillan Publishing Co., 1974.)

[7] Ibid., p. 104.
[8] Ibid., p. 126.
[9] Ibid., p. 135.

There is now also a standardized test, a "scale of mental development," based on the theory of Piaget.[10] It contrasts with the traditional Stanford-Binet in that it looks at intellectual development in terms of the stages described by Piaget. The Stanford-Binet is more highly structured, with a tally of "right" and "wrong" answers giving an average mental age. The Montreal test contains fewer test items, but each is designed to more carefully test the quality of the child's thinking. There are alternative questions depending on whether the answer to the preceding question is yes or no. A test item might be an experiment similar to those described throughout this text. Such a scale, unfortunately, is considerably longer to administer than the Stanford-Binet.

Interview Technique

Another implication for teacher education is that certain pedagogical skills need much more attention than they are presently being given. One of the most important is developing an effective individual interview technique. This can be done by bringing children, ages five to ten, into the methods classes. As students conduct and observe the interviews with children, they realize the difficulty of an interview technique that asks questions in the proper order and uses words that communicate the idea involved. Many of the photographs in this book were taken in such methods classes.

The teacher of the methods class who has not worked with children in front of her own class of college students will find the children most cooperative. The children consider the experiments a game and enjoy answering the questions. If children from an elementary school are not available, often the teacher will find that her college class can bring in neighborhood children or their own children. When the children are brought to class, they can sit at one side and be called one at a time to try the experiments. Beginning with the younger children, the stages of development are easy to demonstrate. The children should have name cards for identification and informality.

Students also need practice in designing experiments and apparatus that adequately test the mathematical or logical ideas being con-

---

[10] Adrian Pinard and Monique Laurendeau. "A Scale of Mental Development Based on the Theory of Piaget," *Journal of Research in Science Teaching*, 2 (1964), pp. 253–260.

sidered. These should be developed and discussed before the children are brought to class.

Teacher preparation, then, should provide opportunities (1) to conduct some of the Piaget experiments with children of differing ages and abilities, particularly in the five-to-ten age range and (2) to design and administer experiments to test children's understanding of specified mathematical concepts. These may be modifications of the Piaget experiments.   Fortunately for us, the Piaget tests are ingeniously designed to approach fundamental mathematical concepts with very simple equipment and materials and with questions children can understand.

It is necessary in teacher training for the student to work with children on an individual basis.   Students quickly recognize their lack of skill in the proper interview procedure. This is one reason for quoting the many Piaget interviews verbatim.   Teachers must find ways of phrasing questions, whether in an individual interview situation or in a conventional classroom situation, so that the child is not faced with the problem of communication as well as understanding the mathematical concept being considered.   Teachers also begin to recognize a greater need for questioning and then **listening** as opposed to becoming impatient and **telling**. In the Piaget interviews answers are **not** given.   If assistance is needed, the question may be: "Would this help?"

When the child asks questions, what is the role of the teacher?   In order that the child develop his own structures, it may be advisable to answer questions only with "yes" or "no" and not attempt to explain, since explaining will not develop the necessary structures in the child.   The child must then develop his own explanations or theories for the yes or no answer of the teacher.   This is the procedure of Suchman in the Illinois Studies in Inquiry Training.[11]

The Classroom as a Laboratory

Many of the experiments, such as those on conservation, involve a change or transformation in shape or direction.   Such transformations cause a conflict between perception or sensory impressions and the logic of conservation or invariance.   It is an important assignment for

[11] J. Richard Suchman.   "The Illinois Studies in Inquiry Training," *Journal of Research in Science Teaching,* 2 (1964), pp. 231–232.

the teacher to help the pupil investigate transformations using physical objects as a basis of moving from a perception to logical thought level.

The development of children's concepts are important in terms of the **time** at which various ideas in mathematics and logic should be introduced and the **manner** in which they should be introduced. The diagnostic tests determine **time.** But when the child is ready or at the concrete operational level, the learning of mathematical concepts is still an individual process and occurs at a different point in time for each child.

Individualized instructional procedures should be a part of the school program. Programmed materials or assignment cards may be a partial answer—that is, programs carefully structured to questions and materials as a basis for developing the concept being considered. Materials in a laboratory setting are necessary. **Carefully** programmed and illustrated materials are necessary to provide sufficient aid for each individual pupil to proceed on his own or with his laboratory partner. The teacher then is free to move from child to child as help is needed.

The new emphasis on a mathematics laboratory classroom situation for learning with free use of many materials is an important contribution to the nature of learning as envisioned by Piaget. Children from five to ten or eleven must first operate on objects to develop abstract ideas, since they are in or moving toward the concrete operational stage of development.

Social Interaction and Lesson Planning

Stress has been placed on children's being allowed to perform actions on objects as a basis for developing the necessary intellectual structures or elaborations. The math laboratory is one vehicle that shows promise in this direction.

But should the children work only individually in the mathematics laboratory? Piaget remarks that " . . . without interchange of thought and cooperation with others the individual would never come to group his operations into a coherent whole . . . ."[12]. There is a necessity of action with people as well as action upon objects in the

---

[12] Jean Piaget. *The Origins of Intelligence in Children.* New York: W. W. Norton & Company, Inc., 1963, p. 193.

educational process. In lesson planning provision should be made for group activity, which encourages questions and the interchange of ideas. It may be advisable to have the children work in groups in the mathematics laboratory as well as on individual projects. The word "cooperation" (rather than "competition") in the quotation above is worth noting. Emphasis should be placed on cooperation, rather than competition, in the group process.[13]

The quotation above is also worth considering in terms of the present trend toward completely individualized programs of instruction, which do not allow for social interaction except with the teacher.

Acceleration of Learning

In Europe it has been said that 1 hour is only 40 minutes in America. Can the teacher accelerate stages of development in children and thus "teach" them at an earlier age? Piaget calls this the "American question"; he reports that he is asked it every time he comes to America.[14]

Stated again for emphasis because of the frequency of the "American question," Bruner classifies Piaget as "unquestionably the most impressive figure in the field of cognitive development."[15] Yet Piaget does not agree with Bruner on acceleration. In a speech at New York University in March 1967, Piaget comments as follows:

> A few years ago Bruner made a claim which has always astounded me; namely that you can teach anything in an intellectually honest way to any child at any age if you go about it in the right way. Well, I don't know if he still believes that . . . . It's probably possible to accelerate but maximum acceleration is not desirable. *There seems to be an optimum time.* What this optimum time is will surely depend on each individual and on the subject matter.[16]

[13] P. G. Richmond. *An Introduction to Piaget.* New York: Basic Books, Inc., 1971, pp. 95–96.
[14] Frank Jennings. "Jean Piaget, Notes on Learning," *Saturday Review,* May 20, 1967, p. 82.
[15] Jerome Bruner. *Toward a Theory of Instruction.* Cambridge, Mass.: Harvard University Press, 1967, pp. 6–7.
[16] Jennings, op. cit., p. 82.

The New Math

Studies made by Piaget furnish a basis for the conclusion that a study of number, using symbol notation such as $3 + 2 = \square$ and $3 + \square = 5$, should begin after seven years of age for the average youngster. First-grade teachers are having a difficult time attempting to teach such new math notations. Even after seven years of age the less able will still not understand.

Other concepts, such as those necessary for measurement, the notion of lines as sets of points, the null set, and perspective and Euclidean space relations, do not become coordinated until nine to eleven years of age.

The new math has made important contributions in mathematics content and in the appreciation many teachers and students have of what mathematics really is. As in many new movements, however, the movement may have gone too far at certain points, the primary-grade level, for example. As Elkind reports,

> In building materials for the New Math, it was hoped that the con-struction of a new [precise] language would facilitate instruction of set concepts. . . . It is likely that the new language created to teach the set concepts failed because it was geared to the logic of adults rather than to the reasoning of children. Attention to the research on children's thinking carried out [by Piaget] might have helped to avoid some of the difficulties of the "New Math" program.[17]

Concerning Elkind's conjecture that using the research of Piaget might have avoided some of the difficulties of the new math pro-grams, it should be pointed out that some of Piaget's works relating to mathematical concepts were not published in English until the 1960s. *The Child's Conception of Geometry* was not published in the United States until 1960, *The Early Growth of Logic in the Child* not until 1964, and *The Child's Conception of Time* not until 1969.

Educational Philosophy and Psychology

Piaget, being concerned with the nature of knowledge involving such ideas as reality, time, space, causality, and logic operates in the field of philosophy. In his basic concern with how the human

---

[17] David Elkind. "Giant in the Nursery—Jean Piaget," *New York Times Magazine*, May 26, 1968, p. 59.

organism incorporates such ideas, he is classified as a genetic epistemologist. Piaget has much to offer in both educational philosophy and educational psychology. For the person whose philosophy of education is that of growth, experience, and accommodation, Piaget's psychology of concrete operations and operational thought structures provides the very foundation it needs. Also, language must be geared to the reasoning of the child, because reasoning is not determined by language.

If much of knowledge comes from within rather than without through the forces of the child's own logic (equilibration) and knowledge is not a copy of reality but a reconstruction of it, as maintained by Piaget, the teacher must see her responsibility in a new light. A basic responsibility will be to provide a physical environment and a questioning technique that provokes the logical processes necessary for concept development. Testing will determine the optimum time for such procedures to be meaningful.

The Acquisition of Knowledge

In Chapter 4 three levels of knowledge were discussed. Differentiating between them is essential for the teacher in planning his program of instruction. What does the typical adult consider knowledge to be? Furth[18] describes the position as beginning with knowing things "as they are" based on perception by our senses. Perception gives us a "copy" of reality. Knowledge is thus a copy of reality. By the principles of association and conditioning, perceptual and motor knowledge are constructed. Intellectual or abstract knowledge, then, begins with our senses or perception, but from where does our logic or reason structure come? Is our logical structure present in the child but not effective until a later date? Or does logic result from many conditioning or practice-type activities?

Logical rational knowledge is considered by many not to be different qualitatively from perceptual knowledge. This means essentially that logic is generalized or developed through being taught certain habits by practice or repetition and verbal instruction. Through a process of association and conditioning chains of appropriate responses are built. Language or verbal explanation often is the medium of this type of learning. Such a simplified approach may

---

[18] Hans G. Furth. *Piaget and Knowledge.* Englewood Cliffs, N.J.: Prentice-Hall, Inc., 1969, p. 183.

mean the teacher need only be concerned with teaching perceptual motor habits. But logic is a more complex mechanism than this interpretation allows.

In teaching children of five to eleven years of age we are concerned with developing knowledge of the physical world and logico-mathematical knowledge; but for the latter the child is limited developmentally or biologically speaking in that he does not develop certain thought structures for abstract logical and mathematical reasoning until about twelve years of age.

Knowledge of the physical world and certain types of logico-mathematical thought is possible from five to twelve years of age but must be obtained by a physically active process—by acting or operating on objects. Verbal instruction is not the answer. The importance of knowledge, as Piaget conceives it, to the teacher of the child from five to twelve is difficult to overestimate. Furth asks: "Who dares to guess how our primary education would change if teachers took seriously Piaget's proposition that knowledge is an operation that constructs its objects?" [19]

In summary, knowledge of the physical world is not a copy of reality achieved exclusively through the senses and verbal instruction, as is commonly thought. Reality or knowledge to the child is primarily what he can construct internally from actions he performs on objects. The quality of this interiorized or internal action or equilibration by which the child structures his world is dependent on his stage of development and on his biological heritage. The teacher becomes an important factor by providing an appropriate physical environment and asking appropriate questions when the child is ready for a higher level of thought.

Teacher Training

The problems of education as Piaget conceived them were explored in Chapter 3. One is the setting of standards by people or bodies who are not professionally qualified, whether it is the board of education, the governor, or the legislature. This is in contrast to the medical profession, for example, where standards are set by boards of professionally qualified doctors.

[19] Ibid., p. 7.

Unfortunately, teaching has not become a science. We have not done the necessary research to be recognized as professionals.

In teacher training provision should be made for (1) the development of initiative, (2) freedom to explore and inquire, (3) a better foundation in child psychology, and (4) a better foundation in research. Research involves learning how to question children, to record facts, and to make reports of research.

"In a word it is by and through research that the teachers' profession ceases to be merely a trade."[20]

---

[20] Jean Piaget. *Science of Education and the Psychology of the Child.* New York: Orion Press, 1970, p. 125.

Appendix

Diagnostic Activities

Index

Jean Piaget dictating letters to his secretary.